They Rob from the Rich....
and Splurge in the Hood!

THE
ROBBIN'
HOODS

ERICKA WII

D1293038

This is a work of fiction. All of the characters, organizations, and events portrayed in this novel are either products of the author's imagination or are used fictitiously.

E-Sharan Publications

ISBN-10: 0615474322

ISBN-13: 978-0615474328

Cover Design: Dashawn Taylor:
Ultimate Media.TV
www.erickaw.com

www.erickaw.com
Email Address: Erickawilliamsinfo@yahoo.com
Twitter: @AuthorErickaw
Facebook: Ericka Monique Williams
Ask Ericka: http://askericka.blogspot.com/
Contact Phone #: 212-201-9329

Acknowledgements

In this, my fifth novel, I still must thank God first. I will always acknowledge and glorify my Lord and Savior, Jesus Christ. Without the grace and mercy that He has bestowed upon me, this would not be my fifth novel. This novel would not exist. My charge is to hold his name high and, through my works, give Him all the glory. Thank you, Father, for using me as a voice to speak to those who may not believe in you. Your blessings are apparent through the fruits of my labor.

Of course, had it not been for my mother and father, who I must always revere, this would not be possible either. Although our family has been broken for many years, I am a product of the love that you two once shared. I love you both and thank you for loving me enough to raise me right.

I would like to acknowledge my family members who have supported me. You know who you are. I love my family. I hope that I am a great example and I hope that you are proud of me.

I have many friends; however, not all have been a part of this journey. I have had to understand that, to some, this is just my job and not something that you feel the need or desire to be a part of. I do not measure my friendship with those in terms of whether they have read my books or not. We may be friends for different reasons, but if you have been there for me and consider us friends, I thank you. For those others who have taken on this plight with me and pushed me in this challenging profession, I thank you even more. I do not want to name names and offend any. I appreciate all of my true friends.

Lamartz Brown. You are my right hand. You are the force behind me. You keep this ship tight. You make this work. You are the best partner that I could ask for and I love you as my brother in Christ, my business partner, my friend, and confidante. I appreciate and thank you from the bottom of my heart for pushing me and staying by my side, through thick and thin. We will get there!

Kita McCrimmon, thank you for the arduous task that you have as the event coordinator for ESharan Publishing, and thank you for being a team player in taking on the tasks that I request of you.

Katt, you are my everything. You do it all. You hold me down. Love you.

To Brandie (Editor; Typesetter), Dashawn (Cover Design), Davida (Design Artist), Kellie (Design Artist), Lou and Tazzy, (The Best Readers Ever) all of you have made this project the best that it could be and I sincerely thank you for working with me. You are important and I do not ignore that fact. Thank you.

I want to shout out Life Changing Books and my fellow authors and label mates.

To my brother, Cap, you have gone through a lot. I hope this story makes you proud.

To Unique Mecca Audio Hall and Greg Williams, thank you for the insight on prison life.

Last, but not least, my family. My love, Life, you are my heart. My son, Tori Sharan. I hope that I continue to inspire you to be great. My daughter Saniya Rain, you are a star already, girl! My stepchildren, Seven Sincere and StarAsia, I love you two!

I must remember always, to thank myself, for not giving up. It is hard to try to face failure. It is hard to put your all into this type of work. I am proud of myself, and I should be.

To all of my readers and fans, as always, this is for you! To the bookstores that held me down from the beginning, thank you!

May you all be blessed!

Dedication

This is my first book with male main characters. I dedicate this book to the men of the world who have had to take to have, raise themselves, be strong with no help, and who love without ever being taught how. I am here to tell the world that your struggles have influenced your choices and that some make mistakes because they choose to, while you have been judged by the circumstances that have been out of your control. Some of you have never been given a break, only the ones that you have had to take! Here's to you, you keep pushing, my brothers!

1988
Chapter 1

Boom!
The front door of a modest home in Teaneck, New Jersey drops from the force of Chance kicking it in and crashing through. He and two of his boys, Supreme and Star, storm in and go their separate ways, frantically ransacking the three floors of the house. Chance runs into the master bedroom and over to a closet, where he checks the pockets of jackets. He roughly sticks his hand into the pocket of a man's suit. He pulls out a wad of bills and smiles.

"That's what I'm talkin', 'bout, baby. Come to daddy." He puts the money in the pocket of his leather jacket.

Meanwhile, Star stands at a woman's dresser, picking up jewelry that is neatly laid out on a mirrored perfume tray. He grabs a handful of the gold and modest, inexpensive diamonds that are displayed, winks at himself in the mirror, and begins to check her dresser drawers for hidden money. He, indeed, finds some.

Supreme is in the family room of the strangers' home, disconnecting a VCR. He finds a duffel bag in the hall closet and puts the VCR and a portable stereo "box" system in the bag, along with a collection of VCR tapes. He then goes into a boy's room and steals his baseball collection.

"Let's go!" Chance screams after about 12 minutes, and the three teenagers meet at the back door. They run through several backyards and over three blocks to Supreme's house.

 2

It is the middle of the day and Supreme's mother is at work. His siblings are at school where the two 16-year olds should be. Chance was 19 and had dropped out of high school at 17 in his junior year.

It was the fall of 1988 and none of the boys were thinking about school. Fast money was their only motivation.

They walk into Supreme's kitchen and Chance opens his refrigerator.

"Yo, man, get out my refrigerator! My moms would have a fit, nigga!" Supreme yells.

"Nigga, shut the fuck up! Get me something to eat, then." Chance moves to the kitchen table and sits, leaving the fridge door open. Supreme slams it shut without taking any food out.

"See, that's why y'all niggas both don't know about surviving," Star says, and whips out a package of Oscar Mayer bologna that is unopened. "Just give us some bread and mayo, can you at least spare that, broke ass? I shoulda took the steaks them people had in they fridge, but I was too hungry to want to cook it and wait to eat it," Star says, waving the lunchmeat.

"Yo, shut up," Supreme says, "My moms ain't got no money. She's raising four of us on her own. Every other year it seems like she's talking about she's about to lose this house. She'll know if we eat up any of that food." Star laughs and Chance shakes his head.

"Well, this should help her out!" Chance takes the wad of cash out of his pocket that he stole from the house while Supreme starts to make the sandwiches.

"And she ain't about to take no dirty money from me neither!" Supreme announces, sitting down and giving them both sandwiches on paper plates. They begin eating without saying another word.

Chance eats his sandwich almost completely, and then proclaims, "Well, my mother don't give a shit. Money is money, nigga, and it don't make no sense to have a whole bunch of pride and no money to pay the bills with. Money makes you proud; tell your mother to get with the program."

They all go into Supreme's basement, where his room is, and take the money, jewels, electronics, and baseball cards out. Chance looks over everything. He counts the money, which totals 700 dollars. Star rolls up a Philly blunt with weed and they begin to smoke.

"Okay, Star, Roderick can take the jewels and the baseball cards and VCR and radio to get rid of. We keeping the cash," Chance directs. Star agrees by nodding his head.

"Well, damn, I wanted to keep the VCR; I ain't got one down here. That's why I took the movies, too," Supreme whines.

"A'ight, nigga, then it's coming out of your money. You get 150 instead of 200. It's no biggie. I won't charge you full price 'cause it's a used joint. You know I get whatever's over an even split, so I gets 300 and y'all niggas get 200. I found the money, so I get more," Chance proclaims.

"Nigga, we know. That's why I get to keep whatever jewels I want, and I want this here necklace to give to my girl," Star announces, and picks up one of the necklaces from Supreme's bed.

"So what? That shit is light, nigga. I'll wait 'til we come across some heavy jewels," Chance jokes, running his hands through the inexpensive jewels on the bed.

They call Roderick who immediately comes to pick up the loot. He gives the boys an additional 100 dollars apiece for all of it, which they gladly take. He also brings them a bottle of Pink Champale and Apple Malt Duck. He leaves and they await some girl company.

They then beep three girls who are almost out of school for the day. The girls come to Supreme's house. Their names are Crystal, Nina, and Janet. The girls join the three boys in Supreme's basement. Supreme gets ice for the paper cups and makes drinks for them all. He pops in a movie for the pairs to watch.

Janet speaks first. "Yo, why y'all don't never be at school anymore?"

"Yo, school don't pay the fuckin' bills. I ain't gon' be no doctor, no lawyer, no fuckin' teacher. The life I live don't require a high school diploma, just some muhfuckin' heart.

And I got that." Chance sipped his drink, eyeing the girls to see which one he was going to try to crack.

"Damn, you ain't tryin' to prepare for your future?" Crystal asked.

"They kicked me out of Teaneck High School. I was supposed to sign up for that alternate school for muhfuckas that are bad, but I never did." Chance said, unconcerned.

Nina asked Star a similar question.

"What about you Star? I ain't seen you in school either." She looked intently at the juvenile delinquent; awaiting what she knew would also be a smart response.

"I just came home from Juvy. I was in the detention center for the last six months for some bullshit. I ain't got time for school; I got money to make, bitches to fuck, and drugs to get high off of," Star says, laughing, and the rest join him.

"Star, you a funny nigga. Y'all niggas is my homeboys and shit, but I can't go out like that. I take my days off here and there, but the school be calling your house when you don't show up. My mother ain't playing that." Chance and Star look at each other and smirk, ridiculing Supreme.

Chance is the first to make a move on Janet. He puts his arm around her. He leans over, kisses her on her cheek, and whispers in her ear, "Come with me to Supreme's mother's room upstairs." Chance gets up and Janet watches him walk before following.

Chance is a handsome, medium brown-skinned, black teenager with a nice grade of jet-black hair, and perfect teeth that own a devilish smile. He is a conniving criminal, who looks as such. His eyes are dark and slanted and his mustache is finely trickled above his lip like a man. He has been through more in 19 years than some men go through in a lifetime. He looks more mature than his age and carries himself like he's in his late twenties. He has charisma and charm, with a well-built body that comes naturally, without the help of any gym. Chance is an old soul.

Chance winks at Supreme and walks upstairs with Janet beginning to follow.

"Yo, man, remember y'all gotta be out of here before five o'clock! And don't use my mom's room!" Supreme calls up the stairs as he hears Chance reach the top of them.

"Man, shut the fuck up; I got this," Chance responds. He waits for Janet and grabs her hand, leading her into Supreme's mother's room. He closes the door behind him and throws Janet on the bed. She laughs and sits up. He pushes her down on the bed, on her back and gets on top of her. He begins to undress her while kissing and grinding on her. Janet sits up on the bed and begins to remove her shirt. Chance stands up, drops his jeans to the floor, and steps out of them. He pulled down his boxers as Janet wiggled out of her jeans, while still on her back, and then pulls her panties down. Chance, with his shirt still on, enters Janet. They begin to have sex on top of Supreme's mother's blanket.

Meanwhile, Star and Supreme have not figured out which girl is for whom.

"So, what you wanna do, girls?" Supreme asks, dryly.

"I wanna fuck," Star states, and downs his drink.

"Damn, boy, you gotta say it like that?" Crystal asks. "Why you gotta be so rude?" She sips her drink, intrigued by Star's frankness.

"You must wanna do it, too, don't you?" Star reaches over and squeezes Crystal's breast through her shirt. "Come on." He gets up and pulls her up.

Supreme, agitated, says, "Don't go in my mom's room." He thinks about how he is going to get some from the remaining girl sitting on the edge of his bed, Nina. He notices that she has had three drinks and is pretty tipsy.

Star takes Crystal into Supreme's brother's room, pulls out a condom, and puts it on. He does not take off his pants, but drops them to his ankles. He turns Crystal around, unzips her pants, and pulls them down. He enters her from the back after pushing her, face down, on Supreme's brother's bed. She remains quiet while Star roughly thrusts into her, hard and fast. He put his hand on her back as he groaned and moaned, allowing himself to climax quickly. He got up, pulled his pants up, and walked out of the room. He went and knocked on the door to the room where Chance and Janet were. Crystal, feeling horribly used, pulls her pants up and went back down to the basement.

Chance came out of the room in his boxers with his jeans in his hand. He put them on as he walked into the kitchen. Janet got dressed and walked past the two teenage boys in the kitchen. They grab their coats off the kitchen chairs and leave Supreme's house, without saying a word to him or the three girls downstairs.

They walked outside, laughing.

"Yo, Supreme is a wack nigga. I know he ain't get no pussy." Chance fixes his jacket on his shoulders and counts the 400 dollars in his pocket, thinking of what to do next. He checks his watch, which reads 4:30.

"Hell no, that nigga's too much of a momma's boy. Shit, I just like hanging by his house 'cause it's close to the school. What you wanna do now?"

"Let's go to the pizza shop. I'm still hungry. Let's see what girls ain't make it home from school yet and see whose house we can go chill at." Chance and Star continue walking down the hill, toward the local pizza shop where all the high school kids hang out. Star is tall, dark, and handsome, while Chance has a stocky build. Star has dimples in his cheeks that the girls can't resist. He is of Jamaican descent, but is an Americanized, young gangster.

The pizza shop is crowded, as usual. When they walk in, they are greeted as the popular teens that they are. They go to an open table for two and sit across from two girls named Lisa and Kelly. The girls acknowledge them.

"What's up, Chance? Hey, Star," Kelly says.

"What up? What y'all about to get into?" Chance asks, and winks at Kelly.

"We about to go to her house," Kelly answers.

"Can we come? I got some weed if y'all do that," Star said.

"I don't," Lisa quickly replied.

"Well, there's a first time for everything," Star replied.

Chance leaned over and started talking in Kelly's ear. He and Kelly had been intimate on a few occasions. She was one of the neighborhood girls who were down with all the bad guys. She knew what Chance was up to and was willing to cooperate to get her cut. Chance leaned back in his seat and winked at Star, who then tried to appeal to Lisa.

"You was always smart and shit, anyway. I remember we were in the same math class in elementary school," Star said to Lisa, who smiled.

"Yeah, she's helping me study for a test we have tomorrow. You know I don't do my damned homework and if I fail, they not gonna let me graduate. So, I'm going to Lisa's. Lisa, can they come for a little while, before we start to study?"

Lisa was intrigued by her new set of company. She wasn't used to being around troubled teens. She was always a good girl who hung around good kids. She was excited and looking for some adventure.

They walked down the main road toward Lisa's house, with the girls in the front and the boys in the back. As they were passing Chance's apartment building, he told them to wait for him. He went inside with Star and woke up his 15-year old brother, Sparks, and told him to follow them, without being noticed, and wait in Lisa's backyard.

The teens got into the home of the honor roll senior and she had no idea what she was in for. She took them to her family room and Chance asked to use the bathroom. The bathroom was close to the downstairs back door. As he walked toward the bathroom, Chance checked to see if Lisa was paying attention. Star was distracting her and Kelly was looking his way, giving him the head nod to go forward. Chance unlocked the top and bottom locks on Lisa's door and went into the bathroom.

"So, you have brothers and sisters?" Star asked.

"No, I'm an only child," Lisa replied.

"Who do you live here with?" he pried.

"My mother and father, but they don't get home until around seven o'clock." Lisa felt like she was doing something special by being devious. Chance came out of the bathroom and joined in the conversation.

"So, show me the house so me and you can play house, Lisa." Chance walked over to Lisa and pulled her chin up for her to look in his eyes. He winked at her.

"Yo, why don't y'all go to the store or something?" Lisa looked nervously at Kelly. She was scared, but not scared enough not to be adventurous for once in her life.

"You gonna let them leave us alone for a little while, Lisa, so I can show you what a hoodlum feels and tastes like?" Lisa blushed. She couldn't imagine that Chance could really like her, but the illusion of it felt good. He went and sat on the couch and started changing the TV channels. Kelly pulled Lisa to the side and coaxed her gently.

"Girl, you better take advantage of this. Chance is picky and he don't ask twice. We'll go get some liquor from the store or something. Walk me and Star to the door, Lisa." Lisa walked Kelly to the door and locked it behind them. She checked herself in the mirror in her foyer, wanting to be a sexy girl. She didn't know what to do. Chance met her upstairs, grabbed her hand, and put it on his penis. He helped her squeeze his dick and she could feel it quickly grow. He held his hand over hers and continued to squeeze and let go a few times.

"You wanna meet my partner, square girl?" Chance looked intently into Lisa's eyes. She nodded and looked away. He took her face in his hands.

"Look at me when I'm talking to you. You a virgin, girl?" he asked, and Lisa nodded yes.

"Okay, I'll be gentle with you. I want to make you feel like you never felt before. Take me to your room." Chance followed Lisa up to the next level in her house and she took him to her room. He closed the door behind them. No sooner than he closed the door was his brother, Sparks, quietly coming through Lisa's downstairs back door. He covered his hands with his sleeve to open and quietly close the door behind him; and then he tiptoed up the stairs. He could hear the radio coming from Lisa's bedroom.

Sparks found the master bedroom and went through Lisa's mother's jewelry box first as Lisa was in her room being seduced for the first time in her life. Chance sat Lisa on the bed and stood in front of her. He zipped down his pants and pulled his dick out of his boxers. Sparks picked up a diamond wedding band and matching engagement ring and put them in his front jean pocket. He opened a tiny drawer in the jewelry box and saw a brooch that looked like it was very old. He wasn't sure if it was real or not, but he put it in his pocket anyway. Chance took Lisa's hand and put it on his erect penis.

"Kiss it, Lisa," he said. She held it in her hand and looked at it. It looked clean to her. It looked nice. She gave it a kiss.

Sparks took a pair of diamond earrings and a gold bangle that was also in the jewelry box. He noticed another drawer and opened that up, too.

"Now, stick your tongue out and lick it like an ice cream cone, slow and gentle, though." Chance loved being in control. He loved turning girls out.

Lisa licked him from the bottom to the top.

Sparks closed the jewelry box, making it look the way it had before he rummaged through it. He then went over to Lisa's father's side of the bed and opened the drawer to the end table. He knew that men didn't have jewelry boxes and usually kept their important belongings carelessly available. He opened the drawer and saw a wad of cash sitting on top of a utility bill. He shook his head and said, "Nigga shoulda paid the bill when his bitch asked him to." He pocketed the cash and saw a watch, one of those old watches that have a chain on the end of it and is kept in a man's pants pocket. He pocketed that as well. He saw nothing else of value in the drawer and closed it.

Chance was thrusting his body into Lisa's mouth as she was sucking on him. She didn't have any idea what she was doing, but he was happy with her cooperation and effort. He knew that once she found out that her parents had been robbed, he would have to bribe her not to tell, so this would probably be the first and last time for them. Under different circumstances, he would have made this one, one of his flunkies because she was going to be in love with him when he got through with her.

 10

Sparks tiptoed past the room and noticed a guest room, which was plainly decorated and seemingly empty of anything worth stealing. He then noticed an office with a desk and opened the middle drawer to a jackpot. There were three credit cards in there that he took for a shopping spree. That would have to take place before Lisa's parents noticed them missing. He quietly walked down the stairs and back out of the back door without locking it, purposely.

Chance's instinct had him knowing that Sparks was out of the house and he was concerned with blowing the joint after his blowjob was done, and after popping Lisa's unpopped cherry. He moved back and removed himself from Lisa's mouth. She looked up at him innocently, wondering what was going to take place next.

"Was I doing it right, Chance?" she asked, with love in her eyes.

"You will learn with practice, but I want you to feel it inside of you. Take your pants off." Chance stepped out of his jeans. He dropped his boxer shorts to the ground.

"You're not gonna wear a rubber?" Lisa took her pants and underwear off and got under her covers, after realizing that she was a bit uncomfortable being naked in front of a boy.

"For what? You need to feel the real thing. I ain't gotta worry about you burning me; you ain't never fucked before. And I ain't got shit, so you ain't gotta worry." He took his shirt off and then pulled hers over her head, unsnapped her bra, and threw it to the floor. He got under the covers and on top of Lisa. He cupped her pretty breasts and began to suck on her nipples. Lisa had been touched before, but not this way. She had let a boy touch her, but she was about to give her innocence to someone more guilty than she could have imagined. Her legs opened up as Chance began to rub on her secret treasure. He kissed her neck and again, her breast. He looked over at her alarm clock and noticed that he had been 10 minutes over his 30-minute deadline. He knew that Sparks, Star, and Kelly would be waiting for him around the corner. He lifted himself up and deposited himself into her. He gave a gentle push and forced open her tight gate. Lisa tensed up and he whispered in her ear for her to relax.

"Open your legs, cutie." Chance's charm was ahead of his 19 years. He was a natural womanizer. Lisa did as she was told. He decided that he did not have time to make sure that she climaxed, although he would give it a shot. The thought of having a virgin turned him on and his gentle strokes quickly became hard ones. Lisa tensed up again. Chance forced her legs open with his hands and gave up the phony concern he had tried to exhibit for a desire to cum in her.

"It's hurting a little bit. Can you not do it so hard?" Lisa squeezed her eyes shut. She didn't know if it was supposed to feel better than it did or not for the first time, but she just wanted this first time to be over.

Chance didn't listen. He pounded on the naïve robbery victim and grunted as he felt himself getting closer to his goal. Chance threw himself as deep inside of her as he could and stayed there for a few seconds, while he relieved and released his wrath on the poor girl. He kissed Lisa on the cheek and said, "I gotta go."

Lisa sat up, feeling nowhere near the way she thought she would. Suddenly, she knew that she had not only done something wrong, but also felt that she would be paying for her bad decision later-somehow, some way. Chance abruptly lifted himself up, stood up, and began getting dressed.

Lisa thought of a movie where the woman would never hear from the guy she had let fool her, again. She knew that she was that girl.

"Am I gonna see you again?" she asked, already knowing the answer was yes and that it would probably only be in passing. Still, she awaited Chance's response.

"I'll be around," Chance said, inconsiderately. He got up and got dressed. "Why? You wanna try this dick again, huh?" He laughed and Lisa didn't find the humor. She gave it another try.

"Isn't Kelly and your friend coming back?" Lisa sat up, holding the blanket around her to keep her covered.

"Oh, yeah, if they do, tell them I had to leave. Star probably won't; he ain't got no patience and he probably bounced. Tell Kelly that I'll see her later." Chance walked to Lisa's bedroom door, opened it, and walked into the hallway. He looked back at Lisa, who was looking dumbfounded.

"Don't worry, girl, the first time is never good for a girl. It'll get better for you; you just need practice." Chance closed the door behind him and she heard his footsteps go down the hallway and out of her front door. She didn't want to walk him to the door naked, but as soon as she heard the front door close, she jumped up.

Lisa ran to her bathroom down the hall. She didn't notice anything different about her house, just herself. She felt a bit of a loss of pride in herself. She didn't know if she should be disappointed in herself or forgiving. After all, she felt that she had been pressured into allowing those juvenile delinquents into her home. *Where was Kelly*, she thought.

As she was washing herself up, her doorbell rang. She ran to her room, put her clothes back on, and looked through the peephole to see Kelly standing at the door, alone. She opened the door and did not like Kelly instantly, for leaving her alone with such an aggressive monster.

"Damn, girl, you was getting it in, huh?" Kelly walked in, laughing.

"He basically forced me," Lisa replied, and Kelly got defensive.

"What? What you trying to say, he raped you or some shit? 'Cause that ain't Chance's style. Chance gets all types of pussy, so if you ain't want to fuck him, you shouldn't have."

"Uh, Kelly, you are the one who wanted them to come here. I didn't say he raped me. I'm just saying that it's obvious that all he wanted to do was get in my pants." Lisa was agitated, but she held her composure.

"All right, well, you better be clear on what you are saying because you coulda told me not to go to the store; you ain't gonna blame me now." Kelly was acting way too defensive and Lisa didn't yet understand why.

"Damn, girl, I was just saying. I should have seen it coming." Lisa walked back downstairs and started studying with Kelly, but she couldn't focus. Not only had she sold herself short, she had also not protected herself. She tried to keep

her mind on her studies and Kelly could tell that she was upset. She decided to act as if she was concerned. She knew that
once the robbery was found out, Lisa would suspect that she
had something to do with it.

"Girl, listen. Boys will be boys. The earlier you experience that, the better off you will be. You don't want to learn
that as a grown woman. Chance is a 'hood nigga, but he ain't
as bad as people think he is."

"I just thought they wanted to come and hang out. I
didn't know he was gonna try and have sex with me." Lisa
wanted answers from Kelly and Kelly had to spare her the
truth.

"Well, was it that bad? I heard he's good in bed. If you
gonna have a first, why not have a stud? At least you have
bragging rights." Kelly playfully pushed Lisa to make her feel
better and Lisa smiled. She hadn't thought about it that way.

They finished studying and Kelly left.

Chance, Star, and Sparks got a ride with Star's older
sister to the mall. They were going to use the credit cards that
were in Lisa's mother's name and they needed a female adult
to represent the card owner. They went to MACY*S department store and ran up the card there. They each got clothes
for themselves, including items for Kelly and Star's sister,
Daphne. They never accompanied Kelly to the register and
she had on a wool cap and shades for the cameras. She did not
have a record and her facial features were covered. There
would be no way for the police to identify her if they did an
investigation at the mall, which does not always happen.

They then went to Paterson, to the 'hood, to buy electronics with the MasterCard that Sparks had found. They
each picked the latest gadget that was a must-have. Beepers
were the new trend and they wanted to be ahead of the game,
so all four of them got one. They always had to be the youngest in the streets with all the new fads first.

Roderick had trained them well on how to live an underground life and conduct business in the "illegal world."

Chapter 2

L isa's parents came home and her mom immediately started cooking dinner. Lisa was nervous, knowing that she had done something that would upset and disappoint her parents. She had always made them proud. The family ate dinner and talked about their day, as they did daily.

"Don't you have a test tomorrow?" Lisa's mother, Evelyn, asked her.

"Yes, Mom. I had a friend from school come and study with me today." Lisa felt that if she told part of the truth, it would be better than hiding all of it.

"Oh, that's nice. How come we haven't met her? You need to start making more friends. You have to have some fun, too." Lisa's strict father shook his head in disagreement.

"She's fine just the way she is. She doesn't have time to fool around with these lowlife kids in the neighborhood. Let her get her education, graduate from college, and then play when she makes a six-figure salary." He patted his mouth with a napkin.

They finished eating, watched the news together, and Lisa excused herself to her room. She took an early shower. She didn't know how to feel. As she was putting her pajamas on, her mother startled her by yelling her name. "Lisa! Get in here right now!"

Lisa rushed into her mother's room and her parents were standing there, looking angrier than she had ever seen.

"Who is the girl that you had in this house?" her father asked, shaking with fury.

"Her name is Kelly, Dad. What happened, Mom?" Lisa was clueless.

"My jewelry is missing and the only reason I didn't wear my wedding band and engagement ring today was because I was rushing this morning; now they are gone! Who is this girl and where does she live?" Lisa couldn't imagine when Kelly could have stolen the jewelry because she was in her presence the whole time Kelly was there. She then thought about Chance. He was in her presence the whole time, too.

"Lisa, answer me! Where does the girl live?"

"Mom, she was with me the whole time. There wasn't any time that she wasn't in my presence." Lisa kept thinking about it and Star stayed in the family room and then left with Lisa. She had jumped up right after Chance left, so he couldn't have possibly had the chance to go across the hall to her parents' room without her seeing him. Her father began to search through his drawer to see if there was anything missing from there as well.

"Goddammit! The money I had for the light bill is gone! It was right here in my drawer. He kept rummaging through the drawer and then began to frantically search. "My watch! The watch that my father gave me; it's not in here!" They both looked at Lisa.

"I don't know where she lives, but I will talk to her tomorrow. I really don't think she did it, though," Lisa said, sorrowfully. She couldn't figure it out, but deep down, she knew that all three of them had something to do with her parents' belongings being stolen.

Lisa's father began to search through the house with her mother. She heard her mother scream, "My credit cards are missing, too!" She heard her father calling the Teaneck Police Department. Lisa was scared. She didn't want to be questioned and then slip up. She was not going to say anything about Chance or Star. She was going to keep saying that Lisa stayed in her presence the whole time. That's all she could say. She sure couldn't say that she had two thugs in her house.

The police came and started taking fingerprints. They noticed that the back door was unlocked. They began questioning Lisa and it seemed that they didn't buy her story.

"So, you're saying that you had a friend here to study, but you don't know how your back door got unlocked, right?" Lisa shook her head and then said yes after being reprimanded by her father for not saying "yes" instead of nodding her head. The detective continued questioning her.

"Did you know that there are teenage boys in Teaneck, who seduce unsuspecting girls into going into their bedrooms, while their friends go in and rob them? You're not the only young girl who's had company and then, all of a sudden, her house is robbed right under her nose." Lisa stared blankly at the officer. She didn't want him to read into her thoughts and see her disappointment in herself for allowing herself to be tricked and played. She believed that Kelly knew all along what Chance and Star were going to do. She figured that Chance must have unlocked her back door when he went to the bathroom and that maybe Star came in when they were in her room. The light bulb went off in her head, *they did it while he was having sex with me.* A tear almost came to her eye, but she had to push it back so they wouldn't see her guilt.

"Young lady, I don't know whether you set your parents up to be robbed or not. You seem like a good girl, from a good home. You need to get that girl's name and number tomorrow and give it to your parents. We will handle the rest. We will tell her that your house was robbed and that we must ask her some questions. We may be able to crack her. It's not your job to interrogate her or accuse her. Remain her friend, just get her number so that we can call her parents and have them bring her to the station. Now, if you do not do that, you might have to answer a few more questions yourself."

The detectives left and Lisa's parents continued to drill her. She stuck to her story, but promised herself that she would at least get Kelly's number because someone who would do what Kelly did to her, would never be considered a friend in her eyes.

 17

The next day at school, Lisa found it hard to pretend that she was not furious at Kelly. She spoke to her, though, as if nothing happened.

"Girl, I bet you dreamed about Chance all night," Kelly laughed, which made Lisa's blood boil.

"How do you know; did you ever sleep with him?" Kelly's face gave away the positive answer.

"Hell no, he's just cool," Kelly lied.

"Yeah, right. You probably did. But, anyway, let's hang out sometimes. What's your number?" Lisa asked. Kelly hesitated, but didn't want Lisa to get suspicious that she was all of a sudden not trying to be her friend, after acting like she had wanted to be. Kelly didn't know what the status of the robbery was, or if Lisa's parents were aware of being robbed yet, so she had to play along. She gave Lisa her house number. Lisa wanted to tell her that she knew Kelly had let her house get robbed, but the detectives had forbidden her from saying anything.

By the time Kelly got home, the detectives were waiting for her. Her mother had let them in to wait for Kelly to return home from school. They questioned her, but she did not give them any information about the robbery. She stuck to her story that she went to Lisa's, studied, and went home. She was not going to give up Chance, Star, or Sparks. The police were going to have to do their jobs; she had no intention of doing it for them.

The police spoke to Lisa's neighbors and most of them were not home from work at the time in question when they could have seen any of the boys coming out of Lisa's house. They were awaiting the credit card company's report to see if they could find out where and who had used Lisa's mom's credit card.

After the mall, Chance went to Star, Roderick, and Daphne's parents' house where Star and Daphne lived, after dropping Sparks off at home. Chance did not allow Sparks to go on night jobs with them and Roderick; he only let his brother do petty robberies. Chance and Star were still learning the ins and outs from Roderick who had a crew his age, in their mid-twenties, who did local burglaries. They ate dinner with their parents and then Chance and Star left with Roderick in his car. They drove to a home in a nearby town.

All three men got out and Chance and Roderick stood, hidden behind two different trees. Star rang the doorbell and planned to pretend to be looking for a classmate's home should someone answer. No one answered and Chance walked around the house to see if there were lights on, or if someone could be in the bathroom. He made sure that no one was home.

Roderick came around the back and burst through the back door. They all ran in. Roderick had his stopwatch on and they only had 10 minutes to work. Roderick led the two boys through the house, showing them hiding places and how to move quickly, in and out, to rob a house. They took mental notes on how to move and common mistakes that people make with their possessions.

There were a few modest pieces of jewelry, which they took, and only a hundred dollars cash on a bedroom table. As they were about to look in another bedroom on the ground level, Roderick spotted a pocketbook on the kitchen table and figured that the owner must not have been too far-maybe at a neighbor's house or walking a dog. As he grabbed the purse, they heard the front door open and they all bombarded the back door and ran through it as the homeowner was screaming behind them. They split up and ran through backyards to get to Roderick's car, which was parked around the corner.

Roderick took off and crossed into another town quickly, knowing that the city of Bergenfield would be sending out a few patrol cars to the woman's surrounding streets. Star searched through the pocketbook finding nothing of value in it, besides credit cards, which would not be able to be used as the owner was probably calling the companies to report them stolen at the same time. Roderick pulled over to a garbage can and Star disposed of the bag.

Chance is dropped off with his clothes from the mall and new pager. He goes into the small apartment where he, his mom, and his younger sister and brother reside. His mom is in the kitchen, cooking, with a half bottle of gin on the table. He walks in and takes his bags straight to his room that he shares with Sparks. He comes back into the kitchen, puts 200 dollars in her back pocket, and sits at the table.

"What's up, Ma? You drank that whole half a bottle *today*?" Chance's mother, Vonetta, turns around, flashes a big smile at Chance, and shakes her head no. She counts the money, smiles, and puts it back in her pocket.

"Good, the light bill is due," she says, cheerfully.

"I know you lying, Ma, that bottle wasn't in here yesterday. I'll give you some more money in a couple of days for the rent. Did you hear back from that job yet?" Chance asks as Vonetta turns back around to continue cooking and, again, shakes her head no.

"What? The cat got your tongue or you don't want me to hear how slurred your voice is?" Chance jokes, and his mother cracks up laughing.

Chance is the oldest of Chante, who is 16, and Sparks, whose real name is Corey, who is 15. They have only been living in New Jersey for a year because his mom fled an abusive boyfriend. Chance entered their home in Brooklyn one day, interrupting a fight that his mom and boyfriend were having, and pulled out a gun on him. His mother knew that eventually Chance would probably kill her ex, Jonny, so she moved the family to New Jersey to avoid her son going to prison for murder, and to give them a better life in the suburbs. Teaneck, New Jersey was only 10 minutes from Manhattan and a place where many black families who "moved on up" migrated to.

Vonetta had a long existing dependency on heroin and was trying to kick the drug for good. Her husband, Chance's biological father, was serving a life sentence for murder when he died after a gang fight.

"Ma, you know you gotta get a job to keep you busy. It'll help you get your life together and stay off that damned shit." Chance was more like his mother's brother than her son. He had seen so much drama, even as a toddler, but he loved his mother very much and did not judge her. She had her problems, but she was a loving mother. She did not ever neglect her children. She did the best she could, considering their life's circumstances.

"I'm trying, Chance. I know I'm not gonna find anything out here in Jersey. These people are bourgeoisie. They don't like city people, even though most of them came over here from the city and forgot where they came from." His mother stirred the rice and took a sip of her drink.

"Bourgeoisie or bougie people are stuck-up. They think they are better than others. They are a part of socialites who put on airs because of their degrees or job titles. The black people who were educated enough to become professionals who turn their backs on their relatives that are still in the ghetto, struggling." Vonetta shook her head and began to make the dinner plates.

"I know what you mean, Ma. You talkin' about Uncle Harry and Aunt Jennifer. You know when we go to their house we can't hardly sit in their living room. We gotta go downstairs, but when they have their club meetings, all those people get to sit on their good couches." Chance's mother shook her head in agreement.

Chance continued, "So, what, Mom, fuck 'em. I'm gonna make sure you are comfortable one day. You gonna have a nice house, too, don't even sweat it." Chance got up, hugged Vonetta, and helped her make the plates for his siblings.

"Chante and Corey, come and eat!" Chance beckoned them to come to the kitchen for dinner from their rooms. He didn't mind playing the father figure. His family was all he had and he took care of them.

His siblings came running in, pushing each other and joking about something that had happened at school that day. They both went to Teaneck High School and were a sophomore and junior.

"Hey, stop playing in the kitchen!" Chance shouted before his mother could. She shook her head and smiled on the inside that her son was so concerned with his family's well-being. She placed the plates on the table and they all sat down.

"Chante, say the grace," Chance ordered. They all folded their hands and waited.

"Lord, I like living in Jersey. It's clean out here and there's not drug addicts laying on the streets. We don't have a pissy hallway in this building and it's not the projects. I like only having 12 families living in a building…" She was interrupted by Corey.

"Hurry up, I'm hungry," he said, and Chance told him to shut up and let Chante finish. Chante continued.

"Lord, thank you. Thank you that we got away from Jonny and that Mommy is getting herself together. Thank you for this clean apartment building in a clean neighborhood with nice houses around it. Lord, thank you for this food. Please don't let anything bad happen; we are starting a new life. Amen."

They all said amen, ate, and talked. When they were done, they all went into the living room to watch their favorite show, Benson, together as a family. They had their laughs and when the show was over, Chance got ready for the rest of his night.

Chance had already robbed three homes in one day, taken a girl's virginity, gone shopping at the mall, enjoyed family time at home, and it was only 10 o'clock at night. The rest of his night would be even more adventurous.

Roderick, Star, and their brother, Malcolm, honked the horn at 11:30 and waited for Chance to come outside. They were going to an after-hour gambling spot in New York to gamble, get high, and try to sell some of the stolen property that Roderick had acquired from the last couple of days' robberies.

New Jersey was quiet and the streets were empty. They crossed over the George Washington Bridge into Harlem, New York, "the city that never sleeps". The streets were alive and bustling with danger, trouble, and fun. They joined the people who still conducted business after hours in an underground world that existed apart from what is called "normal life".

Roderick parked on 145th St. and 8th Ave. Their first stop was an after-hours gambling and drug den called T&T,

which had everything that men loved to live on. Chance and Star ordered drinks and sat at a table, while Roderick and Malcolm went in the back to speak to the "money man" who purchased all the stolen goods he chose, for resale purposes, of course. They had stereos, the baseball collection, the jewels, and Lisa's grandfather's watch, along with other items that were sentimental to the owners that lost them in their robberies.

On this particular night, Teddy Thomas, the buyer and owner of the "spot", was agitated and uninterested. He didn't want anything but the antique watch.

"What's the matter with the rest of these jewels, man? Why you don't want them?" Roderick asked, since he was the one that always sold the stolen property, while Malcolm was the muscle who stood quietly and ready for any altercations.

"Listen, muthafucka, the house just lost 10,000 to a wise-cracking punk out there. I'm not spending no money on shit tonight 'til somebody takes a loss to the house. Be glad I'm getting this shit here for my grandfather. It looks like something he may have had in his time, so here." He threw a hundred dollar bill on the table and reached for the watch. Roderick gave the nod that signaled Malcolm to get involved.

Malcolm slapped his hand on top of Teddy's and suddenly Teddy rang a buzzer that immediately alerted two ex-cons who were a part of security to come busting through the door. Teddy put his hand up for them to wait to make a move.

"Listen, Teddy, you ain't gotta do all that. We do business all the time and you know I'm not trying to fuck wit' you, man, but, come on, a hundred for an antique watch? Why you tryin' to rob me, man?" Malcolm slowly removed his hand from on top of Teddy's and Teddy took his hand off the watch, leaving the money and the watch next to each other on the table.

"What did I just tell you, man? I just forfeited 10 Gs, man, about 10 minutes ago."

"Yeah, but that's an heirloom, man. You know that watch gotta be worth thousands, Mr. Thomas. I can't take a hundred for that. I got four guys to pay for that job. I can't take it, man. If you don't want it, I understand." Roderick reached to get the "Old Timer's" watch and Mr. Thomas pulled out a wad of cash, counted 900 more dollars, and put it on top of the one.

"Thank you, Mr. Thomas. I'm gonna go put some of this on the table and maybe lose a couple hundred for the house." Roderick and Malcolm walked out the door of the back office and over to Chance and Star, who were on their second drink.

"Yo, he ain't want none of this shit. Hold the duffel bag," Roderick instructed Star and Chance.

"Yo, Roderick, get us a 50 of coke, man," Chance requested, in more of a statement than a question.

"Y'all niggas got money. Go see Papoose; he in the side room." Roderick began to walk away. Chance stopped him.

"So, he, Mr. T, ain't buy jack from you, man?" Chance challenged, knowing that Roderick was always trying to be slick because he and Star were younger. He would get over on them whenever he could.

"He got that old bullshit watch," Roderick answered, agitated.

"So, what's up? Where's our loot? That was me, Star, and Sparks on that joint." Chance was not scared of Roderick like Star was of his older brother, so he usually did the talking for them.

"Y'all little niggas better go 'head." Roderick again attempted to walk away.

Chance stood up. Roderick was a tower compared to Chance's height. His size was intimidating. He wasn't tall, dark, and handsome; he was big, black, and ugly. Roderick was 6'4" tall and 265 pounds, compared to Chance, who was 5'10" and 225 pounds. But, Chance had the heart of a lion and the roar to match. He would cut someone if he had to. He believed in the motto, "The bigger they are, the harder they fall."

"Yo, Roderick, give me my money for me and my brother. If your brother wanna let you play him like a sucker, then that's on him." Roderick was in no way intimidated by Chance, but he knew that Chance would fight dirty, and he also knew that they didn't know how much money he had gotten for the watch. Chance and Sparks were supposed to get the biggest cut, $700, and Star and Roderick should be splitting the remaining $300. Roderick took the knot out of his pocket, peeled off 400, gave it to Chance, and went over to the Craps table.

Chance put the money in his pocket and Star got mad.

"Yo, where's mine, man?" he asked, expecting money from Chance.

"You better go ask your scheming ass brother. I asked for me and Sparks' money. I'll buy you a package, though. Here's 80; go get us two forties." Chance put the rest of the money back in his pocket. He was freshly dipped in Ralph Lauren and a new pair of Jordan sneakers.

Star went and got the coke and came back with two foil packets. They had another two drinks brought to them by the barely dressed waitresses, in charge of their section. The place was dimly lit and decorated with cheap, old furniture. It was not a luxurious or finely furnished establishment. It was a hole in the wall. A place where grimy activities were performed.

Teaneck, New Jersey was supposed to be the escape from the trouble of the big city life, but it had only been the initiator of Chance's criminal life. Chance had never robbed anyone or used hard drugs until moving to the suburbs of New York City. He had only smoked weed when he lived in New York, but New Jersey was a place where privilege opened the door for more exposure to bad things. Ever since meeting Star and his brothers, Chance had been introduced to burglarizing homes and sniffing cocaine. It was more opportunity to do more negative things, in Chance's case.

Chance took a matchbook off the table and folded it in half. He used it to scoop some of the powder from the foil envelope, transferred it to his nose, and then sniffed it into his system. He immediately felt the rush of euphoria that is short-lived and makes a cocaine user want more. Star began to use his package as well. In minutes, they were feeling the effects and talking a mile a minute.

"Chance, my brother's over there winning money off my money, man." Star was scared of his eldest brother and Chance laughed at him.

"I'm glad I got my money. Nigga, you soft. Your brother is always gonna do that to you until you stand up to him."

They stayed in the gambling spot until three in the morning. Roderick was drunk and high off cocaine, like the rest of them. He was driving recklessly back to New Jersey when a police officer noticed the four black men in a car that was swerving into other lanes.

"Woop! Woop!" They heard and all got shook. No one turned around to see the police car that they knew was there. They were all high and out of sorts. They could see the lights flashing behind the car, Roderick panicked, and started driving faster as Malcolm dumped the cocaine that he had into the floor and rubbed his feet in the carpet to make it disappear. The four hard-core criminals were as shook as children about to get a beating by their parents. Chance turned around and noticed that a second police car had joined the pursuit.

They were speeding across the George Washington Bridge with the Port Authority Police and now the Fort Lee Police on their tails. Chance started hollering at Roderick and banging on his headrest from the seat he sat in behind him.

"Yo, pull the fuck over! You know these Jersey cops will be ready to shoot this car up! Fuck it, nigga, we going to jail tonight!"

"I got shit in the car!" Roderick screamed back.

"Shit like what? Malcolm got rid of the coke!" Chance kept looking behind them, hoping not to see guns come out of the windows.

"I got stolen property in the trunk!" Roderick looked in the rearview mirror to see how close the, now four, cars were to them.

"Fuck it, man! Pull over!" Malcolm said. Roderick listened because Malcolm normally never said much.

The car came to a complete halt and the four black men were surrounded by one black, one Hispanic Port Authority cops and four white Fort Lee officers. They had their guns drawn.

"Get out of the car!" All of them yelled.

The four men piled out and were grabbed and thrown to the ground and handcuffed.

"Officer, why are we being handcuffed? What did we do?" Star asked, humbly.

"Well, for one, your driver will be charged with eluding police. Why didn't you pull over?" the officer yelled at Roderick, who had a crazed, paranoid look on his face. When they noticed his eyes that seemed poked out of his eye sockets, they detected that he was under the influence of drugs.

"What's the matter, buddy?" the white officer asked. "You been flyin' on a kite tonight?" The other officers laughed as Roderick buried his head in the ground.

"Can you tell us why we were stopped?" Chance asked, raising his head off the ground.

"I suggest you be quiet and let us ask the questions," another officer responded.

The four of them were lifted up to stand and were each placed separately in the back each of the four police cars. They watched in awe as the car was stripped and the stolen items were taken out of the trunk. One officer must have noticed the residue of the drugs in the floor mat because the floor mat was also removed and bagged for evidence.

Chance watched and began to think about his father. He hadn't ever had the chance to know his father because he had been in prison since Chance was very young, and then he died there. Chance finally felt a connection to his dad. He was not ashamed, but proud. He felt like he was about to get his stripes, as if he was about to become a man.

The white officer driving Chance returned to the car and began to taunt him.

"Hey. You guys must work at Sotheby's, huh?" the officer laughed.

"Yeah, we do," Chance answered, sarcastically.

"Nigger, you probably don't even know what Sotheby's is," the officer answered, angrily.

"Nigga, yes, I do. It's an auction house where they sell expensive shit for rich people. And I work there." Chance was not intimidated by the police. He knew that, as a black man, he would always be on the other side of the law, whether he was breaking it or not.

"I suggest you watch who you are talking to. I can always add more charges to your jacket." The officer turned around and looked directly into Chance's eyes with disgust.

"Whatever you say, officer," Chance responded and smiled.

The four men were taken to the Fort Lee Police Department. It was five o'clock in the morning when they reached there and, by 10 in the morning, Star was taken to the juvenile detention center in Paramus, NJ. Chance, Roderick, and Malcolm were taken to the Bergen County Jail Annex.

Roderick received most of the charges because he was driving and it was his car. He was charged with driving while under the influence, eluding police, drug possession, and receiving stolen property. He was even charged with endangering a minor because he Star, 17, was in the car. The charges were trumped up so that they could at least guarantee some jail time, in case some of the charges didn't stick.

The prosecutor contacted the adjoining localities to inquire about recent burglaries. The woman whose house they had robbed identified her pieces of jewelry as well as Roderick, Chance, and Star. The homeowners in Teaneck where the baseball cards were stolen from also identified their cards. Finally, Lisa's parents were able to get her mother's engagement ring and wedding band back.

Roderick's friend, Jason, bailed him out. His bail was set at 50,000 dollars. He got out and bailed Malcolm out, who really had no charges but was being held under suspicion of conspiracy to commit burglary. Roderick's parents picked up Star. Chance had to remain in the annex for a few days until his mother could convince her brother, a school superintendent, to put up the bail money for him.

When Chance got out, Roderick returned the money to Chance's Uncle Harry. Star and Chance were being held on a $1000 bail, with minor charges. There was not much that they could be charged with except juvenile delinquency, but Roderick influenced them to take some of the weight, because they were minors and would not receive the stiff sentence that Roderick would for the stolen property. Chance and Star were found guilty of burglarizing the homes and possession of the stolen property.

A couple of months after their arrests, Chance and Star were sentenced to 18 months in two separate prison camps. Chance was sent to Pennsylvania to a prison camp in Lewisburg, PA, which is about an hour and a half from Teaneck, and Star went to Bordentown, which is in South Jersey. This is when their lifetime of going in and out of prison began.

Chapter 3

Chance sat in the courtroom while the judge sentenced him to 18 months at Lewisburg. He showed no emotion and the judge noticed his arrogance.

"Young man, I hope you use this as a lesson. I hope to never see you in my courtroom again." Chance shrugged his shoulders and smirked.

"Your Honor, I'm just a black man trying to make a dollar out of 15 cents," he said, sarcastically.

Judge Warner, a black man himself, was disappointed in Chance's attitude, but it was something that he saw very often from misguided black youth who were bucking a system that they felt had it out for them. He knew the frustration that Chance probably felt, but he also knew that it was a cop out.

"Young man, let me tell you something. In this life, you make your own way. You make choices that no one can make for you. No one told you to choose a life of crime instead of being a young scholar. My parents were both dead by the time I was 15. I went from foster home to foster home. I made the choice to be a judge, not a loser. You may think you are a man now, but you will be when you return home to your mother. I hope you will change your direction before you ruin the rest of your life."

Chance remained quiet, but did not take heed. He turned around to see his mother, brother, and sister behind him. His mother and sister were crying. He winked at her and fought back a lonely tear that wanted to fall, not for himself, but for his family. He knew they needed him, but he had to go and become a man. He had to pay his dues.

Sparks looked scared, but tried to look strong. Chance saw right through the bravado that his little brother was trying to exhibit. Sparks knew that he was going to have to take his brother's place; he just didn't know how he would be able to do it. He fought back the tears that he wanted to shed.

Chance was led out of the courtroom in handcuffs. Vonetta and her children followed him out, and the officer taking him to the bus for transport to Lewisburg allowed them to hug Chance before letting him go to deal with the consequences of his actions.

Chance was put on the bus, which had about 20 other teenage boys from different towns, backgrounds, and criminal activities. Out of the 20, most were black, then Hispanic, and then there were four white teenagers on the bus as well. They were all going to camp and many of them thought of the situation as a vacation and not a punishment. To them, it was part of the game of crime. *You do the crime, do your time, and come back and start all over again.*

Chance sat alone and looked out of the window. He wondered what it would be like. He wasn't scared; he just wanted to get it done.

"Yo, why you going to Lewisburg?" a black boy in the seat in front of him turned around and asked.

"For robbing houses," Chance answered, flatly.

"Word? Damn, nigga, that's cool. Shit, I was only stealing cars. You was bold to go up in a muthafucka's shit? Peace, I'm Mellow." The two boys nodded heads since their handcuffs did not allow them to shake hands.

"Where you from?" Chance asked.

"Newark. You know, the grand theft auto capitol of New Jersey. We learn to steal cars from the age of five." The boys laughed.

"This your first time? How old are you?" Chance immediately liked Mellow; his persona seemed comedic. Chance knew he would need comic relief while he was there, so he would try Mellow out for friendship. He was interested in Mellow's story.

"I'm 16, but I'm really 25. I been on my own since I was like, 12. My mom is in prison and my dad is cracked out. I steal cars to eat. This my third time doin' a bid and it won't be my last," Mellow joked. Chance shook his head.

"This my first one." Chance really did not know how to feel about it. He had already dropped out of school, so it wasn't like he was missing his chance to get ready for college. He really had no plans for his future. He was just taking it one day at a time.

"Well, where you from?" Mellow probed.

"I live in Teaneck, but I just moved over to Jersey from Brooklyn." Chance thought about his life in Brooklyn and, even with going to a prison camp, it was better than being in the projects where death seemed to lurk and threaten everywhere someone went. There were plenty of nights that Chance would wake up to gunshots and hear about the murder of someone he knew the next morning. Where he was at that moment in his life felt safe for him.

"Oh. Teaneck is where all them rich, professional blacks live. The white-collars. Newark got the blue-collars. Your family got money?" Mellow asked.

"Nah, my mom moved here because I have a rich uncle who told her she needed to move me and my brother and sister out here for a better life. But, she can't find no job and the nigga ain't trying to help us. That suburb shit looks good, but if you ain't got money, you just a poor nigga around people that got so much more than you. And it makes you want to get it any way you can." Chance wished that he had the upbringing that his cousins, Uncle Harry's kids, had been born into. They had both of their parents, who were professionals with good jobs, a nice home, and no domestic violence. Chance had been born into a life of minuses, while they had all the plusses that a child needs to have a good head start in life.

"Yeah, at least in Newark, everybody is poor and struggling in the 'hood. But, that don't stop us from wanting to get it anyway we can, too. Shit, it's the American myth of having the American dream. It was all a dream..." Mellow said, re-citing the line from the Biggie Smalls song.

Chance continued the line, "I used to read Word Up magazine..."

The continued together, "Salt and Pepa and Heavy D up in the limousine, hangin' pictures on my wall, every Saturday Rap Attack, Mr. Magic, Marley Marl. Way back..." They were interrupted by the officer manning the bus.

"Hold it down! This ain't no party!" The rest of the boys, along with Chance and Mellow, started rebelling and complaining about why they couldn't just sing a damned song, until the officer stood up with his taser, ready to shock someone into submission and use them as an example to calm down the rest of the rowdy bunch. They all quickly became extremely quiet for the rest of the ride.

"Yo, these cops kill me. You would think we was in the Civil Rights Movement. I'm surprised he ain't bring out a water hose, " Mellow whispered to Chance and Chance nodded his head in agreement.

Chance fell asleep for the rest of the ride and was awakened by the nudge of the officer to get off of the bus. It was hard to walk in the shackles that were on his legs and he was glad that they came off once he got inside of the secured detention center.

The housing unit was not like prison with individual cells. There were large rooms, like cabins, where 20 boys each slept. Chance was sent to Cabin C and was glad that Mellow was sent to the same location.

They received an orientation of what their days would entail. Their day consisted of school, chores, and two hours of television and game time before their six o'clock dinner, cleaning detail, and bedtime at 9 p.m. After dinner and clean-up, they had another hour of recreation before bed.

Chance was not used to that amount of structure or discipline. He was a grown man in a teenager's body. He made his own rules and did what he wanted to do. He was the head of his household. Now, he was a ward of the state.

The first day was the worst. Chance was angry that he had agreed to take the weight for Roderick, but he knew that

Roderick hadn't forced him to begin robbing houses. Chance and Star had begged to learn the "business". He also knew that he wasn't innocent. He had taken some of the property that Roderick's trunk contained and Roderick still had to serve time, two years, for the other charges that he had been found guilty of. He knew that they would all be getting out around the same time. He was glad that they all would do their part and that it didn't just fall on one of them. Malcolm even had to serve a year because he had violated his parole for being in the car with stolen property and drugs.

The second day, Chance was awakened at the required wake up time of 6:45 a.m. He wanted to curse someone out.

"Easy, partner," Mellow warned. "You can't be getting infractions for having a smart mouth. It ain't worth it. They will use the littlest thing to take away your privileges."

"What privileges? Shit, I feel like I'm in kindergarten. Shit, I can't imagine what prison must be like."

"Aw, man, it's gotta be a hell of a lot more fun!" Mellow joked, and Chance shook his head, laughing.

By the second week, Chance had accepted the reality of his circumstance and decided to just deal with it.

Chance and Mellow went to the cabin where breakfast would be served. They were able to walk the grounds freely because there was nowhere for them to get lost and officers to oversee their every move. The grounds were open, but they were in the middle of nowhere.

"Yo, it's so open, though. We could probably bounce if we wanted to," Chance observed.

"Trying to escape would be like choosing to go tempt a coyote to have your ass for dinner, man. Don't even think about it. The bars are invisible, but they are there. They will have a shotgun crew out for you in no time," Mellow warned.

As they were getting in line to eat, a boy bumped Chance. Chance turned around and put his hands up.

"What's up, nigga? You don't know how to watch where you walk?" The boy threw a punch at Chance and they started throwing blows. Within seconds, four officers were separating them and taking them to a cabin that Chance had never been in before.

They sat the two down and the other boy, named Stacy, said that Chance had stolen his snacks the night before. Chance denied the accusation. He knew the boy was just trying to get off the hook.

There was no proof that Chance had stolen anything, but he was charged with an infraction of fighting. Because it was his first offense, he only had to stay in the isolation cabin for a week. He was confined to a small room with no windows, a bed, a toilet, and a sink, similar to a jail cell, without the bars. He used the bit of money he had in his account to buy some paper to write letters.

Chance missed breakfast that day. He lay on his cot until lunchtime, just thinking. He drifted off to sleep and began to dream.

Slam! The door to his project apartment closed and he heard two voices.

"Why are you doing this, Charles? Why are you putting us in harm's way?" The voice was Vonetta's. Chance got out of his bed, looked in the other bed, and saw little brother sleeping. He tiptoed into the living room and peeked in. He saw his father counting a lot of money on the coffee table.

"What the hell are you talking about? I am making sure we have dinner on the table," Chance's father replied.

"But, Charles, you can't rob from people you know. Those men are in the mafia. They will come after you." Vonetta was crying.

"They won't know it was me. This is not your concern. Just get dressed and go to the market and get some food for my kids to eat." Charles put the money together and gave Vonetta half of the pile. He then took the gun from the inside of his jacket and hid it on the top of the China cabinet.

Chance was awakened by the opening of the wood door of the cabin that contained him. The officer brought in a tray of what looked like mush. It was slop: beans, corn, and what was supposed to be meat loaf. The meat loaf looked like it had been made weeks before. Chance ate the corn and stale, hard roll and left the tray by the door. The tray remained by the door for about an hour, while Chance tried to write a letter to his mother. He was starving and his stomach was knotting up from the hunger. He put his pen down, picked the tray back up from the floor, and forced the cold, disgusting food down. He almost threw up three times, trying to swallow. He put the empty tray back by the door and went back to his letter. It read...

Dear Momma,
It's so boring here. I have to work on the field. I clean the grounds and stuff. It's not like prison. There's no bars. It's a big campground with cabins, but it's like living like a pilgrim. Everything is wood and shit. I get up early as hell and then I have to go to school and then I do my job. It's a lot of other towns and cities where these muhfuckas came from. I met one his name is Mellow he's from Newark. He's my boy. He is funny as hell. After we do our jobs, we get some time to ourselves and then we go to bed so early. I'm in isolation right now for fighting some crab nigga. He tried to say I stole his soap or some shit. What's up with y'all? I miss y'all. Keep your eye on Sparks, don't let him think he runnin' the house and shit. Don't let him be hanging out late and shit. Watch who his friends are. Chante don't be no problem. I know she is gonna do good in school and stuff. It's Sparks I'm worried about.
Mommy, I had a dream about you and Daddy. He had all this money. I think he had robbed somebody. I was little and I woke up and peeked in the living room and saw him counting all this money. And he put a gun up. Was that real, did that really happen or did my mind just make that up? I want to remember more stuff about him. I feel like him, in jail. It's some things that men just have to go through that women don't understand. Black men don't live the same type of life that white boys do when they are growing up. We gotta do what we gotta do to survive. Did you find a job yet? Don't worry; I will take care of the family when I get back home. Just get something to help you for now.
Write back to me and let me know what's going on. I love you, Mommy. Don't worry about me. This ain't the best thing but it's just boring, it ain't that bad. It is bad, but I can handle it. I want y'all to come see me soon.

Love, Chance

Chance put the letter in the envelope and addressed it. He wanted to see outside. He couldn't tell what time it was, if it was getting dark or already dark outside. He thought about what Star, Roderick, and Malcolm were doing at the same time. He was hoping that his brother, Sparks, was not going to start getting into trouble because he wasn't there to keep him under control.

He started thinking about the girls that he had been messing around with before getting into trouble. There was Janet. She had big titties that he loved to look at and rub on. He would go to her house when no one was home and make her walk around without a bra. She was a cute girl, too, but he didn't care about her looks. He just cared about the control he had over her. He could tell her to do anything and she would do it. She wasn't smart enough to really intrigue him beyond sex. She was one girl that would always be around to use at his disposal. Janet was good for looking at.

Then there was Kelly. She was similar to Janet. She was even more willing to follow his commands. Janet wouldn't be involved in setting up robberies or having sex with other boys for Chance, like Kelly would. Kelly didn't have as sexy a body, or as cute a face as Janet, which is why she was down for whatever. She was a wannabe. He could have sex with Kelly and then tell her to have sex with his other two friends and she would do it. Kelly was a girl that Chance would never admit to messing around with and she knew not to tell. Kelly was just a dumb whore.

Then there was Danielle. Danielle was a smart girl who came from a good home. Chance really liked Danielle and had respect for her. She was a girl that he dreamed of being good for. He did not want to mess over Danielle. He knew that he was no good for her, but she showed him a different life. She tried to take the time to inspire Chance. They had met in English class when he was in tenth grade. He immediately liked her when he heard her read a poem to the class. He fantasized about what it would be like to be able to get, and keep, a girl like Danielle. She was not the type to take anything from a boy just because she liked him. She had respect for herself, which made him admire her. They had sex one time and she told him that she couldn't be with him again, because she knew that he would hurt her.

Chance lay down and put his hands in his khakis to feel his manhood. First, he imagined Janet, walking around with her bra off. His dick got hard and he began to play with it. He then imagined Kelly having sex with him and his boys and he began to grope himself harder. He wanted to give himself time to think about Danielle. He imagined Danielle, with all of her clothes off, lying in her canopy bed, with her legs wide open, waiting for him to enter. Chance was ready to bust. He turned on his stomach and humped the bed as if he were humping Danielle. He began to ejaculate and humped until he was done cumming. Then, he drifted off to sleep.

The whole week consisted of Chance eating nasty food, masturbating, and daydreaming. He was bored out of his mind and was so happy to see light again at the end of the week. He walked out of isolation feeling 10 pounds lighter. It seemed like, when you were in isolation, they purposely brought you cold food.

After work, he returned to his cabin. He was happy to see Mellow.

"Yo, you made it, huh?" Chance and Mellow gave each other a pound.

"Yeah, I must have jerked off a thousand times, nigga; my sperm count gotta be on empty right now." They laughed.

"I want you to meet my man, Dex, from my 'hood." They walked over to the recreation room and Mellow introduced Dex and Chance. The three of them talked about their lives and talked about the rest of the boys in their cabin.

"Listen, you see that dark as night nigga right there? I heard that nigga molested his little cousin. He a fag. Nigga over here trying to play hard; he wears a skirt. Don't fuck with that nigga, they'll think you like balls in your butt." They clapped and laughed.

"And that big, sloppy nigga over there, his name Kee Kee. He ain't a nigga to fuck with. He got a big family out in Trenton and that's real close. There's about 10 of his family in here right now. They some crazy ass muhfuckas, just let that nigga be." Mellow knew all there was to know.

"Damn, nigga, you was doing a lot of work while I was in time-out," Chance joked.

"Yeah, you got to. I ain't trying to add no unnecessary time to this shit here. It's best to eat, do your job, and beat your meat until your time is up."

Chance took heeded that advice. He was not interested in school, so he would sit in the class and daydream. He never took his GED test because he didn't think it would matter. He did not intend to get a job. Jobs didn't bring in enough money for the lifestyle that Chance planned on leading.

Chance did his job on the campgrounds, enjoyed recreation time with Mellow and Dex, and looked forward to the visits from his mom and siblings that took place every other month. Janet came to visit with his family a few times and he snuck a few squeezes of her titties.

It was 1990 when he was sent home and the saga would continue.

1991
Chapter 4

Chance returned to Teaneck shortly before his 22nd birthday and was ecstatic to be home. He spent the first week catching up on the sex he couldn't get for 18 months. He made Sparks sleep on the couch in the living room while his mother's apartment door revolved with girls, in and out, paying him with their bodies to welcome him home. He had made sure that his sister, Chante, got in touch with the girls that he wanted to see two weeks before he came home, and got their numbers all ready for him to beckon them to his sex room.

The first day he was home, he called Kelly. He knew that he could wear her out for hours and hours and do whatever he wanted with her. She stayed at his mother's house for two days straight.

He called Janet as well and she came over and spent the next two nights. He felt like a maniac, trying to get as much pussy as he possibly could.

The fourth day, he called Danielle.

"Hey, pretty. I'm home." He didn't want to just ask her for sex. He wanted to know how she was doing.

"I know, I heard. My cousin told me that your sister had wanted my number and I was happy to hear that you were coming home. You know I'm away in college, right? I'm majoring in criminal law at Hampton University." Chance smiled when he heard that.

"Why, because of me?" Chance knew that Danielle had always really cared about him, but she cared more about herself to leave him alone.

"Yes. There are far too many of you out here." Danielle was always brutally honest with Chance, which he also loved and respected.

"What does that mean? You know they broke the mold when they made me, Dee Dee." Danielle's last name was Donalds and everyone called her Dee Dee.

"Chance. You have always been pessimistic about life. You have never given yourself a chance to see what doing good feels like. You feel that you have to be bad because you think that is the only way that you can be." He began not wanting to hear anymore of her truth, knowing how right she was.

"Danielle, you weren't raised like me." Chance was beginning to get offended.

"Chance, stop copping out. I hope to see you when I come home on break. Stay out of trouble, okay?" Chance got angry.

"If I do, will you represent me?" he asked, in his normal, sarcastic way.

"Yup, because I love you and I want you to have a good life." Danielle hung up. Chance wanted to call her back and ask her if she really meant that statement, but he knew that she did, just not the way he wanted. Danielle's love was a caring love. She didn't want to see anything bad happen to him. She didn't love him enough to be in his life and ruin her own.

Roderick and Star hadn't returned home at that point. They would be home within months, but Chance was ready for the streets. He got in touch with Jason, Roderick's friend, to find out what he'd been missing.

Jason picked Chance up and they rode around and talked. The business of robbing houses had been put on hold for Jason while he waited for Roderick and Malcolm to come home. There were other burglary crews, but Jason kept his loyalty to the brothers.

"Yeah, you know these Englewood niggas is trying to be like our crew. They starting to do B & Es, (Breaking and Enterings) too. And then, you know Marquise, Rock, and Po Po be goin' out on their own since Roderick left. I'm laying low right now. I'm gonna let them niggas get the shine and get caught up. They will get busted and get all the heat."

"Yeah, but when they go in, Roderick and Malcolm will come out and the cops will be looking at us all again," Chance responded. He had a good point.

"True. I mean I can't pinpoint when these niggas will fall, but the thing is to lay low for a minute. We gotta be better than them niggas, do it better. They got some tight cliques and they are getting it done. I'm not going to be envious and make no moves until my dawgs is back out here." Chance nodded his head in agreement.

"So, what you doing for money, then? I gotta eat." Chance was broke. He needed clothes and money to live.

"I got this chick. She holdin' me down right now. I give her this good tool and she takes care of me." Chance was surprised to hear that and looked stunned.

"You livin' off a woman, dude?" Chance shook his head.

"Why not? Fair exchange ain't never been robbery." Jason was a good-looking character. He had been a ladies' man from the age of 14. He was light-skinned with fine, curly hair, chinky eyes, and a smile that melted girls and women alike. He had "it".

"Let me introduce you to this chick. Her man just got locked up and left her with a whole bunch of stash money. Let me see if you can pull her. She likes young niggas and she will definitely spend that cash."

Jason drove to a nice house in Teaneck. There was a Benz and a Montero truck in the driveway. He and Jason looked at each other and smiled.

"Hey. I'm just putting you on to her, but you gotta do the work." They got out of the car and walked up her porch steps.

"How old is she, man?" Chance asked, feeling unusually nervous. He was never scared of anything, but he liked how the house and cars looked and he wanted to successfully achieve this feat. He was glad that Jason had given him the shot; now, he had to make sure he slam-dunked it.

"She's 32. She got three kids. Seven, 10, and 14. But, don't worry about that. Her husband had bookoo dough and he's doing life in prison. He was a big-time Harlem hustler. You know they all move out to Jersey when they hit it big. You better lasso this ho."

They both laughed as the woman came to the door. Chance gave her a look, up and down, and decided that looks didn't matter. She was not ugly; she just wasn't a beauty queen. She was a bit overweight, but she had a nice style. She was honey-brown with nice hair and a nice smile, but the stress of her situation with her husband was written all over her face. She looked like she had been through a lot and Chance knew that meant she would need some good loving to get her by. She opened the door, smiled at Jason, and then looked at Chance. She gave him the eye and that was all he needed to see.

"Hey, Jason. Damn, where you been? You said you was comin' by yesterday." She stepped to the side and let the two men in. She closed the door behind her and looked out of the window in her door to make sure no one was outside watching her house.

"Nadja, this is Chance. This is my man. I see you still all paranoid and shit." Jason made fun of Nadja. She again looked at Chance with wanting eyes before speaking.

"Hi, Chance. Nigga, you know the cops be trying to harass me and shit. Trying to intimidate me and sit outside my house, like I'm doing something wrong. They just mad 'cause they couldn't get a conviction on me, with my husband. But, he made sure I was never involved in any of his shit. Y'all hungry?"

Nadja took some food out of her refrigerator to heat up while they sat at her kitchen table.

"Y'all want lasagna?" Nadja began to make three plates as the two men nodded their heads yes. Chance was checking her out, waiting to start his attack.

"I hope you cook good because I need a girl who can cook." Jason winked at Chance. Nadja smirked and ignored his statement.

"So, Nadja, what happened with Dip?" Jason was pulling for information for Chance to overhear.

"Ain't shit. He got baby momma drama and I am not pressed. He moved back in with her last week." Nadja put the hot plates of food in front of Jason and Chance and sat down with her plate.

"So, that means that you are free and single to mingle?" Chance butted in and asked. Nadja looked into Chance's eyes.

"I sure am. I do what I want to do." Nadja put a forkful of lasagna in her mouth.

"So, what if I want to change that?" Chance asked.

"Why would you? I mean I don't know anything about you and you don't know anything about me. So, what? You see a nice house, two cars outside, and you think I'm an easy target because my husband is locked up?" Nadja had an attitude and was quick at the tongue, however, Chance was not intimidated. It only made him more ready for the kill.

"First of all, I do know about you. You are 32, you have three kids, your husband is locked up, you just broke up with a nigga that's trying to play you to the left, you sexy, and you look like you need someone to hold you. Now, as for me, I'm 21, I have no kids, I'm tired of these young, silly girls and I have nothing but time on my hands to make you feel loved. Why you? 'Cause you grown and you got style and you ain't got nobody right now, so why would I wait until you find another man to try my hand?"

Nadja was caught off guard. She didn't know that Chance would have the quick wit that she had. She did know that he looked good and she liked that he had no kids. He being young was a turn on-that he would even be interested in her. She had been married for 10 years and did not like being alone. She would give Chance a try; she just wouldn't let him think that it was going to be easy.

"You know, you Jersey cats kill me. Y'all really think you can outsmart city girls." Nadja smiled.

"I'm not a Jersey cat. I'm from Brooklyn." Chance responded.

"Oh, maybe that's why I immediately liked you. These Jersey niggas think they got more game then they really do." Nadja and Chance both laughed.

"Hey, what's all this shit here? Why New York muhfuckas always gotta try and rag on Jersey when this is the first place y'all run to when you get some cheddar?" Jason said, offended. "I'm tired of people always saying how Jersey is this and that, when all of us came over here from the same place. My parents were from the Bronx, so dead that bullshit."

"Damn, nigga, okay; we ain't mean to hurt your feelings," Nadja said, laughing.

"I'm about to blow this joint, Chance. Let's go." Jason got up and put his plate in the sink.

"I'm staying," Chance replied.

"Oh, nah, baby, you ain't. You can have my number, though, and we can do the phone thing for a minute so I can see where your head is really at. All that talk I've heard a million times before." Nadja wrote her number down on a piece of paper and gave it to Chance.

"Okay, I will call you, honey brown. I wanna spend some time with you."

"I bet you do." Nadja walked them to the door, and shut and locked it when they were outside.

Jason couldn't wait to get in the car to talk about Nadja.

"Yo, nigga, you in. I saw how she was looking at you and I thought she had you when she said you was only interested in her because of the house, but you was *The Comeback Kid* on that shit. You gets dap for that!" Jason gave Chance a handclap.

"Yeah, I'ma get that ass. I need a place to stay. I'm about to be 22; I can't be living with my moms and shit. I just did time. I'm a grown ass man."

"Oh, a'ight, I'll set you up with a hotel party. We'll get some stripper, hooker chicks to come and bless us with some good head and pussy and shit. I got you, homeboy." Jason pulls up to Chance's apartment building, gives him some more dap, and pulls off when Chance gets out.

Chance goes in his house and his mother is lying on the couch. No one else is home. He gets something to drink out of the refrigerator and is about to go in his room, but he notices that his mother is not sleeping, she is in a drugged stupor. She is nodding out and drooling. He snatches her up.

"Ma! What the fuck? I knew it! I knew it when you came to see me that you were getting high. You didn't look right. I just didn't want to ask because I couldn't handle the truth from in there. Why, Ma?" Vonetta is unaware of what's going on. She is in another world. Chance hugs her and begins to sob. He rocks his mother back and forth, not knowing what else to do. As he is sitting there on the couch, holding onto her, he begins to remember a day in Brooklyn that was similar to this one.

Sparks was sitting on the floor, crying, when Chance came in from school. His mother was lying on the floor. Chance ran over and noticed his mother's eyes rolling in the back of her head. He told Sparks to go and call a neighbor, Miss Rhonda, over. Miss Rhonda ran in the apartment and told the boys to get out. She made them go into the apartment with her kids. He remembers peeking out of the door and seeing the EMT workers taking his mother out on a gurney. He recalled his father and her female friend keeping them somewhere else for a couple of days. His mother had overdosed and his father kept the kids at his girlfriend's house until his mother's release. He remembered not liking the woman and thinking that she was mistreating him when his father was not there. The memory was very faint, but he did remember.

Chance came back to reality and noticed his mother had drifted off to sleep. He laid her in her bed and went to sleep next to her. He awoke in the middle of the night when he heard his brother coming in. It was 1:00 in the morning, on a school night.

Chance got out of the bed. He checked Chante's room and she was sound asleep. He went into his and Sparks' room and punched his brother in the chest.

"Where the fuck you coming from?" He asked, sternly, without being loud enough to wake his mother or sister.

"A bitch house. Why?" Sparks had grown to be taller than his brother in the almost two years that he had been gone. He was 18-years old and felt like he was a man. He didn't feel like he had to answer to his brother anymore.

"Why? You ain't got school tomorrow?" Chance looked at the clock.

"I don't go to school no more and you can't say shit. I'm grown. You left me a boy and I became a man on my own, without our sorry ass father's help, or yours." Sparks was towering over Chance. He was about to take his brother down, but he knew that all it would be was a fight. He no longer had control over his brother or his mother. He wondered what would be the next story with Chante. He knew that it was time to leave his mother's house. He had to make his own way. They were going to do whatever they were going to do with their lives because he had shown them that he would do the same. Chance realized the example that he had set for his brother and knew he couldn't expect Sparks to follow a straight path when he hadn't been able to.

"I just want you to be all right, man. I didn't want you to be like me," Chance said, and retreated to sitting on the bed, feeling hopeless.

"Like you? How different am I from you? We came from the same mother and father, the same circumstances. What would make me think different or be different? I am you." Sparks looked at his brother and Chance had a tear in his eye. "Maybe if you would have been different, I would have become different. I always wanted to be like you and now, I am."

"I hear you, man. Well, that wasn't what I wanted for you. I wanted better for you." Chance walked out and came back in.

"So, Ma been getting high a lot?" Chance didn't want to hear what he knew he was going to hear.

"Yes. Ever since you left. She's a lost cause. I don't even care anymore. She might be better off dead," Sparks said, uncaringly.

"Don't say that, man. I'm gonna get her together. What's going on with Chante? Please say she hasn't started getting high?" Chance sat back on the bed as Sparks started to undress and get into his bed.

"Nah, she straight. She the only good thing we got. She's doing good in her community college. I wish she would have gone away to school, but she didn't want to leave Mommy in her condition. That shit ain't even fair to Chante. Ma couldn't even do right so her daughter could better herself."

"Well, I'm gonna make this all better." Chance felt guilty and responsible.

"Chance, you ain't Daddy. You need to do you and let us do us. Everybody chooses their path in life."

"Well, I'm gonna talk Chante into going away and put Mommy in a program."

"Whatever, man. Save the day if you can. I'm going to bed. I don't give a fuck." Chance was so shocked that his little brother had become so hard.

"I'm sorry I let you down," Chance said, and closed the bedroom door. He went back into the room with his mother and laid next to her, after making sure that she was still breathing. He cried himself to sleep.

The next morning, he woke up early to go and talk to Chante before she left for school.

"Good morning, pretty girl." He gave Chante a kiss and hug, which she returned.

"You see Mommy's a mess, right?" Chante asked.

"Yeah, why you didn't say anything in your letters to me?"

"For what? To make you suffer even more? There was nothing that you could do." Chante put her jacket on and Chance followed her to the door.

"Well, I want you to go away to college. You have halted your life enough. I will take over now. You get out of this environment before you end up knocked up and drop out or some shit. You got a boyfriend?"

"There's this boy that I like who likes me, but it's not serious like that yet." Chante blushed at the thought of the person.

"Damn, you grinning from ear to ear. You know I have to approve him first." Chance stood at the door and watched his sister walk down the steps.

"No, you ain't scaring him away. When I know for sure, and when he likes me enough to deal with you, I will introduce you two. Bye, Brother. I love you." Chante blew Chance a kiss like she always had since she was very little.

"I love you, too. And I'm very proud of you. Being the first to graduate *and* go to college. You go, girl!" They both laughed as Chante disappeared.

Chance went back in the apartment. It was 10:00 a.m. and his brother and mother were still sleeping.

He went and made breakfast: waffles, turkey sausage, and scrambled eggs and called them both when the food was done.

"Corey! Ma! Come eat!" He sat down and thought of what he was going to say to them.

They both came in, looking like they had hangovers. He didn't smell alcohol on Corey when he had come in the night before, but he looked disheveled and out of it. His mother looked like she had awakened from being dead. He fought back the tears.

"Ma, what are you gonna do?" Chance asked, before his mother could take her first bite of food. She stopped, looked at him, and put the food in her mouth.

"I'm gonna eat my damned food," Vonetta replied. She laughed as if she had no shame. Sparks looked at Chance and shook his head. "Did I hear you call Sparks, Corey? You haven't called him that since he was seven and you gave him the name Sparks. You trying to be all brand new and shit since you came home." Sparks laughed and Chance couldn't help but laugh because of how she said it.

"Ma, you really look like a damned druggie and you said that shit like a real junkie. That's what you wanna be? And I remember when Corey was little and he always used to wanna play with firecrackers and I told him that he would blow his hand off one day and he stopped because he said he couldn't be a racecar driver if he blew his hand off. So, I started buying him posters every time Mr. Rogers would let me sweep up his barber shop for dollars. I would buy him all his favorite NASCAR drivers' posters and, when I asked him what his name would be, he said he wanted me to name him. I named him Sparks because he liked the firecrackers and he gave those up for the chance to, one day, burn rubber instead. But, now, that's not the case."

"Listen, Chance. I know you are disappointed. I know you wanted us to be okay while you were gone, but shit just kinda fell apart. We needed you," Vonetta said, matter-of-factly. "At least Chante held it together, but *Sparks, Race Car Driver*, over here, dropped out of school and he don't wanna do shit with his life. At least you was bringing in money. He always got his hand out and shit."

"So tell him you been letting Jonny come over here." Sparks ratted on his mother.

"So what? He been giving me money."

"Oh, word is bond, Ma? So, what? Well, that shit is about to stop and you are going into rehab. And Corey, yo' ass is going back to sign up for school." Vonetta and Sparks started laughing.

Chance got up and walked out of the kitchen. He went into his bedroom and slammed the door. He picked up the cordless phone that was in there and called Danielle.

"Hello?" Chance smiled at Danielle's sweet voice.

"Chance, what's wrong?" Danielle knew him so well.

"I need to see you." He would get up the money and take a bus, or train, or plane to see her. He didn't care.

"You gonna fly down here?" Danielle smiled, thinking about Chance's handsome looks and personality.

"Yeah, I'll fly to California or China; where you at?"

"I'm in DC, at Howard University. A HBCU."

"Okay, I'll call you when I get the flight. I'll call you back."

Chance used Chante's credit card to book a one-way flight to Washington, DC. He didn't know how long he would be there. He would be leaving the following day. He would have to make sure he had money to wine and dine Danielle while he was there.

Chance took Nadja's number out of his pocket and called her.

"Hello?" Nadja answered.

"What's up wit' you? It's Chance." Nadja could detect that Chance was upset.

"What's the matter, Brooklyn boy?" she joked.

"My family is all fucked up. My moms is a dope-head and I don't know what's wrong with my brother. I guess he would be called a loser. I'm just tired of trying to take care of them."

"Well, you gotta look out for you. Family is stressful. They work on your nerves." Nadja sounded genuinely concerned.

"So, do you mind if I come over?" She actually lived only about four blocks, in walking distance, from Chance's apartment.

"I'm about to go out to the grocery store." Nadja was still playing hard to get.

"Well, come and pick me up, I'll go with you." Chance was desperate to get away from his house.

"Damn, you must really be upset. I ain't never had a nigga want to go with me to the grocery store before. I used to have to drag my husband. You sure?" Nadja questioned.

"I'm sure. Come get me, my *Harlem Highness*. I need you to make me feel better." Chance told her where he lived and Nadja said she would be there in 10 minutes.

Chance wanted an older woman. He needed someone established. He needed someone to mother him instead of him trying to father his family. He loved Vonetta very much, but she had failed as a parent in his eyes. He planned to ask her one day, to tell him the full history and truth of his childhood, and the circumstances leading up to his father's incarceration and demise. She had never been able to deal with it, face it, or explain it to her kids; but he knew that was the root of her suffering and addiction. He needed to know what had gone wrong.

At that moment, he needed to know how to get in with Nadja. He looked at his nearly empty closet. Most of the clothes that he had before he was sent away were outdated. There were new designers and labels that were in and popular. It was June and the summer time required fresh gear. You could get away in the winter because you always had on a coat. He had to take something out of Sparks' closet, which made him feel even more horrible than he already did for being broke.

Chance walked past Vonetta and Sparks, watching TV in the living room, and walked out, without saying another word to them.

He stood on the stoop of his building and looked at the nice houses that lined his street. There were not a lot of apartment buildings in Teaneck, compared to the city, and his was one of only two on his street. Most people owned their own homes, many with nice cars in the driveways to match.

He felt so inadequate and out of place. He needed a come up and Nadja was going to have to be it. Just after that thought, Nadja pulled up in her white Benz. Chance strolled to the car, feeling as though he was about to hit the jackpot.

"Hey, Miss. Thank you for coming to save me." Chance got in, leaned over, and gave Nadja a kiss on her lips.

"Yeah, you sounded real bad. I felt sorry for you. At least you care about your family. Most niggas only care about themselves." Nadja pulled off and headed to the grocery store.

"All I have is my mom, my brother, and sister. I need someone else to care about," he said, hoping to get her sympathy.

"I know; I do, too. You want to make a deal-that if you care about me, I will care about you?" Now she was talking.

"Yeah, I can do that. I hope you can take good care of me; I need a lot of attention." Chance was enjoying the idea of Nadja.

"Well, we will give it a try. I can't say that I like to deal with more than one dude at a time. So, if I'm trying you out, it'll be you, and only you, until I feel that I should give someone else a shot." Nadja pulled into the parking lot of Path-mark, in Bergenfield, which was right next to Teaneck.

They went into the store and started shopping and getting acquainted with one another.

"So, tell me about your kids." Chance knew that most women expected a man to show some interest, if not, attention and likeness to their children.

"Well, my daughter is 14 and in the eighth grade, but she got the body of a 17-year old, so I have to keep her close to my hip. Grown men be trying to talk to her, even when I'm right there. But, she's not grown, or fresh or fast, so, I'm blessed. My two sons are 10 and seven. My 10-year old is bad as hell, like his father, and my seven-year old is so smart and so good. I guess two good out of three ain't bad."

"What's their names?" He figured, how could he genuinely want to know, and then not care to ask their names. His mind was racing, trying to be a mastermind at conquering her. The nice house was all he needed to see; he was ready to move in that spot.

"Tariyah, Trayvon, and Tevin." She smiled as she thought of her children, who were all she had.

"Wow. You and my mother with the same letter name beginnings. You women are so neat and organized all the time, it makes a man sick. But, I like that ass you carrying." Chance squeezed Nadja's ass as they walked down another aisle. She laughed and went to pick up a box of lasagna. As she was getting the food, another younger, prettier girl walked past and gave him the eye. He checked her assets, which were nice, too.

"Did you like my lasagna the other day?" Nadja walked back and dropped the box in the cart. Chance was thinking about the girl who had just passed.

"Huh?" He had no idea what she had said.

"Did you like the lasagna?" Nadja had no idea what he was thinking.

"Oh, yeah, it was good. Let me go find some deodorant. I forgot I don't have any. I'll be right back." Chance walked away before she could tell him that she had to get deodorant, too. She kept going down the aisle she was in.

 53

Chance walked down the next three aisles, looking for the girl. He saw her getting milk. He walked up behind her and said, "Milk does a body good. You must drink a whole lot of milk."

The girl turned around and said, "Oh, so you snuck away from your mama?" The girl was in her early twenties, sassy, and street.

"Don't be like that. Age ain't nothin' but a number. And your name is all I care about."

"My name is Twinkie and I'm 23. And my number is 201-440-5532. Call me. Now, go, before you get into trouble with grandma. She's obviously much older than you."

"Damn, boo, don't hate. That's my girl," Chance said, without realizing what he said.

"Whatever. Call me," Twinkie said, and walked away.

Chance recited the number repeatedly in his head, before making it to the customer service booth to ask for a piece of paper and pen, to write Twinkie's number down. He then went and got the deodorant and found Nadja. He saw Twinkie walking out of the store as he and Nadja went up another aisle. She winked at him and he turned away. He didn't know her, but she looked like trouble. Trouble that he wanted to get into.

Nadja and Chance finished shopping and went back to her house. When they pulled up, he looked at the Montero. He knew that he would be driving that truck soon.

"That's your husband's truck?" Chance asked, not so sure of his last thought, considering the question at hand.

"No, his cars and trucks were confiscated in the drug raid. These cars are in my name and I own four Laundromats in the city, so I have legitimate income."

"Oh, that's good for you. They probably wanted to snatch up your house, too," Chance probed.

"Yup."

They carried the groceries in and Chance took the groceries out of the bags as Nadja put them away. She loved having a man's help. It hurt her to be without her husband.

"Did I tell you how nice you look today?" Chance flirted.

 54

"No, but thank you." Nadja was starving for attention.

"I like that sweat suit. But, I'm going to like it better, off." Chance was ready, but Nadja was not that easy.

"Oh, yeah? I hear that." She finished putting the groceries away and invited him into her plush living room, where they began to watch movies and continue talking. Chance decides not to push the sex issue because of Nadja's response to his statement about taking her clothes off.

At 3:30, the doorbell rang. Nadja got up and let her two boys in who had just gotten off of the school bus. She introduced them to Chance and sent them into the kitchen to start their homework, advising them to call her if they needed help.

Chance couldn't picture himself as a stepfather, but he liked kids, was good with them, and could be their friend. He started thinking about Twinkie. About an hour later, Tariyah came home. She was a pretty girl who did not look 14 at all, but one thing Chance was not, was a child molester. There were enough women of age; he was not a monster that would be lusting over a little girl, no matter how cute she was. Chance was a ladies' man, not a pedophile.

Nadja introduced Tariyah to Chance and she said a humble hello, spoke to her brothers, and went to her room to do her homework.

"So, what you about to do?" Chance asked, feeling somewhat uncomfortable and out of place.

"Just hang out. You letting my kids scare you away, huh?" Nadja detected Chance's discomfort.

"Nah, I got something I got to do. Let me use your phone." Chance called Jason and asked him to pick him up.

Jason rushed over to hear the latest developments with Chance and Nadja. Chance was not a bitch-type nigga who was going to report everything to a dude about him and a girl.

"It's nothin', man, I'm working my way in. But, that's not why I called you. I need some money. We gotta do a house." Jason looked at Chance intently and knew he was serious.

"Them niggas will be home next month. You can't hold tight?" Jason liked his crew, and he and Chance had never done anything with just the two of them.

 55

"It's either that or you gonna have to give me some cheddar. I ain't got shit. I been home, like, two weeks. It's about to be my birthday and I don't even have clothes to wear on my back. What type nigga is you? You was supposed to hit me with some cream when I hit the streets anyway. And I need a new pager." Jason drove to Chance's house and parked outside of the building so they could finish talking.

"So, you wanna do a house? A'ight, fuck it; let's do it." Jason knew what to do and he was ready. "I'll pick you up as soon as it gets dark. We not messing with Teaneck, Bergenfield, or Englewood. Let's hit up Hackensack. They got some nice, big houses, too. Why not?" Chance smiled.

"Yeah, that's what I'm talkin' 'bout. Get some black gloves and some black hats. No one will be identifying me again." Chance went inside to get ready.

He went inside and Vonetta's door was closed. He put his ear to the door and heard Jonny's voice. He got ready to bust in the room and throw him out, but he needed to get rest and not be preoccupied. He needed to be mentally poised, alert, and his senses needed to be sharp. He was about to get some much needed cheddar.

Chapter 5

Chance took a four-hour nap. At 9 o'clock, he was awakened by a knock on his bedroom window. He looked out of it and saw Jason, dressed in all black. He snatched one of Spark's black hoodies and went outside.

Jason and Chance rode through a few dark, desolate streets of the capitol city of Bergen County, New Jersey. Hackensack was another town on a different borderline of Teaneck. They felt safe because they knew many different routes to get back across the line to make it safely home.

"Look at that one." Chance pointed to a completely dark home. The two houses on both sides of it were dark as well, which was better.

"Hey, you called it; let's get it." Jason parked around the corner and they noticed a very large fence that they would not be able to jump. He drove back around to the street and parked a few houses down the block on the other side of the street. They got out of the car one at a time.

Chance crossed the street while Jason remained on the other side. Chance went to the back door, while Jason went and rang the doorbell. There was no answer. He put his gloves on and met Chance around the back. The back door had a storm door that was locked. They looked at each other and Jason pointed at Chance. That meant that Chance would have to be the one to enter through the front door. He would have to bang it open and place it back on its hinge quickly so that no one would see a dark house with the door open. They didn't choose another house because, once you chose, you had to follow through or fear and anxiety could creep into the mix.

Chance checked to make sure no one in any of the other homes in his view was in any of their windows, watching him. The front door did not have a screen, which would have made it impossible to hold the screen and put enough force through the front door. He ran up the porch steps and, in one kick, kicked the door in. He rushed in and put the door back in place. The alarm to the home began to sound and he ran back out and saw Jason, booking a foot ahead. Jason jumped in his car and started it. He swung the passenger door open for Chance to jump in as he pulled off.

"Damn! I didn't know they had an alarm. They didn't have that ADT sign outside!" Chance screamed.

"Nah, it was one of those old alarms that sound like a damned cowbell. It's not linked to the police department or anything. It's really to alert the neighbors to call the police. You can't tell with those old ones. I figured the house was old and they probably didn't keep it on. You just never know!"

They saw four speeding police cars with their lights flashing and sirens blaring going in the opposite direction of them, toward the house they had just broken into. They looked at each other and smiled.

"We back home," Jason said, as he crossed back over into Teaneck.

"So, what we doing back home? Let's go to another house!" Chance was desperate.

"Nah, nigga, that's a sign. We done for the night. Shit, I told you we needed to wait until Roderick and them come home anyway."

"Then what am I gonna do for money? I can't ask Nadja for money yet, nigga!" Chance was furious.

"Why not? Tell her you fucked up. Tell her it's a loan. Then, by the time you supposed to pay the shit back, you'll be in and you won't have to," Jason plotted for Chance.

 58

"Yo, take me to the mall and get me a beeper or a phone and something to wear for my birthday then!" Chance wanted to fuck Jason up.

"The fuckin' mall is closed. I'll take you tomorrow, shit, you all whinin' and shit. Nigga, you ain't a bitch. I don't take care of no muthafuckin' men. It's every man for himself." Jason started driving toward Chance's house. The last place he wanted to be was in that crowded apartment.

"Yo, stop at that pay phone." Jason pulled over and Chance got out to call Twinkie, after taking her number out of his jean's pocket.

"Yeah, what up, it's the nigga from the grocery store, Chance. Where you live at? My man about to drop me off there."

Jason took Chance to Lodi to an apartment complex where Twinkie and her female roommate, Peaches, lived.

Twinkie came to the door in short shorts and a wife beater with no bra. She was smoking a blunt and had a drink in her hand as she opened the door. Chance looked around the shabby apartment as he walked in.

"Nigga, what you lookin' for? You think you about to be ambushed or some shit?" Twinkie closed the door and introduced Chance to her roommate, Peaches. He figured that they were either strippers, whores, or both.

"What's up? I wanted to see if you could back up all that slick talkin'." Chance had no place else to go and he planned on staying the night.

"Can you back up that broad back? I figured you all wide and shit. You must have some power behind your strokes. Is that true?" Twinkie passed her roommate the blunt.

"I guess you will find out in a little while. What y'all bitches do? Sit around half-naked all day and talk shit?" Chance sat down on the couch that was covered with a dingy sheet. He already didn't like the place and would have preferred Nadja's house, but, beggars can't be choosy.

"We get money, however we choose. As a matter of fact, you got money to pay for this visit?" Twinkie said, and started laughing.

"I don't pay for pussy. I get paid for my dick; don't get it twisted."

"Well, we will see about that, whether you good enough to get some free stuff. You smoke?" Peaches passed the blunt back to Twinkie who passed it to Chance. He took it and started smoking it.

"Damn, I ain't smoke in a minute. Almost two years. What kind of weed is this?" Chance was immediately high.

"That good shit." Twinkie answered. She did not let Chance know that there was crack laced in the blunt and Chance didn't pick up on the smell because Peaches started spraying air freshener through the room, to keep the neighbors at bay. Their apartment was the subject of many conversations in the complex and the neighbors would love to see them put out. There had been many dramatic events. Chance did not know just how much trouble he was truly going to get in from deciding to play in Twinkie's garden. He was playing with fire and he would be getting burned.

"Let's go in my room. I got drinks in there for us." Twinkie led Chance to her bedroom, which looked like a room out of a porn tape. She had a red, heart-shaped bed with a red veil covering that had showbiz feathers on the bottom. The room was pink and she had small mirrors glued to different spaces of the ceiling and walls. She also had a clothing rack on one wall with different pieces of cheap lingerie hanging from it, out in the open.

This chick gotta be a trick, Chance thought. He did not intend to pay for what he was sure was dirty and used up pussy. Twinkie was a yellow, Twinkie-colored girl with light brown hair and light brown eyes. She wore her hair in box-braids, pulled up in a ponytail, and had big, doorknocker earrings in her ears. She was somewhat petite, with a cute shape. Her breasts were normal-sized, and she had a cute, little, round ass. She had a slutty look to her, which most men secretly liked.

"So, what's all this going on in your room? You a stripper?" Chance didn't really care anything about her. He was just passing the time.

"Yeah, why? You got a problem with that?" Twinkie asked, while pouring his drink.

"I don't give a fuck; if you like it, I love it." Chance took the drink and downed it. His plan was to get fucked up, fuck that whore, and get some sleep. That's what he planned.

"I hear that. You may not care, but you got a girl and you are here." Twinkie poured him another drink, which he took his time to sip. He was feeling extra mellow. He figured he'd better take his time. He could see she was a troublemaker.

"Listen, don't worry about none of that. I'm here to get in that ass. You know that. My girl ain't got shit to do with it." Chance took his dick out of his pants and held it. "Now, what you gonna do with this? Come make it hard. Put it in your mouth," he sang like the Akinele rap song.

"Fuck it. I knew it would go down when I saw you coming toward me in the store. So, it ain't no need for frontin'." Twinkie walked over to the chair that Chance was sitting in and put her mouth around his soft dick, which became hard in seconds. He was in ecstasy, instantly.

"Mmmm. You know what you doin', girl. You gonna make me cream too fast."

"Why you think they call me Twinkie? I make your cream filling come out." She put her mouth back on him and went back to work.

"Well, it's about to cum out! Uggggggh! Yeah! I like that!" Chance pumped his body up and down and released into Twinkie's mouth. She held it in her mouth and went to the bathroom to spit it out. She went back in the room and Chance was sitting there, in a daze.

"Not a bitch like you not swallowing." Chance didn't even want to have sex with her after that. He was good for the moment.

"Nigga, I don't swallow if I don't know you like that. You lucky I didn't put a condom on that shit. I just wanted you to see my real skills. But, we sure ain't fuckin' raw."

"I ain't gotta fuck you right now, anyway. That shit was spectacular." He smiled.

"I know." Twinkie opened the curtain to her bed and sat on it. She picked up her television remote and started changing the channels.

"So, what's the deal with you, homey? You and your girl having problems or you just another nigga that wants to have his cake and eat it, too?" Twinkie was the type of girl who didn't give two shits about men but, for some reason, she was intrigued by Chance.

"I'm a nigga that wants what he wants and gets it. I ain't married and don't ask me about my girl. I ain't no bitch ass nigga; you think I'm gonna sit here and talk to you about my girl? So you can use some shit against me later? I know how y'all skeezas do." Chance felt that Twinkie had too much mouth.

"Hold up. Why you gotta call me names and shit? I'm a girl that does what I do; you ain't have a problem with it a minute ago."

"Yeah, you right. Pardon me, boo."

Twinkie went outside, laced another blunt, and came back in. Chance smoked it with her. This time, he could tell what was different about her "weed".

"Yo, what's in this blunt? You put coke in here?" Chance had told himself when he was away that he would leave the coke alone when he came home.

"Yeah, just a little powder. It makes the high mellow," she lied, not admitting that it wasn't powder, but crack-rock.

Chance would not have been able to tell the difference without actually seeing it because the smell was the same.

Twinkie's beeper went off and she took the phone outside into the living room to make a call. Chance took his pants and shirt off, and lay down in the bed. The drug had him feeling woozy and he just wanted to go to sleep.

Twinkie came back in the room and said, "I gotta go pick my sister up. She needs a ride home from her job." She threw some jeans on over her shorts, put a jean jacket over her wife beater, and left. Chance drifted off to sleep and Twinkie went to handle a client.

At about three in the morning, three hours later, Twinkie got in the bed with Chance. He was dead asleep and she didn't wake him. She got under his arm and drifted off to sleep, too.

The next morning, Chance woke up and realized where he was. Twinkie was next to him, naked. He pulled his boxers off, put on a condom, and started fucking her. She woke up and let him get his shit off. They went back to sleep.

At about noon, there was a loud knock at Twinkie's bedroom door. They both jumped up and, before she could put some clothes on, a dude busted through the door.

"Oh word, bitch?" The dude walked over to the bed and Chance jumped up to grab his boxers. The nigga put a gun to his face.

"Yo, nigga, I just met her! You ain't gotta bus' no cap in my ass, if this your girl, pardon me, homeboy. She ain't tell me she had a man." Chance was calm. He did not want to excite the man any more than he already was, considering that he had a gun to his face. He did not make any more moves. He pointed to his boxers and the dude nodded, giving him the okay to get them.

"Yo, this bitch ain't my girl, but she a ho, and she got me for some dough! Where's my fuckin' money, Twink? Don't fuckin' play with me. I told you to take 500 and you snatched a G? Bitch, where's my money? And you thought I didn't know where you lived? Bitch, I been knew where to find you. I was just waitin' for you to try to do some slick shit. Give me my muhfuckin' money! Now, 'fore I blow your brains out! And you slipped some shit in my drink to make me sleep so you could rob me? You better get it right now!"

Twinkie got up slowly, walked over to her pocketbook, counted 500 dollars, and put it in the guy's hand. He turned around and walked out of the door after letting him know, "You better watch your back, nigga, that is a grimy ass bitch right there. Ain't no head or ass enough to deal with that shit right there. Bitch trying to rob a nigga." Just as the guy said that, Chance got an idea. He figured if Twinkie was bold enough to rob somebody in their face, she wouldn't have a problem robbing somebody when they weren't home. Or, at least, being his driver and getting paid for it. He then had a purpose for her, which he would share with her when the time was right. He needed to work on Nadja to fulfill his other purpose.

"Yo, you wilin'. Why you take that cat's bank like that? You on it like that?" Chance asked Twinkie, who still looked shook. "You ain't think he would come looking for his cash?" Chance laughed at the frightened look she had on her face.

"I ain't know the nigga knew where I lived at. I was just gonna never let the nigga catch up to me again. And I ain't put shit in his drink. He know I blew his brains out and put him to beddy bye." Twinkie laughed.

"Yo, you shot out. I got something for you to do, though, if you wanna make some paper. But, right now, I gotta go. Take me to my mom's house. And let me hold 300 'til later." Nadja knew that *hold something shit*, she knew that was a *crock of shit*.

"Come on, nigga, I ain't dumb. Why should I believe you gonna give me this money back?"

"First of all, I'm fucked up. I just got out two weeks ago and I ain't got no clothes. I need you to do me that favor. I ain't trying to get over on you. Word is bond; I will give it when I get it. I told you I got a way for us to make some paper, anyway."

"So, why you don't get it from your girl?" she asked.

"Because my girl held me down when I was down," "Chance lied. "I'm out here now, I don't wanna keep asking her for money. I'm a man. I gotta get my own." Chance wanted Twinkie to think that he had been with Nadja for a while, so that she wouldn't think that he would want anything serious with her. On the other hand, he wanted her to feel like there was a place for her to fill as well; that, although he had a girl, he needed Twinkie, too. That would make her think they had their own bond, outside of what he had with Nadja.

They got dressed, got in her Honda Accord, and she drove him to his mother's house. Twinkie passed him a stack of bills, which he counted as 500 dollars when he got inside. Chance got out of the car, without giving Twinkie a kiss. The rule is to treat a ho like a ho, so she stays in her place. Chance went inside and no one was home. He took a shower and called Nadja. Her answering machine came on and he left a message.

"Nadja, it was good spending time with you yesterday and meeting your kids. They seem cool. Yeah, I felt a little uncomfortable, but I'll get over it. I thought about you all last night. I hope I can see you when I get back from DC. I'll call you when I get back."

Chance packed a bag and took the bus to New York and the train to LaGuardia airport where he boarded his flight to Washington, DC. He had $700 from Twinkie, his mother, Jason, and Chante.

Chance was surprised when he got outside by the taxi stand and saw a driver holding a board with "Chance Major" on it.

"Uh, I am Chance Major."

"Okay, sir, follow me."

Chance received a chauffeur-driven drive to Danielle's apartment building. She shared a two-bedroom apartment off campus with a girl from Houston, Texas. He followed all of Danielle's instructions and rang her doorbell when he got out of the car.

Chance was buzzed in to the building and found apartment 4J when he got off the elevator. Danielle opened the door and jumped into Chance's arms. He held her tightly and carried her inside.

"Damn, girl, you that happy to see me?" Chance put his bag down and gave Danielle a long kiss. That was something he didn't do much, kiss a girl on her lips or with his tongue. He had to really like her to kiss her, or have an ulterior motive.

"Chance, I think about you all the time." Danielle held his hand and led him to the couch where they both sat and she put on Video Music Box.

The video "Love Makes Things Happen" with Pebbles and Babyface came on.

"So, how's these college niggas treatin' you?" Chance stroked Danielle's cheek while she looked deep into his eyes.

"I don't have time for niggas, college or not. I'm on a mission to succeed. I'm gonna be a lawyer. I see my future and that's all I'm focused on."

"Do you see me in your future?" Chance asked, gently.

"I don't because I see what you future is going to look like if you don't change your present."

"Danielle, I'm gonna be a'ight. And I'm gonna make you my wife."

"Well, I will believe it when I see it. I need a strong man like you, but one who is not a slave to the streets. The streets gets you nothing but death or jail."

"Listen, we are not gonna get into this conversation. I came here to spend some time with you, baby girl. Take me to see Washington, DC." Chance wanted to jump Danielle and dick her down, but he knew she deserved more respect than that. He would wait until she made the first move.

Chance stayed in DC for three days. The first day, Danielle took him to the National Air & Space Museum. Chance had always liked airplanes from a very little boy. As they walked through the museum, holding hands, Chance looked at the Wright Brothers' plane and World War II planes.

"You know what, I never told anyone but my family? I wanted to be a pilot when I was a little boy. I always used to love to see airplanes flying up in the clouds." Danielle squeezed Chance's hand.

"Well, you can always work for an airline. You can have the experience of working on planes, or near them. Or, even on them. You don't have to fly them. And I'm only saying you can't be a pilot at this stage because you will have to finish high school and enroll in flight school. You could do that if you put your mind to it…" Danielle was an optimist.

"Danielle, you are such a dreamer. You know that I can't be a pilot now." Chance wrapped his arm around her neck in a gentle chokehold while playing with her hand.

They visited the National Mall and then Danielle cooked steak, potatoes, and fresh spinach for Chance while they watched Goodfellas, Another 48 hours, and Flatliners. They talked for the rest of the night and fell asleep in each other's arms.

The next day, Chance went with Danielle to her criminology class. He enjoyed the experience. He also liked the topic that she was studying and her major, criminal justice.

They also went to a sociology class, Human Deviance, which was about the anti-social behaviors of human beings. Chance enjoyed the college experience. They went to the Student Center where everyone hung out and Danielle introduced Chance to her college crew, who were from different parts of the country, but mostly the New York area, like her. Chance felt comfortable around them.

"Yo, they're not nerds. They're cool peoples," Chance whispered in Danielle's ear. Danielle shook her head at Chance's ignorance.

"Chance, it's cool to be smart, handsome."

That night, they partied at a college party, got drunk, and had a ball. Chance was not one to dance, but he enjoyed dancing and was enjoying himself with Danielle. She made him feel free from the rat race of the streets. He could be another person when he was with her.

That night, they were both too drunk to do anything, but Danielle made up for that on the last morning. Chance awoke to Danielle straddling him. She had no clothes on and her breasts were sitting up and beautiful, and Chance cupped them. She rode him slowly and gracefully, all while looking intently into his eyes. Her mind was talking to her, though.

Damn, Chance. Why do you have to be so lost? You are the only man I want. I see the greatness in you. You are not like everybody else, you just choose to be. I love you.

Danielle moved her hips back and forth like she was riding a pony. She licked her lips and then suddenly, she started screaming, "I'm cumming; I love you. I love you, Chance."

Chance pumped on her and ejaculated into the condom. He wished that he didn't have one on, but Danielle had put it on him before she got on top. They lay in bed, cozy and intertwined, all morning and early afternoon.

An hour before Chance was to be at the airport, they got up and got ready for his departure. Danielle had ordered a car that would be at her place in an hour. Chance was glad that he had visited her. He had had the best three days of his life, or that he could recall.

"I'm going to come once a month, okay?" he said, after getting out of the shower and getting dressed. Danielle sat at her computer desk and looked at Chance for a few moments before answering him. She took a deep breath and forced herself to answer the way she knew she had to.

"Chance, I want you to get your GED. I want you to go to either a community college, or go to the airports and apply for jobs there. Maybe you could be an air traffic controller. Maybe you could get your Commercial Driving License and drive for a private car service. Or..."

"Danielle, there you go again, telling me what I should do. You said you love me. Do you love me, or what you want me to be?" He stopped putting his sneakers on to look into her eyes for his response.

"I love you for what you have on the inside, not your street image. I love what you could become. I am trying to tell you that you have choices and options, Chance. You just did a bid, but you can recover from it. You're not considered a career criminal yet." Danielle took a deep breath and continued. "Chance, I don't ever want you to feel like I was judging you or not appreciating you for you. But, I love you enough to let you go be what you choose to be. I just can't bear to watch you destroy your life. You can't come again. Please get your life together, Chance. I love you enough to keep being a nag about it. You think I like to have to always lecture you? That's just how much I care."

Chance grabbed Danielle's face and held it. He moved his face right in front of hers and whispered.

"Danielle, you are the only good thing that I know. I need you in my life."

"And I need you to be the man I need you to be, so that I can be in your life. Is that too much to ask? For me to ask you not to do things that will take you out of here, either way? For me to ask you to be the best man that you can be, so you can hold your head upright and be proud to be the man that you are?"

"Danielle, this is who I am. And I don't hate it. I'm good." Chance kissed Danielle–long, soft, and hard to try to convince her to change her mind and decision.

"Okay, well then, I wish you the best."

Danielle and Chance embraced and kissed one more time when his car beeped for him to come out. Danielle refused the money that Chance had offered for their weekend every time he tried to give her some.

"Chance, I work at a law firm, part time. This trip was my gift to you. I'm glad you came and got to see the college experience. I'm glad you got a minute to get away. I hope this trip will always mean something to you."

"It will," Chance said, as he got on the elevator to leave. He winked at Danielle as he stepped on.

Chance got on his airplane and was back in Jersey within three hours. He slept the whole flight and was ready to hit the streets when he got home. As soon as he got home, he called Nadja. She didn't answer, so he went home. The next day, he called Jason.

Chance called Jason to hold him to his word of taking him to the mall to see if Jason would look out for him.

Jason picked Chance up in a different car than he had been driving the other times Chance had seen him.

"Damn, nigga, this a different bitch's car?"

"Yeah, I'm telling you, these women out here are desperate. All the black men are dead or in jail, so they say." Jason and Chance laughed. "That makes it better for the ones who are out here. Shit, women used to not be havin' it if you cheat, now, they know they got so much competition, they just deal with it. You better get on your job, nigga."

They went to Garden State Plaza Mall and to a Motorola booth. Jason and Chance asked about the cost of the phones. The cheapest phone was $500.00. Jason was not about to pay that much for a phone for Chance when he didn't even have one.

"Just get a pager, then." The sales clerk told Jason and Chance that cell phone prices would soon be going down and would be the next "big" thing because, when people get paged, they need to make phone calls, so the demand for portable phones was going to decrease the cost of them, the same way pagers had went from being used by doctors to everyone else.

"Okay, let me get a pager, then." Jason paid the 100 dollars for the Metromedia pager and Chance signed up for the monthly rate.

They then went to MACY*S department store. Chance picked out two FUBU outfits, two pairs of Levi's and Guess jeans, with shirts to match. The bill came to $500 and Jason refused to pay it.

"Nigga, you buggin'. You ain't got no dough at all?" *Chance was gonna have to be happy with a FUBU outfit*, Jason thought.

"Yeah, I got 300. Damn, nigga, you know I'm good for it." Chance pulled out all the money he had and Jason dropped two 100 dollar bills on the table for the rest. Chance smiled and gave Jason a pound. "Thanks, Duke, you my man. I will never forget this. Cuz that 'every man for himself' shit is wack."

"Yeah, a'ight. You better have my back if I need you, muhfucka. I don't wanna hear nathan!" They both laughed and Chance proudly took his bags off the counter and they started walking out of the store.

Two white girls were walking past them and Jason started speaking to them. Chance didn't know what he was up to, so he kept his mouth shut until Jason gave him the cue to speak.

"My name is John. This is my man, Rob. Rob, that's Arielle. And this is her friend, Katelyn. Katelyn is mine. We going with them to lunch." The girls giggled. Chance said hello to the girls.

They walked to a restaurant in the mall and ate and talked. Chance knew what Jason was up to. He just wanted to bone these girls and Chance wasn't going to go against that idea. *Why not fuck some dippy white chick in the middle of the day?* He thought. But, as Chance hears Jason ask certain questions, he realizes that Jason is planning to rob one of their houses. Chance got even more excited. The girls were very open with their business after the two drinks each that Jason quickly ordered, before even ordering their food.

The girls were friends who lived in Saddle Brook, a rich town right next to the mall. Jason had a way with words and girls. He knew how to manipulate them and get what he wanted out of them. He had the gift of gab that was genius.

"So, where we going, girls? Whose house won't have parents coming home any time soon?" The girls were giggly and giddy. They were interested in playing with the boys because they liked the thrill of doing something bad.

"We can go to my house," Arielle said. Chance didn't know how Jason planned to pull off the caper, but he knew that he would fill Chance in on the drive to the girl's house. He made sure they had another drink after they ate, so they wouldn't be "on the ball". All Jason needed was about 10 minutes away from all of them to go through the bedrooms. He was only going to be able to take jewels and money.

The girls told Jason how to get to Arielle's house, which was three blocks from the mall. They finished their drinks, Jason paid the bill, and they went their separate ways to get their cars and meet up.

When Jason got in the car, he told Chance that they would have to get the girls naked and then Jason would act like he had to go to the bathroom. Chance would have to start having sex with both of them to keep them occupied and not thinking about how long Jason was taking in the bathroom.

"They're white girls, they will be down for it. They love black dick and they are freaky as they wanna be. We couldn't get no black chicks like that, but white girls love that shit."

"Fuck it, then. I'm down." Chance had never fucked a white girl before, but there was no better time or reason than the present.

When they pulled up to the address they were given, both of their mouths dropped. The house was a brick mini mansion. Jason smelled money. He just didn't know how he was gonna find it in that big ass house with the girls in there. He told Chance to follow his cues and that he would take his time to find out as much as he could from Arielle before venturing out on his own. They funny thing was that he was probably going to have to do it with no clothes on. He would have to start the orgy and then act like he had to use the bathroom so they really wouldn't be suspicious. He knew that he was going to leave out of there with something.

The girls were in the house waiting. They had no idea what Jason and Chance were really there for. They were ready to get some black dick. As soon as Jason rang the doorbell, the door swung open. Both girls were standing in the foyer in anticipation of what they were about to get.

"We decided that we don't want to have to choose. We would both like both of you," Jason said, as he walked through the door. Both girls laughed.

"We decided the same thing," Katelyn joked. "Come on in. Let's go up in my room so we can play a sexy game. We got a bottle of Tequila from the bar downstairs."

"This house is hot to death. Can you show it to us? I've never been in a house this big." Chance really wanted to see the house, genuinely. Jason patted him on the back for his sincere statement and for assisting Jason in the job he would do.

"Oh, sure, everyone loves my house," Arielle bragged.

"Shut up, cunt, you are such a boastful bitch," Katelyn replied, jokingly. "Shit, my house is nicer."

"Yeah, right. Your house looks like a trailer home," Arielle teased her friend.

The girls took Jason and Chance on a tour of Arielle's lavish home. They were dumbfounded by the wealth. Although it was apparent from the outside that this was an extravagant home, they had no clue as to the amount of expensive furnishings, accessories, and trinkets that were filling each wall, floor, and volume of this fancy habitat. Her house was like a museum or an expensive, upscale department store.

They started from the bottom and worked their way upstairs, which was good for Jason and Chance. The basement had a mini bowling alley in it. It had three small lanes that really worked. On the other side was a bar area. It had a sunken in lounge area with a plush carpet and matching, cushioned swivel chairs, a large television, and entertainment center. The room was all red with red lighting. Chance thought of the difference between this and Twinkie's low-budget, red bedroom and he smiled to himself. What was so fascinating was the statues, sculpture, and artwork that adorned the empty spaces. Where there was no furniture, there was a high-priced object.

The lower level also had a laundry room and a mini home theater. There were about 20 reclining chairs and a projector screen in it. The back door led to a pool area, small house for changing, and a tennis court.

The next level was the family room and a library.

The next level was where the front entrance, foyer, kitchen, living room, and dining room were. The furniture in the living room had to cost a mint. There was a case that caught Chance and Jason's attention in the living room. It was full of different ornaments. Most importantly, there were about a dozen different Faberge eggs. Jason knew that he would be taking those, for sure. He was pretty much set. He would look in the master bedroom for cash and jewels and then grab the eggs and that would be it.

They then went upstairs to the fourth level where all the bedrooms were. There were five bedrooms each with their own bathroom in it, not next to it. Each bedroom was like a master bedroom, but they wanted to know which was *the Momma and Poppa Bear*'s bedroom.

"Okay, so there is the guest room. That is my brother's room. That is my sister's room. That is my parents' room up those stairs, and here is my bedroom." Arielle pointed to all the rooms she told about and each of the doors were closed. Her parent's room had a penthouse effect. It was the only room on the top level. She opened the door to her bedroom and it looked like the room of a princess. It was exquisite and spotless. He knew, without a doubt, that they had a maid.

"Damn, I wish I was your brother," Jason said.

"Shit, I wish I could marry into this family, but I'm sure they wouldn't have that," Chance joked.

"My parents aren't prejudiced," Arielle defended.

"They may not be, but that don't mean they wanna see you with a black dude." Chance sat on Arielle's bed and patted it for her to sit next to him. "I want to kiss this princess." Chance took her chin and stuck his tongue gently in her mouth. He wanted to appear gentle and not aggressive. He would save that for the sex-making. Arielle kissed him back, softly.

"Okay, stop the romantic shit. Let's play a game," Katelyn said.

"Yeah, let's get this party started," Jason said, eager to get his *robbery* on. He did want to have some fun with the girls, but he had bigger and better things to do. "What time will your parents be home?" he asked.

"We've got time. It's only 2 o'clock. Don't worry, not 'til like six." Arielle put her arms around Chance.

"Okay, so we are going to play a game. Girls versus boys. We ask a question and, if neither of you get the answer right, you both have to take a piece of clothing off. And vice versa." Katelyn poured the liquor in four cups with ice and passed the glasses out.

"Okay, ladies first. I ain't scared," Chance said.

"Okay, what is the capital of Nevada?" Katelyn asked.

"Carson City," Chance answered, and all three of them were surprised. He saw the look on their faces. "Damn, I ain't no dummy. I did go to school." They all started laughing.

"So, girls, take off something. I got the answer right." Jason gave Chance a high-five.

"That wasn't the rule, but fuck it; I'm ready for the real fun!" Katelyn took off her pants and Arielle took off her top.

"Okay, what is the name of the rap group that sings 'OPP' or I'll give you another chance, what does OPP stand for?" The girls started jumping up and down.

"Oh, my God, I can't think of their name! Is it Raw Nature?" Katelyn yelled out and Arielle got mad.

"Oh, my God, it's Naughty by Nature! Why did you yell it out? Can we get that since I got it right?" Arielle pleaded.

"Nope! She said the wrong answer," Jason answered, and he winked at Chance who cracked up laughing.

"Let's go, ladies," Chance urged.

Katelyn took off her shirt and Arielle took off her pants. They were both in their underwear and Jason and Chance were fully clothed.

"Listen, we will do you girls a favor. Chance will help you take the rest of your clothes off and I will help you, Katelyn. Then, we want to see you girls dance together naked. Put some music on." Jason had everything all planned out.

The girls were good and drunk. They put on music, rap, at Jason's command and started touching on each other. Chance took his clothes off and lay on the bed. Jason took his off and sat on the couch. He was going to get something done to him before he went to work and he wasn't going to pass up a white girl's claim to fame. He was going to get that first.

"Katelyn, come on over here and suck on this here." Jason lifted up his tool and waved it at her. Katelyn approached and obliged him on her knees.

Chance called Arielle over to the bed. He laid back and she climbed on the bed and took him into her mouth as well. He closed his eyes and imagined that it was Nadja sucking him. He was never attracted to white girls and he didn't want the thought to interfere with the pleasure. It felt so good that he had to open his eyes and deal with the reality that this white chick was making him feel like he never felt before. Her mouth was working magic. He heard Jason groan and he released just as quickly.

"Told you white girls give the greatest head!" Jason stood up and clapped. "Let's give it up for the bunnies! Oh, shit! My stomach! I gotta take a shit! I ain't going in here with y'all, I'm gonna stink up the whole room. Can I use the guest room?"

Arielle nodded yes.

"Chance, take care of Katelyn while I'm gone. Go 'head and get up there with them." Jason led Katelyn to the bed and she went willingly. "Get my man hard, eat your girl Arielle out and let him watch." Arielle giggled. "Come on, you know you want to." Jason went out of the room butt-naked.

"He must really gotta shit, he ain't even put his clothes on," Chance reassured. "Come on, girls, give me a show so I can give both of y'all some of this big, black dick." Katelyn laid Arielle on her back and caressed her breasts as she began to stick her tongue out and lick on Arielle's clit.

Jason tiptoed, but ran, up the steps and opened the master bedroom door. It was immaculate and exquisite like all the rest of the rooms. He noticed that her parents had separate walk-in closets. He went to her mother's side first and to the dressing room type table and mirror, with lights going around the mirror. He opened the drawers, looking for a jewelry case. All he saw was makeup. He searched the closet for the same thing but saw nothing but shoes, clothes, and furs. He wished that he were there at night. He would clean her out of these luscious minks. They looked as soft as cotton and as rich as Bill Gates. He was sick that he couldn't snatch one.

He went to her room and looked in all the drawers and still couldn't come across a jewelry collection. He knew she had one, but he couldn't figure out where it could be. He stood in the middle of the room, bare-assed, and kept looking around. He knew that his time was running out. He had been gone about 10 minutes.

Chance was in the room watching the girls play with each other, while he played with himself. He grabbed Katelyn and made her suck on him. He wanted to compare the two girls and see who was better. He told Arielle to sit on his face, at the same time, so she wouldn't go looking for Jason. He began to taste the white girl and she was loving it. Before he came, he wanted to fuck them. He told Katelyn to ride him, while he continued to feast on Arielle. Arielle couldn't take it anymore and released into his mouth. He told her to straddle him and hold on to Katelyn from the back, while she continued to ride him. He had to keep his stamina up so he kept changing positions. He told Katelyn to get off of him and made Arielle lay down on her back. He fucked her missionary style while Katelyn lay on her stomach and teased his balls with her tongue, while he pumped up and down on Arielle. *This nigga Jason better hurry the fuck up*, he thought.

Jason stepped into the male closet and opened the dresser drawers. There was nothing. He checked every drawer and there was no sign of any money. He passed the linen shelf and took a pillowcase. He would at least get those Faberge eggs from the living room. He threw on a pair of Arielle's father's pants and a shirt. He slipped on a pair of his shoes and went to the living room and took six of the 12 eggs. He knew that it would be too obvious if he took all of them and he didn't want Arielle noticing before they got out of the house safely. He quietly opened the front door and put the pillowcase in his trunk. He always left his car door open in the event of having to make a fast break.

Jason ran back in the house and back into the bedroom. He took her father's clothes off and was about to walk out of the room when he noticed two paintings over each of their end tables next to each side of their bed. He went to the painting on her mother's side and pulled it. It opened and revealed a safe behind it. He tugged on the handle and it was open. *Jackpot!* He opened the small safe door and it revealed what looked like a diamond mine. There were four shelves of jewelry on stands. He grabbed a pillow off the bed and took the case off of the pillow. He took every last piece of jewelry that was in the safe. He ran to the other side to see what Daddy had on his side. He tugged on the handle but the safe was locked. *Damn!* He thought. His time had run out. He didn't have time to get dressed and go back to the car. He had to think fast. He looked out of their bathroom window, which was on the side of the house. He opened the window and dropped the pillowcase out of the window and it landed behind a bush. He would get it when they left.

Jason ran down the stairs and back into the room. Chance was fucking Katelyn.

"Oh, my God, are you okay?" Arielle got up and walked over to him.

"Yeah, I had to wash up and stuff. I used one of the washcloths that was folded on the towel rack."

"Oh, that's fine." Arielle looked at his penis and back at him. She smiled. He took her hand and led her to the couch. He bent down, put her tittie in his mouth, and started fingering her. She was already wet and aroused.

He turned her around and bent her over. He entered her from the back and fucked her until he came. He was ready to go.

He removed himself from her and put his act back on.

"Damn, my stomach is still cramping. Yo, Chance, we gotta go man. That food in that restaurant fucked my stomach up. I gotta go to the emergency room or something." Jason looked serious and made himself look ill.

"Damn, I was enjoying Katelyn over here. You sure you don't wanna go take another dump?"

Jason raised his voice, "Nah, I gotta go. My stomach is killing me. Get their numbers; we will come back another day. I ain't gonna be having the runs and shit on this girl's floor."

"Ill, that's nasty," Katelyn replied. "You better go."

Jason and Chance got dressed as fast as they could without making themselves seem suspect. They were both nervous. They would not be comfortable until they were out of the house. Anything could go wrong on the way out. The girls could look in the China cabinet and notice the missing eggs. He didn't even know if he remembered to close Arielle's parent's bedroom door back. He just wanted to get out of there and snatch that pillowcase from the side of the house and be out!

The girls walked them to the door with no clothes on. They gave them fake kisses and promised to call. They wanted to run and jump in the car, but the girls were peeking out of the door waiting for them to pull off. As soon as they closed the door, Jason pulled up a bit a few doors down and told Chance to run back to the side of the house and get the pillowcase, which he did. Chance ran close to the other houses, so they girls wouldn't be able to see him if they were looking out the window. He snatched the pillowcase and ran back to the car. Jason pulled off slowly and then picked up speed.

Chance looked into the pillowcases and couldn't believe his eyes. His eyes widened like he had just hit the lottery.

"Jackpot! Damn, nigga, this looks like a fucking jewelry store! And the eggs, they worth money, too?" Chance was excited and screaming. He felt like a millionaire.

"Hell, yeah! Them shits cost paper!" Jason peaked into the pillowcases and shouted, "Whoo Hoo! We should go straight to New York right now!"

"Fuck it, let's go!"

Chapter 6

J ason drove the girl's car over the George Washington
Bridge and straight to see Mr. T. They got out of the car
and each put a pillowcase in their plastic bag from the
mall. They walked into the *spot* and asked for Mr. Thomas.
Mr. Thomas came out and motioned for them to come into his
office. He remembered Chance and knew that they had gotten
locked up leaving his place two years before.

"Hey, young buck. I see you made it home safely.
Where's the rest of the boys?" Mr. T. gave Chance a slight
hug and pat on the back.

"Oh yeah, I had to go away and become a man. They'll
be home soon. And, look, I'm a man now. I graduated."
Chance and Jason put the pillowcases down.

When Jason and Chance dropped the contents of the
pillowcases out onto the table, Mr. Thomas just sat there for a
few minutes looking at all of it. He shook his head.

"What's the matter, Mr. Thomas, that's a lot of shit,
right? We finally got some rich people shit, not that old rinky
dink shit from our town. We hit an expensive town this time,"
Chance bragged. Mr. Thomas continued to stare. He didn't
even touch what was on the table.

"What's the matter is that I don't have anyone that
could buy this stuff here. The stuff you guys used to bring me
I could sell right back to the old men and women who would
hit the number and have a few extra dollars to spend on some-

thing small. This is a whole 'nother league you guys are playing in. It's nice though, real nice." Mr. Thomas still didn't touch one piece of the jewelry or the eggs.

"Come on, T, man, you gotta know someone that we can take this stuff to, though," Jason pressed.

"You boys need to find you a Jew. They run the diamond district. They ain't no less crooked than anybody else. But, I can't help you there. I'm a Harlem boy. I do business with the poor, or the ghetto rich," Mr. Thomas laughed. "I tell you, the money regenerates itself right here. We don't see that clean money or that white money. Our money circulates back and forth between us."

"Okay, what about all the drug dealers? These hustlers out here in Harlem got mega bucks. They like Daddy Warbucks. I know you know somebody like Richard Porter, RIP, or these niggas that got that Alpo money. They wasn't the only ones doin' it." Chance was getting frustrated. He thought that Mr. Thomas just didn't want to help them.

"Yeah, I do. But they don't want no used white people's jewelry. You know they gotta buy the dookie rope chains. This ain't their style. And you know how y'all are. You would rather spend all of your money and go broke than be frugal like the hustlers of the old days. Man, you guys got it all mixed up. There's old men who made a lot of money and knew they wouldn't see Social Security or pension for being hustlers, so instead of buying fancy cars, they kept it in a mattress and they are still living off of it. This new breed, man, y'all are just plain greedy and dumb." Mr. Thomas shook his head.

"Okay, Mr. Thomas, we don't want to hear a history lesson. What can we do?" Chance asked.

"I told you. Go on down to the diamond district in midtown and make friends with one of those Jew boys. They can send that stuff anywhere in the world. It will never be seen again."

"Yeah, but we can't go down there and just ask who wants to buy stolen property. They might call the cops on us." Jason was not about to do that.

"You gotta feel them out. You gotta do business with them. You gonna have to spend some money first. I don't know, but I can't help you. Now, I gotta go. Just be careful with that stuff. Y'all hear me? Don't go flaunting that stuff around up here; somebody is bound to try you for that stuff. Shit, I would if I was still wild like I used to be. I would have sent somebody to shoot you for that stuff there." Jason and Chance looked at each other and Mr. T started laughing. "See, you guys are not as tough as you think. Now take this stuff out of here before somebody tries you guys. I'm the last one you gotta worry about."

Chance and Jason put the loot back in the pillowcases and watched their backs as they walked down the steps, onto the street, and into their car. Chance locked his door when he got in.

"Damn, you ain't no punk; what you scared for?" Jason asked.

"Punk? Ain't about bein' no punk, nigga, we got thousands of dollars' worth of shit and I ain't fightin' no bullet and I don't wanna give this shit up. I'll be a punk right now, 'til I get some money for this shit." Chance shook his head at Jason's stupidity.

"I hear you. Damn, calm down. We gonna make it happen," Jason reassured him.

"How? I don't have no Jewish friends."

"But, I know Jewish chicks! Ha ha! There were some down by law white girls that I went to Teaneck High School with and they gotta have brothers or cousins or something. I will do my homework. Just hold tight." Jason started driving back to Jersey.

"Yo, make sure you drive slow and shit. The last time I came across this bridge, I ended up doing 18 months in a camp." Jason and Chance were both paranoid. They had never had jewelry and items worth so much money in their possession. It was the first time that either of them had robbed such a rich home. Usually, they stayed close to home, in their comfort zone.

"Shit, nigga, it's my birthday tomorrow. Let's do the hotel shit tonight so I can bring my birthday in, in some fat,

 82

slutty pussy." They both started laughing and Jason called three stripper/hookers who met them at the Radisson Hotel. Jason supplied the coke and liquor and the girls supplied the orgy.

They had a private party with two men and three women. It was sex, drugs, and music. The girls had their routines. They dressed up and dressed down and performed three "shows", which included foreplay on each other while Jason and Chance both watched with rock-hard dicks.

Chance couldn't take it anymore. He zipped his pants down and pointed at one of the girls, Bambi, to come and serve him.

"Come here, bitch, and do something to my dick. And do something good, too. Take all that skimpy shit off! All of y'all, get naked. As a matter of fact, Tasty, come play with this bitch while she fucks or sucks me or something." Chance laid his head back.

The girls went to work. They used toys on each other and Chance to make his experience outstanding and mind-blowing, which it was. Chance didn't think he could feel so good in his life. He looked over at Jason and put his thumb up to him while one girl sucked on the other, who was sucking on him. Jason gave him a wink and closed his eyes to enjoy his real fantasy that was taking place at the same time.

When the girls left at three in the morning, Chance and Jason crashed and slept until half past noon, when the hotel lobby called to tell them they were late for checkout. Jason paid extra for a late checkout and they came back from the dead at three pm and checked out.

Chance did not want to go home. He stopped at a pay phone and called Nadja. She answered and said that he could come over. Her kids were in New York at her mother-in-law's house. He was hoping that he could get some affection, or at least some sex.

When Jason pulled up to Nadja's house, Chance thought about the stuff.

"Yo, nigga, what about the shit? Let's split it up." Chance may have been cool with Jason, but when it came to money and loyalty, he was skeptical. He knew that you couldn't trust a thief; they are no different than cheaters and liars. He also knew that if he was the one with the stuff, that he would be stashing some of it for himself.

"I got it. Don't worry about it. I'm going to get in touch with the girls I know. I will have a connect for us in a couple of days." Chance looked at Jason sideways. He wanted to take something with him.

"Well, give me one of those eggs, at least. I don't want to have to fuck you up, nigga. Let me in the trunk.

"Hold up, young buck. Who the fuck you threatenin'? That was my setup. I put you on. If I wanted to, I wouldn't have to give you half. I can give you what I want to give you. Don't let that Brooklyn shit go to your head, you in my town. I run this joint." Jason put the car in park and put his hands up. Chance wasn't moved.

"Look, nigga, let me get one of those eggs. As a matter of fact, I'm taking two. If I wasn't with them Barbie dolls, you wouldn't have been able to get shit. Let's not get it fucked up; it took both of us. Pop the muhfuckin' trunk."

Chance jumped out the car and walked to the back. Jason popped the trunk and remained in the car. Chance looked in the pillowcase and took two of the Faberge eggs. He peeked to see if Jason was going to get out. He quickly reached in, grabbed a diamond brooch from the other pillowcase, and stuffed it in his jean pocket before closing the trunk. He walked back around to Jason's driver's side, showed him the eggs, and gave him a pound. He didn't care. Jason should have known to get out of the car and watch him.

Chance walked up the steps to Nadja's house and she opened the door. She had on a pair of leggings and a tight t-shirt that showed her figure. She was a big girl, but she had a nice shape. She had enough ass for him to grab, titties that would fill up his mouth, and he knew the pussy was fat to go along with that. She kept herself up and was clean. Her hair was always freshly done, which made up for the fact that she wasn't pretty. *Shit, who needs pretty? Them pretty bitches are too into themselves*, Chance thought. *I want this bitch to be into me!* He laughed.

"What you laughin' at?" Nadja asked, as she stood to the side and let Chance in. She waved to Jason and closed the door.

"I was thinking about how I'm gonna tear that pussy up," Chance said, getting his bid in early. He was not about to not get no pussy this time, especially since her kids weren't there. He was staying until they came back.

"And it's funny?" Nadja walked into the kitchen. "You want something to eat?" She took a bottle of champagne out of the refrigerator and made a mimosa.

"Damn, you drink champagne like it's juice, huh? I wanna live like that; that's that good living." Chance walked up to her, took her champagne glass, put it on the counter, and put his arms around her, grabbing her ass. He kissed her long and hard. She kissed him back. He put his tongue in her mouth and roughly occupied her whole mouth. She took his tongue in her mouth and let him stay.

Chance took his tongue out, smacked a big kiss on her lips, and squeezed her ass.

"Damn, I been waiting to do that." He smacked her ass, picked up her glass, and sipped from it.

"I been waiting for you to do it, but I didn't know it would be like that." Nadja leaned in and softly kissed his lips. "So, what we gonna do about this?" She looked in Chance's eyes.

"We gonna be a couple. We gonna give this shit a shot." Chance told her to make him a mimosa and he went in the living room and started changing the channels on the large screen TV in her plush living room. He looked around and was excited. In no time, he would be living there; that was his plan. Her house was a typical drug dealer's house. It had everything.

Nadja came in with a plate of macaroni and cheese, turkey wings with gravy, and collard greens. She put out a tray and put his plate on it. He sat up and started eating. Nadja noticed the Faberge eggs on the table.

"Where'd you get those from? Those are nice." Nadja knew that Chance was running with the burglary crew before he was sent away. Jason had filled her in about Chance the same way he had filled Chance in about her. "You runnin' up in houses again?" Chance finished chewing his food and swallowed. He took his time and cut a piece of turkey. He looked at Nadja.

"I don't own laundromats and shit. I'm a nigga with nothin' but an illegal craft, that's my hustle. I don't have a trust fund. I don't have a diploma. All I got is my word and my balls."

"You got quite an attitude, too, I see." Nadja was used to black men with chips on their shoulders. It was just the state of black men in America, who still thought they didn't have opportunities, who didn't realize that it was their poor choices that were ruining their lives, not "the white man". She didn't feel like explaining it to him. She would save that for another day.

"So, you know where I can sell these at?" Chance was not ashamed. He was arrogant, which didn't leave room for humility.

"I have a jeweler downtown that I deal with. I can probably talk to him." Chance jumped up.

"In the diamond district? Is he a Jew?" She nodded yes to both questions.

"Call Jason." Nadja didn't ask any questions. She called Jason and handed the phone to Chance.

"Yo, Nadja said she can talk to her jeweler. She know a Jew man down at the diamond district." Jason laughed.

"Damn, nigga, okay. We can check him out. I'm still gonna see what I can do. If I can't get nothing going today, then tell her to take us down there tomorrow. Be easy, nigga, stop buggin'. Get some of that pussy and calm ya ass down." Chance got agitated that Jason was taking it as a joke. He hung up.

"You gotta take us down there tomorrow." Chance put his tray to the side.

"What's the matter? You lost your appetite? You so uptight, baby. It's gonna be okay. You gotta relax." Nadja sat closer to Chance and started rubbing his neck and giving him a massage.

"Make me relax. Take your clothes off. Give me some of that pussy. I know it's fat." Chance put his hand between Nadja's legs and moved it up to her crotch. He squeezed on her pussy.

"You want some, baby?" Nadja whispered in his ear.

"Yeah, I need some, too. I want to feel your insides. What we waiting for? Let's make this official. Let's become one." He stood up, took his shirt off, and threw it to the side. He unbuttoned his jeans, dropped them to the floor, and stepped out of them. He dropped his boxers. He grabbed her hand and put it on him. Nadja stroked him and he was instantly hard.

Nadja took her shirt off. She pulled her tights and panties down. Chance sat down on the couch and she straddled him. She put him inside of her and started riding up and down on him. They looked at each other in the eyes.

Chance felt her insides wrap around him. He felt her warmth and her juice. It felt good to him. He put his hands on her waist and pushed himself up into her as he pulled her down onto him. They moved slowly and she moved all the way to the top of him and all the way back down his shaft. She wanted to feel all of him inside of her. She looked at him and smiled.

Nadja leaned down and kissed Chance softly. He felt good inside of her. She wrapped her arms around his neck and kept riding slow and long. Every stroke opened her heart to the chance that he could be the one to fill the void in her heart. She didn't want to think about reality and the fact that he was too young. She ignored the fact that she had experienced so much more than him and that fact would eventually cause animosity between them. She didn't want to think that he would not know how to love her because he didn't love himself. She ignored the fact that he was only out for himself, while she would have his back.

"You feelin' good, baby, I want this dick to be mine." Nadja didn't care that the odds were against them. She was determined to beat the odds.

"It is yours," Chance replied. He grabbed her, thrust into her hard and fast, and came. He pulled her down to his chest and hugged her. He held her for a few minutes. She held him back. It felt right to them both. But, feelings change and sex can mask lust and make it feel like love.

Chance and Nadja enjoyed the rest of the day having sex in the kitchen, to the basement while she washed clothes. They did it on the dryer. They took it to the bedroom and slept in each other's arms.

The next morning, Saturday, Chance woke early. He was ready to get his money for the loot. He didn't even think about what may have been going on at Arielle's house.

The police did their investigation. The girls did not tell anything about the two black men that they knew nothing about, that they brought home for casual sex. Arielle lied and said that she had misplaced her keys and left the door unlocked to go to the mall with Katelyn. Jason had wiped the door handles off with the pillowcase. There were no prints found. Arielle had washed the glasses that they had drank from before she even realized that her house had been robbed. Then, when her mother noticed her safe emptied out, Arielle created the story. She couldn't bear to let her mother know that her stupidity and promiscuity had robbed her mother of many of her dearest and most prized possessions. Not only were they nice and expensive pieces of jewelry, but some had very sentimental value. Some were heirlooms that had been passed down for generations. Arielle would never tell and neither would Katelyn.

Chance woke up Nadja. "Mommy, I need to eat and then we need to go and sell this shit me and Jason got. I'm not feelin' this broke shit. I keeps money in my pocket." Nadja rolled over and looked at the wild buck that she had let into her stable. She had no idea that taming him would never happen.

"Give me some dick first. What you think this is? I don't work for free." Nadja and Chance had slept naked. He got on top of her and gave her some quick morning dick.

"Now get yo' ass up and make this shit happen. You don't want no broke nigga hangin' around in your shit. I'm a man; I pay my way. If I'm with you, you gonna do for me, and I'm gonna do for you. I ain't expecting you to carry me. I just want you to love me and let me stay. Feed me good and don't get on my fuckin' nerves." Chance got out the bed and looked at Nadja, who was turned on by his smart mouth.

"Oh yeah? Don't play no bullshit ass games and I won't get on your nerves. Don't take my kindness for a weakness. 'Cause I will show you a side of me that you won't be able to handle." She got up and walked past him. He smacked her ass and she went into the bathroom and turned the shower on.

They took a shower together. She washed him like he was her baby. She was going to take care of him like he was, too.

They got dressed. He had to put the same clothes on, because he hadn't brought clothes.

"Before we go to New York, I'm taking you to get some clothes," Nadja announced. Chance smiled inside because he knew that his claim that he would hold his own would only make her want to take care of him. Had he asked or seemed like he had his hand out, she would not have wanted to do anything for him. *Damn, I'm good*, he thought.

They ate breakfast and went to the mall. Chance called Jason before they left and Jason told him that he hadn't had any luck as of yet. They told him to meet them at Nadja's house at 1:00 pm to go to the Diamond District.

Nadja and Chance walked around the mall and he racked up. She bought him all named brand clothes and sneakers, jackets, and underwear. He had Tommy Hilfiger, Ralph Lauren, Polo, Nautica, and Karl Kani gear. He also got FUBU, Nikes, Ecko Unlimited, and Mecca.

She bought enough clothes that he could go three weeks without wearing the same thing twice. She spent about 5000 dollars on Chance in one pop. It didn't matter to her. She liked him a lot and she was giving him a shot. Nadja was kind, until you crossed her. When she was mad, you wouldn't want to have to deal with her.

They ate and then met up with Jason. He parked his car in front of Nadja's house. She put the jewels and eggs in one of her husband's old briefcases, one thing that was not confiscated in the raid on her house. It was a rich-looking, crocodile-skinned attaché case. Jason and Chance looked "fresh dressed, like a million bucks" (Slick Rick) and ready to increase their pockets by a couple of thousand each. Chance was thinking big.

"I think we about to get like 10, 000," Chance said and Jason laughed.

"Nigga, we about to make 20 Gs," Jason reassured him.

"Y'all just better be calm and let me talk first, until I can feel him out. As a matter of fact, don't even come in there until I come back out and get you." Nadja was only doing it for them because she had been dealing with the same jeweler for more than five years. She figured that he would either bite the bait or pass on the opportunity; but calling the police on her she didn't suspect.

Nadja parked on 48th St. and 5th Ave and they walked around the corner to 47th St. Chance and Jason waited down the street in a coffee shop while Nadja went to her jeweler's booth.

She approached Harum and Sherim, and the two brothers greeted her. She had done business with them for a while and always found Sherim to be more down to earth than his brother. Harum always was very rigid and reserved and was not flexible with prices like his brother. If she had to guess which one would be more apt to do some illegal business, her bet would fall on Sherim. Sherim was helping a customer and Harum walked over to her.

"Hey, Nadja, long time, no see. Is everything okay? I was reading about your husband in the paper." That was another thing about Harum, he was your typical, rude ass Jew.

"Hey, Harum. I'll wait for you brother." Nadja wasn't going to smile and be phony. If he didn't know not to ask about personal business to someone who is not your friend, then he didn't deserve courtesy; he hadn't shown her any. Harum acted like he didn't hear her, but still walked away. He walked over to someone else who approached their booth. Nadja started looking at the jewels in the glass cases, remembering *back in the day* when the Feds were not a nuisance and the money was flowing in like water. She had been a drug dealer's girl from the age of 16 and his wife from the age of 20. It was a tumultuous life that always involved material things and possessions more than love, honor, and respect. Nadja was Ant's possession. He owned her and she had to deal with whatever he dished out and, oftentimes, his only display of love was through gifts. Nadja would have much rather had her man's full heart and to have been treated with respect. The trinkets became meaningless after numerous run-ins with other women, and the physical and mental abuse that came from his frustrating, dangerous, and stress-filled life.

Sherim startled her out of her zone when he approached and said hello.

"Hey Sherim, how are you? I need a big favor." She decided to play on his sympathetic side, which he had, unlike his brother.

"You know that I've been through so much over the past year, with my husband being indicted and sent away for life. I just need to get rid of some stuff that I have because I have to try to get some of the money back that was spent on my husband's lawyer. I am trying to get back on my feet and not lose my house." Nadja didn't care if Sherim thought she was broke, she wasn't. She decided that it was a better story than letting him know that she was trying to sell him stolen goods. Although she thought he might be down for that, she was going to hold that information until it was inevitably revealed.

"I'm sorry to hear that, Nadja. Anthony was a good guy to me. Well, what do you have?"

"I have a lot of my jewelry and I have some Faberge eggs." She knew that he would know what she had bought from him and none of what they had would be that. "It's just some stuff that I had gotten on vacations or from other jewelers. The stuff that I've gotten from you, I'm trying to hold on to. I love that stuff," she flattered.

"Okay, let me see what you've got." Sherim took out his magnifying glass to check the quality of the stones she had.

"I gotta go get them out of my car. I was just checking to make sure you were here, 'cause you know I don't deal with anybody but you," Nadja tried to continue to submissively manipulate him into cooperation before even showing him one thing.

Nadja went and sat at the table where Chance and Jason were sitting.

"I didn't tell him the shit was stolen. I told him it was my stuff that I had to get rid of 'cause I'm broke, so y'all can't come. Give me the briefcase." Chance and Jason looked at each other. Chance trusted Nadja, shit, she had just spent 5,000 on him was his thought. Jason knew Nadja didn't need to try to rob him, she had her own money. Jason handed the briefcase over to her.

"Let us go back to the car; I'm tired of sitting in here." Chance reached for the keys and Nadja put them in his hand. He and Jason walked to the car as she walked back to see Sherim.

Nadja went back in and requested to go to Sherim's private office, which was across the street. He took her there.

Nadja opened the briefcase and took the 25 pieces of jewelry out of the briefcase. She was just as surprised to see the pieces as Sherim, but she tried to look at them without her shock being apparent. They were very nice pieces.

Sherim picked them up and looked at each piece through the glass. His eyes rose as he looked. The diamonds were clear and of high quality. He picked up all of the pieces and began to use his calculator to tally up what he would offer Nadja for everything.

When he was done he said, "I'll give you 35, 000." Nadja figured the pieces were at least a couple of thousand each, so Sherim would be making a killing. She contemplated questioning that amount and then realized that she hadn't given him the eggs.

"What about these Faberge eggs?" She took them out of the case and laid all six out on the table.

"Well, I will have to look into these. Some of them are very expensive and some of them are not. Would you like me to keep them and get back to you?" Nadja wasn't sure how Chance and Jason would react to that.

 92

"Well, can you take pictures of them and do the research and I will call you in about a week?" She was very quick-witted.

"Sure, I can do that." As Sherim was taking the pictures, she got scared. *What if he tells the police*, she thought.

"Sherim, I have to be honest, though. I didn't buy these. My husband brought them home one day. So, please...." He cut her sentence off.

"Nadja, don't worry. I like you. I always have. If I think that it will be trouble, I will just pass, but I won't bring you any more trouble than what you have already had to deal with. Listen, I'm not like my brother. He thinks everyone should do what's right. I know that I was born into opportunity, while everyone was not. Everyone should be able to live good. And these lawmakers and police officers and judges are crooked. They do not play by the rules because they think they are above the rules. I'm being sincere." He looked in her eyes and she trusted him. He continued taking the pictures and then she put them back in the case. He excused himself from the room and came back with the money, which she counted in front of him. He gave her an envelope to put the money into.

"Thank you, Sherim. I'm sorry that I had to do this, but I am glad that I could come to you." He shook her hand and she put the envelope in the briefcase and closed it. "I will be calling you in a week?" she asked.

"Well, give me three. I'm taking my wife on vacation for two weeks. We are going to Greece and Italy. So, I will look them up and have some information for you when I get back."

Nadja walked back to her Benz. She felt a little nervous, with all of that money on her. It was like déjà vu, reminding her of the many times she was involved in illegal activity with her husband.

Chapter 7

Nadja went to the passenger side and, when Jason saw her, he got out of the car and into the back. Chance was in the driver's seat and she let him stay there. No sooner than she closed the door, Chance was hounding her about how much money she got.

"Damn, can I get in the car good? He gave me 35,000." They both gave each other dap while Nadja continued, "And I'm taking five." Chance and Jason looked at each other and shook their heads. "Y'all got a problem with that?" They both shook their heads no. "Come on, Chance, go straight to the house. I'm not riding around with all this money in the car." Chance drove straight back to Jersey and to her house.

They all went inside where she passed the envelope to Chance. Jason didn't like that, but he knew she did it because she was fucking Chance. Chance counted 15,000 dollars and the remaining 15,000 and passed one to Jason. He then counted the remaining pile, which added up to 5,000, which he passed to Nadja. He then counted his pile one more time, smiling the whole time.

Chance walked Jason out to his car. Jason took the Faberge eggs with him after convincing Chance to let him try to get rid of them another way, but not without Chance persuading him to let him keep the same two of the six. Jason promised that he wouldn't make a move with the eggs without him and Chance again held the two for collateral of that agreement. For all Jason knew, Chance could have the most expensive ones, so he would have to come and get them and Chance before selling them all.

Chance popped Nadja's trunk and brought their shopping bags and clothes in the house.

"So, now you feel better, baby?" Nadja walked over to Chance and rubbed his neck.

"I feel better, yeah, but that still ain't enough money to live off of," Chance complained.

"Chance, you have to learn how to be happy about something. You were just crying broke, now you have some change to play with and you're already whining."

"I know. I'm sorry, mommy. I'm just always thinking ahead. That's all. I will be happy and I thank you for makin' it happen. You wanna do something?" Chance figured it was only right to spend some money on her first.

"All I want to do is go to the movies. I don't ask for much." Chance took Nadja to the movies and was suddenly antsy. He didn't want to go back to her house. He wanted to see what was up with Twinkie. He had been with Nadja for a full day and he wanted to go outside and play.

After the movie, Nadja wanted to go have drinks at the local bar. Chance went along with her, hoping that she might run into her friends and then he would be able to get away.

They walked into Ray's bar and it was packed. A few people had shocked looks on their faces when they saw Chance with Nadja. While Chance was gone, Nadja had moved to the area and become very popular with the local "celebrities". That was how it was in Teaneck, Englewood, and Hackensack. If you were known on the streets of New York, when you moved to Jersey, you were instantly a part of the street culture, and automatically a "'hood star".

Jason was at the bar buying bottles of champagne, flossin'. Nadja and Chance walked up behind Jason. Jason turned around and greeted them both as if he hadn't seen them in years.

"Yo, I got a surprise for you!" Jason walked Chance to the back of the bar and up the stairs where there were tables and a small dance floor. He walked to the back wall and, sitting in the middle of two girls, was Roderick.

"Yo, my nigga is home, too?" Chance asked, as he gave Roderick a hug. He then hugged Malcolm who was sitting on the other side of one of the girls.

"Monday! And then it's on! Jason told me y'all just had a nice come up." Chance nodded proudly. He knew what that question was leading to. He had to hit Roderick off with some cash. Chance took a thousand dollars out of his pocket and passed it to Roderick. Roderick got ready to put it in his pocket.

"That's for you and Malcolm. Damn, shit don't change, you still a greedy nigga, huh?"

"Yup, and we gotta get this money. No more small-time jobs. We ready to go out tomorrow."

"A'ight nigga, I'm down. It don't matter." Chance had a funny feeling in his gut, but he ignored it. *Damn, these niggas ain't been out a week and they already want to rob a house. They need to calm down*, he thought. He then realized that he had been on it the same way when he had come home weeks before.

Chance went back to the bar where Nadja was sitting and talking to a girl that he didn't know.

"Hey, Sariah, this is my baby, Chance. Chance this is my girl, Sariah." Sariah looked at Chance and gave him *the look* and said hi to him. Chance said hello and moved away. *Damn, these bitches out here ain't shit. She's supposed to be my girl's friend and she giving me the "Let's Fuck" look.*

Chance was about to walk back by Jason and Roderick and Nadja called him over.

"What's up?" he asked.

"Get a bottle, baby, let's pop a bottle to us."

"Okay, you right. I got you. You want everyone to see that *we* an' *us,* huh?" Nadja started smiling.

Chance walked to the end of the bar, took out his knot of cash, and bought a bottle of Moet. It was overpriced at the bar for $80. He had it so he flaunted it.

When he turned around to bring the bottle, he saw a dude approach Nadja. He leaned down and was whispering in

 96

her ear. Chance asked himself if he really cared. She had been his girl for all of one day. But, he knew what she had and what she represented and he knew that a lot of niggas would want to be in his spot. He approached the table and the guy stood up. He looked at Chance like he was a *small fry*, and walked away.

"Let's go to this table," Nadja said and she got up and moved to a table so they could have their own private celebration. They sat and Chance popped the bottle. They were getting a lot of stares.

"To me and you, baby," Chance said, tapped her glass and took a sip, while she did the same. "A'ight, who was that nigga? He was all up in your ear."

"That was Dip. The one I just stopped fuckin' wit." Nadja liked that Chance was interested.

"So, what he want?" Chance said, feeling possessive.

"He wants me back. I told him I was with you."

They drank and Chance was introduced to more of her friends. He didn't even want to look around because everywhere he looked, it seemed like girls were coming on to him. He didn't realize that he was giving them the same look that they were giving him. He felt like he wanted to go home with more than just a few of them.

Jason, Roderick, and Malcolm came walking up to their table.

"Yo, homey, we going over the water to celebrate. You comin'?" Roderick asked Chance.

Chance looked at Nadja and she looked at the desire in his eyes. She knew he wanted to go.

"Go 'head. I'm gonna go out with my girls. Y'all be safe." Nadja gave Chance a kiss and he walked out with *the boys*.

Jason drove and they went to a new after-hours spot called Carters on 132nd. It was a brownstone and a step up from Mr. T's place.

This place had private rooms for private orgies and that is what they partook of. Roderick wanted to get some girls, so they did. They got three girls who entertained them while they sniffed cocaine and got drunk. They partied into the afternoon of the next day.

When Jason dropped Chance off at his mother's apartment, he slept for the rest of the day. They had plans to go out and do a job at 8:30 when it would be nice and dark out. Chance rested for work.

At 8:30 sharp, Malcolm knocked on Chance's window and he came out in his dark clothing. They had gloves in the car for Chance. They rode into Paramus, New Jersey and started looking for houses that were empty.

Jason spots three homes that appear to be unoccupied. One was pitch black and the other two had lights on but, from watching, they saw no movement in the house. One light on in a house usually meant the homeowners were trying to make it look like someone was home.

Roderick was eager and he jumped out of the car. He went and rang the doorbell. A car pulled up into the driveway and he walked back down the steps. The homeowner got out and suspiciously looked at Roderick and the other three men in the car. He signaled for his wife to stay in the car as he met Roderick in his driveway.

"May I help you?" he asked.

"Oh, I was looking for a girl named Sabrina. She told me she lived here." Roderick kept walking and got in the car.

Jason pulled off. They knew they had to leave that area because the white man seemed just the type to call the police to report them.

They got on the highway and drove to another town. They went to Fair Lawn, which was next to Paramus, another white, upper-middle class town. They drove around a few blocks just looking at the homes. Many of the houses were nice, but most of them were alive on the inside. They could see people moving around.

They turned down a street and slowly passed the houses. Chance called one. That one looks good. It was a brick house that had nice statues outside and nice landscaping. He figured that meant they had extra money to spend. A lot of money was being spent on the outside of the house, so the inside had to be extra nice.

There were four of them. Malcolm would stay in the car. Roderick, Jason, and Chance would go in. Chance agreed to wait by the window and watch from the inside to see if anyone pulled up. Roderick and Jason burst through the front door and Chance put the door back in place. He went to the living room window to watch.

Roderick and Jason made it through the house in eight minutes. They found nothing in jewels or money, so they started taking paintings off the wall. They took about eight paintings. They figured that there must have been hidden safes but they were unable to find them. As they were leaving with the paintings, a neighbor was coming out of their house.

"Hey. What are you doing over there?" the neighbor yelled and ran back into their house to call the police.

"Pop the trunk, Malcolm!" Malcolm popped the trunk and they put the paintings in. Only about five of them fit. They dropped the other three and jumped in the car. As they were driving down the street, a police car was turning onto the block. They passed the police car that must not have gotten the call yet, because they kept driving past them.

All of a sudden, Malcolm saw the police car do a U-turn and put his lights on. Malcolm put his foot to the floor and began speeding to get away.

"Yo, we gotta get away!" Roderick screamed.

"Pop the trunk! Let the paintings fall out!" Jason screamed.

Malcolm turned another corner and sped, as the paintings slid out of the car. The police car was swerving to avoid the paintings. They made it to the highway and then pulled behind a strip mall. They saw the lights of the police car continuing down the highway. The officer did not see them get off. Then they saw three more cars. They knew that they might double back and start looking in the parking lots. They had to abandon the car.

"Get out!" Chance yelled.

Malcolm pulled the car right along the back wall of the store that was closed. They got out one by one, walked a ways down, and went into a ditch that was behind the strip malls that line the highway Route 17.

 99

Chance got out, checked the trunk, and noticed the bag of Faberge eggs still in there. He grabbed the bag, but did not see that two of the eggs had fallen out. He went over to the three men lying in the mud.

"Listen, I'm gonna walk down this highway and go call Nadja to come and get us. Stay here until I get back. He got ready to leave the bag of eggs, but decided against it. He didn't know if he would make it or if they would be safer than he would, but he had to take his chances because laying there he could not do.

Chance walked along the highway and noticed three police cars on the north side of the highway coming back. He figured they were going to double back on the other side and start looking for the car. He ran into a motel and ordered a room.

Chance got in the room and called Nadja.

"Nadja, you gotta come to Route 17 and go buy the Paramus Park Mall and take the U-turn. When you get to that furniture store, pull off the highway. If you see the cops there, don't stop, but if it's clear, go behind the furniture store. The one next to PC Richards..." She cut him off.

"What are you talking about Chance? What happened?" She couldn't figure out what he was talking about, but she had an idea of what was going on.

"Listen! I'm in the Howard Johnson's hotel next to the Benz dealer. Go get Roderick, Malcolm, and Jason and bring them to room 312. Did you hear where you have to go? Pull behind that furniture store next to PC Richards. They are laying there in a ditch. You will see that Camry that Jason's been driving and flash your lights, or call them and they will come out. I'll be waiting here."

Chance hung up. He looked in the bag and saw that there were two eggs instead of four. He wondered if they were in the trunk or if they had fallen out. He looked at the beauty of the eggs. One was white and encased in a net of gold trimming with crystals or diamonds, he didn't know. It was beautiful. The other was blue and had a gold carriage around it. It looked like the chariot that Cinderella went to the ball in.

Chance dreamt of himself as the Prince that found Cinderella's shoe. He had money. He had power and he wanted the girl of his dreams. He imagined himself driving a Rolls Royce through the neighborhood and everyone standing outside, waving at him as he passed, waving to the crowd. There were plenty of girls waiting for him to stop for them, but he kept driving looking for the girl that would complete him. He noticed a girl in a yellow dress. She wasn't waving; she was just looking. She was looking worried when she saw him approaching, but she smiled. He recognized her face. The girl was Danielle.

Chance was awakened by a knock on his hotel room door. He slowly got up and peeked out of the peephole. He saw Nadja standing there by herself. He opened the door. The look on her face told it all.

"I got there and the cops were putting them in the cars and towing that car. Damn, you lucky." She walked in and sat on the bed. "What happened?"

"That nigga, Roderick, was thirsty. We went one place and the people came home when he was ringing the doorbell. Then we went to another spot and a neighbor saw us coming out with paintings. We got away, but they had to lay and wait for me to get to you. I seen the cops coming back down the highway and I knew they were gonna start searching the back of the buildings because our car just disappeared. Damn."

"I don't know what to say, Chance. What are you gonna do now?" Nadja was hoping that Chance would re-evaluate his life and start to think of other things to do with himself.

"I gotta see how much their bail is gonna be. I hope I don't have to spend all of my money bailing these niggas out. Come over here and give me some pussy; I need some." He grabbed Nadja and stood her up. He pulled her pants down and she stepped out of them. Although there was a bed right there, he pushed her up against the wall, took his dick out of his pants, and started fucking her from the back. He pulled her hair and grabbed her around the back of her neck. Nadja took his rough sex, knowing he was relieving stress more than anything else. When he came in her, she was not worried about getting pregnant because her tubes were tied. From the looks of it, Chance would be going away sooner or later, and this time, it would be prison and not a camp.

They left the room and went back to her house because her kids were there and she had to be there with them. They would be going to school the next day and she would be making the calls to find out about Roderick, Malcolm, and Jason's bails.

Nadja woke up and saw her kids off to school. She had Chance stay in her room. She wasn't ready for them to see a new man in her bed, since they had just seen Dip in there not even a month before.

Chance came down when the kids left and Nadja made breakfast for him. She was in a tight nightie that was not see-through, but tight fitting. Her curves were wide, but shapely. He liked Nadja a lot, he just wasn't totally attracted to her. He was more intrigued by who she was than what she looked like. He knew that being faithful to her was out of the question, especially since he had been thinking about Twinkie since he last got head from her. He knew he would be going back for more of that. Not to mention that he was wanting too many of the girls he saw in the bar. He just wanted to fuck as many girls as he could.

Nadja called the Bergen County Jail Annex and was told that the three detainees hadn't been arraigned yet. She was told to call back after noon.

Chance told Nadja he needed to drive her truck to go to Roderick's parent's house to see if Star was there yet.

"Do you have a license?" Nadja did not want to be linked to any robberies or have any accidents on her insurance that were not covered.

"No, but I won't get into anything. I just need to hold the car." Chance grabbed her and pulled her to him. He was sitting at the kitchen table and he pulled her panties to the floor. They dropped and he lifted one of her legs. He bent over, put his mouth on her pussy, and started sucking it. She lifted her leg up and let his tongue slide inside of her as she started to drip. Chance began to long stroke her with his tongue and she started to move on one leg until her wetness turned into a faucet of running cum. She grabbed his head and made him drink what was coming out of her. He sucked it, swallowed it, and smacked one last kiss on her pussy before sitting back up.

"Hmmmm. That pussy tastes good. That's all the breakfast I need. Where are the keys to the Montero?"

Nadja sat down and pointed to the drawer. Chance got up, took the keys, and told her he'd be back shortly.

"Oh, and keep calling the jail to see about my niggas." He was out the door with a fresh orange Enyce sweat suit and matching Ewing sneakers on. He had 10, 000 dollars in his pocket, which made him feel like a million bucks.

Chance drove past Star's parent's block and jumped on Route 46 to go see Twinkie. He stopped at a pay phone and told her that he was coming. She said okay.

Chance walked in and Twinkie had no clothes on, lying in the bed. He didn't want sex; he wanted head.

"Damn, you waiting for me like that? Or you just fucked another nigga?" he asked, but he really didn't care.

"Nah, I'm waiting for you. You gonna give me some of that dick? You ain't really twist me out the other night, but that's okay. That old lady probably got you all tired from washing her feet and helping her go to the bathroom and shit." Twinkie laughed and lit a laced blunt.

"What I tell you 'bout that? Why you talkin' shit about my girl?" Chance didn't like her talking about Nadja that way.

"Your girl? You mean your ol' lady?" She laughed, and took a hit of the crack and weed and passed it to Chance. He took it and smoked.

"My girl. Just for all that smart talk, you ain't getting no dick. Just suck this here dick and maybe I'll come back and bless you later."

Chance pulled his dick out of his pants and walked over to the bed. Twinkie sat up and wrapped her mouth around him. She sucked on him as if she was sucking the last bit of syrup out of a Dairy Queen Misty. She slurped and spit, and put in that work. Chance stood there pumping into her. His head was in the clouds. Her mouth took his mind to another place. A place where he wanted to stay. It was paradise inside of Twinkie's mouth and he let his waters run free like a waterfall. Then it was like a needle had scratched a record and it was over. He opened his eyes and came to himself. It was time to go.

"Yo, you want me to come back later?" He rubbed on her tittie and squeezed it real hard.

"Ouch, stop!" She pushed his hand away. "Nigga, you can do what you wanna do. I don't sweat no niggas; I just dig you for some reason, that's the only reason why you ain't payin'. But you ain't the only one." Twinkie didn't want Chance to think that he was getting over on her and she was mad that he had a girl, so she had a personal beef with him. One that she planned on winning. Her plan was to string him out and ruin his relationship. *Shit, this nigga think he gonna come here, get his shit off, and go back to his girl? Well I got a trick for his ass*, she thought.

"I ain't payin' cuz I ain't gotta pay. I ain't no duck. I'll call you later." Chance got in Nadja's truck and drove off.

He went to Star's house and rang the doorbell. Star came to the door, all smiles.

"Yo! My nigga! Last night was crazy!" Chance and Star hugged.

"What happened?" Star walked outside onto the porch.

"You don't know? Your brothers got locked up last night." Star looked shocked.

"Damn, my parents are gonna be through with them. What happened?"

"We went to do a house and a neighbor spotted us coming out of the house with paintings. We beat the chase but they caught them hiding. I had to walk the highway to go call my girl. Come with me to my girl's house so we can find out about their bails." Star closed the front door and got in the car with Chance.

"Yo, nigga, you need some up to date clothes. After we find out about them, we gonna go to the mall. Me and Jay made 30,000 on this house in Saddle Brook. And I still got four of these expensive eggs shits to sell. We gotta be smarter when we do this shit. We gotta have a better plan. That shit last night was reckless." Star nodded his head. Star was ready to get some money.

Chance rang the doorbell and Nadja came to the door dressed in DKNY. She had on a jean jumper with high heeled sneakers. She looked like a hustler's wife, for real, with all of her jewelry and fresh gear. *She is a hustler's wife*, he thought. He walked in and gave her a kiss.

"This my wifey, Nadja. Nadja this is Star." Nadja turned around and walked into the living room. Chance smacked her ass. She turned around and rolled her eyes.

"What's the matter?" He pulled her into the kitchen to talk to her.

"I don't go for that wifey shit. That's bogus. I am somebody's wife and I will never be nobody's wifey." Chance smirked. She was taking it too seriously.

"Okay, I'm sorry, boo. I won't say that anymore." He gave her another kiss. "So, did you call the jail? This is Roderick and Malcolm's brother."

"I know. I know Roderick. He was cool with my husband for years. They have a mutual friend. I knew Star when he was little." Nadja laughed.

"You tellin' your age, boo." Chance sat down and turned the channel on the TV.

"I ain't ashamed of my age. Shit, I've done more in 32 years than some people do in a lifetime. Star, you can sit down." Star looked at Nadja and winked at Chance. He could tell that Chance was just in it for the opportunity. "So, the jail said their bails are 200,000 each." She shook her head. "Jersey don't play. Damn, you can kill a nigga in New York and your bail won't be that high."

"Yeah, that's 'cause in New York, they know niggas can't pay low bails," Star said, and they all laughed.

"Damn, 200,000 each is 20,000. I gotta call the bail bondsman. You know any over here, Nadja?"

"They always have them by the jails. Let's go over there."

They went to the bondsman and were told that they had to put up 2,000 for each of them. That was all of Chance's money and he didn't know how much Jason had left of his money to give back to him. He knew that Roderick and Malcolm didn't have any money. They had just gotten out.

"Okay, so you have to go see Jason and see how much he got to give me back. I'll pay for Roderick if he pays for Malcolm." Nadja went across the street to the jail to see when Jason's visitation was, and it was later in the day. She went back to her car, where Chance and Star were waiting.

"Okay, we have to come back later. Where you wanna go?" Nadja didn't want to ride around with Chance and Star while they talked that jail talk. She was not in the mood. All the men she had known from New York to New Jersey were jailbirds and she was getting tired of it. That lifestyle was played out to her; it was just something that she was still tied to, but she wanted to break her own cycle.

"I'm going to get Star a few outfits from the mall. Go to the mall." Nadja did as she was told.

When they got to the mall, Nadja told Chance she would meet him at the car in an hour. She went to her favorite stores and shopped.

Chance and Star went to MACY*S and Chance bought Star a Karl Kani outfit, an Adidas sweat suit, and a pair of Jordan sneakers. They went to the food court and had something to eat. Two girls were walking by their table and Chance stopped them.

"What's up wit' y'all?" The girls turned around and stopped.

"What's up with y'all?" one of the girls replied.

"Well, you're by yourselves and we're by ourselves. So, what y'all wanna do?" Chance didn't see Nadja approaching from behind him and Star didn't have enough time to alert him. "Y'all wanna give up the digits?"

"Word, Chance, you doin' it like that?" Nadja walked up next to the girls, who started laughing and walked off. "I know that we just started calling this a *thing*, but you are already on some bullshit, huh?" Nadja stood there looking at Chance. Chance thought fast.

"I was just trying to get my man some ass. He just came home. Why would I do that and I'm here with you?" Star looked away so that he wouldn't laugh.

"Listen, Chance, I want you to know that I might be older, but I'm not slow. You can take this opportunity and get the best out of it, or you can mess it up. You never played in this league before and I'm giving you a shot. But, don't think for one minute that you can run circles around me mentally. I'm just letting you know, I was driving around the block in a Benz, when you were still crawling. Don't get it fucked up. I'm going to the car. It's time to go to the jail."

Nadja walked away and went to her car. *Do I even want to waste my time with this bum nigga?* She asked herself. *Fuck it, I'll get some good dick until he fucks up, and then I'll kick his ass to the curb.* She laughed. *Niggas are so fucking dumb; they couldn't keep a good thing if it attached itself to their fucking belt straps. He's gonna play himself; they always do.*

Chance got up and Star made fun of him. "Damn, she told yo' ass!"

"So what? She ain't goin' nowhere. I already got her twisted off this dick. It's all good. I bet she ain't gon' do shit." Chance didn't like how Nadja thought she was putting him in his place in front of his boy.

They approached the car and Nadja was talking on a mobile phone. Chance got in the passenger seat and Star got in the back.

"When did you get that?" Chance asked. Nadja put her finger up for him to wait. She hung up the phone.

"I just got it. They had a special. It's better to have a phone than a pager. When someone pages you, you can't even call them back." Nadja was not feeling Chance at that moment, but she was going to play it cool.

"Yeah, but when me and Jason came they wanted like $600. How much did you pay for that?" Nadja wanted to tell him to shut the fuck up.

"Well, the man was saying that cell phones are the new rave or wave or whatever he said. He was saying that soon beepers are gonna be obsolete." Nadja started driving toward the jail. Chance put his arm on her leg and started rubbing her thigh. She looked over at him and flashed a fake smile.

"What the fuck is obsolete mean?" Chance laughed.

"It means outdated. The cell phones are gonna be cheaper and people won't need beepers, but I'm a bad bitch cause I don't have to wait for that. I get shit before regular niggas get it." Nadja instructed trying to shine on Chance.

"Ooh, boo, that rhymed. What's your emcee name?"

"Caramel Queen. I used to rap with Sha-Rock from the Funky Four plus One More. She's my girl." She saw the look on Star and Chance's face and she explained, "She is older than me, but we grew up in the same building. I used to sit on the stoop with her and make up rhymes." They laughed at her. "So what?" Nadja laughed with them. "32 ain't even old."

Chapter 8

Nadja parked around the corner from the jail and left them in the car. She went inside, gave her driver's license and Jason's name, and sat down to wait. Two girls came in that looked familiar to her. She knew one as Roderick's girl. After the girls gave their names, they sat down. Nadja went over to them, leaned in, and whispered.

"Your name is Raquel, right?" Nadja asked the tall pretty girl with long hair and model looks.

"Yes." The girl looked suspicious, wondering if Nadja was going to tell her that Roderick was seeing her behind Raquel's back.

"My name is Nadja, I'm Chance's girl. I'm about to go see Jason to tell him that Chance will bail him and Roderick out if Jason agrees to give him the money back and will come and bail Malcolm out. They want $200,000, so, off the 10 percent the bail bondsman wants $2,000 apiece. Tell Roderick we are working on it." Raquel smiled.

"Thank you. I just had a son by him when he got locked up. I have been so stressed out. He just came home. This is my cousin, Stephanie." Nadja and Stephanie said hi to each other and Raquel kept talking. "My son just is about to be two and Roderick hasn't even been with us for a month." Raquel looked stressed out.

"Girl, my husband is doing life, don't feel bad. These men don't understand that what they do affects everyone, not just them. And then, when they get locked up, the women and children are left out here all fucked up and all they think about is themselves. My husband is not gonna stress me out, shit, all the hell he put me through with other bitches and shit. He can sit and think about that shit now. What goes around comes around. I'm not saying anything bad about Roderick but, girl, look out for you 'cause that's all these niggas do is look out for themselves and give you headaches until they need you. Then they act like they didn't do nothing wrong. Please." Raquel thought about it and knew Nadja was right.

"I'll tell him. But, let me get your number. Maybe we can be friends and help each other stay strong." Raquel took a pen out of her bag.

"No, just give me your number. I'll put it in my new mobile phone." Nadja took her phone out. The officer at the desk spoke to them rudely.

"Hey. Put your belongings in a locker. You're not taking that inside." Nadja looked at the redneck and decided to comply instead of getting a bullshit charge for using her right to freedom of speech.

"What's your number?" she asked, ignoring the officer and punching Raquel's number in her phone as she walked over to the locker. She stored the phone number the way the salesman had instructed her to, put her phone in her bag, her bag in a locker, and locked it using a quarter. She went back to sit next to the girls.

"Shit, they love to treat visitors like inmates." All three girls started laughing.

A few minutes later, their names were called to go to the visiting room. The room was a round room with plexiglass that separated the inmates from the visitors. The inmates were already seated at a phone and the visitors walked around until they found the seat opposite the person they were going to see.

Nadja waved at Roderick and Malcolm and walked past as Raquel and Stephanie sat down to visit them. Jason was a few seats away. Nadja sat down and picked up the phone.

"What happened to you that night?" Jason asked, without even saying hello.

"Hi, Jason. How are you feeling? I came and when I pulled off the highway, I saw the flashing lights and the car on the tow truck. I saw them putting y'all into the cars. Chance had walked to a phone and called me and I came right away."

"Damn, they got the eggs from that other shit," he mouthed to her, knowing that everything they said into the phone was being listened to. Out of his mouth, he said, "They are trying to say I was driving that car and that it had stolen property from two different homes in there. But, I don't own that car. So, they are trying to charge us with robbery when I bought those eggs off the street to give to my girl." Nadja just nodded her head and listened. She knew that whatever charges they had would be reduced due to technicalities like Jason was mentioning. The prosecutor always had to trump up the charges because, many times, the charges wouldn't be able to be proven, so they wouldn't stick. Many charges are eventually reduced or dropped.

"Well, listen, my friend said that he will bail you out and Roderick if you get the money from your girl. It's gonna be 4,000 and then you will have to use 2,000 to get Malcolm." Nadja looked at Jason's response to observe its genuineness. She knew that a caged animal would promise not to bite, until it got out and devoured its prey. Jason could say anything just to get out.

"Word to the mother? He said that? Okay, tell him do it. You comin' back to put it up?" Nadja nodded yes.

"Okay, that's my dude. Tell him my girl got the paper. I'll give it right back to him."

Nadja hung up the phone, walked past Raquel, and told her she would call her. She waved again at Malcolm and Roderick. They were all inside, dressed in orange jumpsuits, looking dusty and crusty. There was nothing cool about a jail jumper.

Nadja went outside and to the car. They went to the bails bondsman and completed the paperwork. The bails bondsmen went through the questioning process and they signed the paperwork. They went over to the jail and went to the side where you go to bail someone out. They waited, paid, and left. It would be hours before they would be released and Nadja was not taking the loyalty that far. She was ready to go home to her children.

"Do you want to wait? Because I'm going home," she told Chance, still holding on to her attitude. He walked over to her side of the car and up close to her.

"Fuck is wrong with you?" He had an evil look in his eyes.

"Chance, I'm hip to your game and I'm not wit' it. I don't like what you did at the mall. Now, I want to go home. You staying with Star or what?" Chance looked over at Star. He knew they didn't have a way to get Jason and Roderick home, so it didn't make sense to wait. He also knew that he wasn't even in good enough yet with Nadja to be fucking up. He hadn't even moved in officially. He had some charming to do.

"Yo, Star, I'm going home with my boo. We will drop you off home, 'cause there ain't no need to wait for them, we can't ride them home on our backs."

"That's cool. Take me home." Star wanted to say what was really on his mind, *Damn, nigga, you got this bitch running yo' ass like that?*

They rode in the car silently and Nadja said bye to Star under her breath. When Star got out of the car, Chase blasted on her.

"Yo, what the fuck is wrong with you? You a grown woman and you're acting like a baby. So what? I spoke to some little dumb pigeons. That's just sport. It don't mean shit. I get numbers all the time that I never use." Nadja felt reprimanded like she was a child.

"Oh, I hear that, playboy." Nadja pulled into her driveway and they went in the house.

As soon as Chance closed the door behind them, he grabbed Nadja and pushed her on her knees. He pulled his dick out of his pants, pulled her head, and forced himself into her mouth. Nadja began to suck Chance off when a key was heard being put in the door. She jumped up just as Tariyah came in. Chance started walking toward the kitchen so that he could zip up his pants. He got something to drink out of the refrigerator, went to Nadja's bed, and fell asleep.

Nadja stayed downstairs with Tariyah and helped her with her homework and her sons, too, when they came in. When they boys left the dining room table to go play, Tariyah confronted her mother.

"Mommy, what is the deal with you and that guy?" Tariyah was a mature 14-year old girl. Nadja always vowed to be honest with her daughter so that she would see life for what it really is, not sugar coat things to set her up for disappointments as an adult.

"I am seeing him. Dip didn't work out, so I'm trying to see if this will." Nadja told Tariyah to join her on the couch in the living room so they could continue their conversation.

"But you know it's not gonna work Mommy." Tariyah flipped through the channels.

"Why do you say that, Ti-ya". That was what Tevin called her since a baby and everyone picked it up.

"Mommy, he seems like he is just gonna play you. Dip seemed like he really cared. He doesn't seem like he does." Nadja didn't want to hear that.

"You have to get to know him; he just has a lot of issues and things that he's going through right now. Plus, younger guys are more moldable. I can work with him; an older man is too stuck in his ways." Nadja didn't realize that she was only making excuses because she wanted things to work out. She also didn't want to be honest with herself that at least an older man would have standards and substance, which a young man might lack, if it wasn't instilled in him from a young age.

"I don't want to get to know him." Tariyah stopped speaking as Chance came downstairs.

"Let me hold the Montero. I just called Star, and Roderick and Malcolm are waiting for a ride." Nadja didn't want to show conflict in front of Tariyah so she just gave him the keys.

"How long are you gonna be?"

"I'm just going to get them and come back. You want me to take your cell phone so you can call me if I'm taking too long?"

"Yeah, because you might get them and they will try to talk you into doing something stupid. You need to get a mobile phone." Nadja passed Chance her phone.

"I know, let's go to the mall tomorrow and get me one." Chance walked out the door without giving Nadja a kiss. She knew that men got bored very fast and the newness wears off very quickly.

Chance went to Jason's girl's house. When he called Star, Star had told him that Roderick's girl had picked them up. Jason gave him the 2,000 dollars back. He rushed from Jason's house. He only had a little bit of time.

He stopped at a pay phone and called Twinkie. She said he could come over.

He walked in and another dude was walking out. He went straight to her room and she was in the bathroom in the shower. He saw that she had some coke in a bill. He picked it up and started sniffing it. His heart started racing right away and he felt like he should sit down.

Twinkie came in the room with a towel wrapped around her. He pulled the towel off her and told her to walk around the room with no clothes on. She sat on the bed next to him.

"Why do you keep coming here like this?" Twinkie grabbed the bill and started sniffing the coke.

"I don't know. I keep thinking about you. You know, every nigga likes a bad girl." He leaned over and sucked on her tittie.

"Yeah. I know. Husbands, boyfriends, y'all niggas ain't shit." Chance looked at the time. He had been gone for 45 minutes. He didn't have a lot of time left. He took his cock out of his pants and played with it. He made it get hard.

"Come sit on me."

Twinkie got up and got ready to sit on Chance.

"Put on a condom." Chance didn't want this bitch to burn him and then he burn Nadja.

"I don't have any." Twinkie backed herself up onto Chance. She opened her legs and sat on his pole. He couldn't resist. He was already hard. As she was pumping on him, the phone rang. He looked at the phone and saw Nadja's house number pop up. He grabbed Twinkie by her hips and pulled her up and down on him fast and hard. He came in her and jumped up. He asked her for some of her cocaine and she gave him some. He left and told her he would call her the next day. When he walked out of her room, she wrote down the number that she saw appear on the screen.

Chance made it back to Nadja's house in an hour and a half. When he walked in using the key, which was on the car key chain, he liked how walking into a house felt. He had lived on a block of nice houses, in an apartment, and the envy was unbearable. When he intruded other people's homes, he felt animosity that they had so much and he had so little. He felt like he had graduated.

It was 11 o'clock and the kids were sleeping. Nadja was lying in her bed on the phone. When Chance walked in the room, she got off of the phone.

"What's up, baby? How'd everything go with Jason and Roderick?" She moved the blanket back and revealed the sexy negligee that she had on. It was a pink, crotch-less, netted one piece, that only reminded Chance of how Twinkie would look in it.

"They good. I got my money back from Jason. I want to sell those eggs. Call that guy downtown."

"He said I have to give him a couple of weeks." She opened her legs up to get his attention. Chance remained at the end of the bed facing the television set.

"Oh, yeah, I got this, too." Chance got up and found the necklace that he took from Jason's trunk and had hid in Nadja's closet. He put it on the bed. Nadja picked it up and put it in her end table drawer. She was anxious to have sex with him.

"Okay, I will take care of it, now come on and take care of me." Chance knew that he could not just fuck Nadja without at least washing Twinkie off him. He would have preferred to wait the three days to make sure he wasn't burning. Nadja would be done with him if he gave her an STD.

"I'm hungry. Make me a plate while I take a shower." Nadja's antennae went up. *Yeah, nigga, you gotta take a shower before you eat?* She thought. *I wonder what you been doing. Women's intuition was not something to play with.*

"Give me some first." She was gonna see how far he would go to avoid her and why. Nadja moved behind him and tried to pull his shirt up over his head. Chance pulled away from her.

"Nadja, stop! I'm stressed the fuck out! My niggas got new cases. I'm hungry; I ain't thinkin' about fuckin' right now, damn! Can you get me something to eat first?" Chance stood up and walked out of the room.

"Oh, okay, I hear you. You stressed? Let me find out that it's something else," Nadja called after him. She put a silk robe on over her and followed him into the kitchen.

Chance was pouring a drink from the liquor bottles that Nadja kept in the cabinet. He poured himself a shot of Remy. Nadja went into the kitchen and sat at the table.

"I thought you were making me a plate." Chance downed his shot and poured himself another one.

"Damn, you *that* stressed over other niggas, huh? You sure that's what it is? Your plate is in the microwave; you can just heat it up." Nadja waited for Chance's response.

"Isn't that what I said?" Chance sat at the table and waited for his food to finish.

"Listen, Chance, I feel for you. I liked you from the moment you walked in the door. I feel your struggle, but I will not be your doormat. You are young. You still have a chance to fix your life before it's too late. You are choosing the life that you are choosing."

"I don't have choices; I have to make it happen or do without." Chance finished his second shot of Remy. He kicked his Jordan sneakers off under the table.

Nadja patted her lap and Chance put his feet in her lap. She started rubbing his feet.

"Listen, Chance. You gotta make your own choices, but the right ones. Why are black men so scared of sacrifice and struggle? What you make fast, will go fast. What you build will give you a foundation. It won't crumble. It will stand on

 116

your hard work, blood, sweat, and tears. What do you want to do?"

"I want to get money. Damn, that feels good, ma." Chance leaned back and tuned Nadja out, enjoying his foot massage.

"Chance, money is not the end; it's the means to the goal. The money can't be the object, just the tool." The microwave signaled that his food was ready.

Nadja got up, took Chance's plate out of the microwave, and put it on the table in front of him.

"I'll be waiting for you in the bed, baby, don't make me wait to long." Nadja went upstairs to lie down.

Nadja jumped up out of her sleep at two am and Chance not only had not touched her, but he wasn't even in the bed. She got up and went downstairs thinking that he might have fallen asleep on the couch, watching television.

Chance was not on the couch. She went to the kitchen. He was not there either and his shoes were no longer under the table.

Nadja started breathing hard. "I know this muthafucka didn't take my car," she said aloud.

She walked to the door and opened it. Her Benz was in the driveway, but the Montero was not parked in front of her house. She went to get the phone to call her cell phone and as she called it, it rang from the kitchen table.

Nadja sat on the couch until 4 a.m. when Chance came walking quietly through the door from seeing Twinkie. He was startled when he saw Nadja sitting on the couch.

"Oh, shit. I had to go handle some business, ma. I didn't want to wake you up." He went to walk upstairs and Nadja called him quietly. He turned around nonchalantly.

"What's up, ma?" he stood on the steps and she motioned for him to come in the living room so the children wouldn't wake up.

"Chance, are you playing me?"

"Playing you how?" Nadja looked at him, as he knew exactly what she was talking about, and, of course, he did. He played the dumb role. "Oh, with a broad? Nah, ma, I'm just out here trying to get this money." Nadja knew that he was lying. She had a trick for him.

"Oh, okay. Because I don't want this to get ugly. If this is not what you want, you don't have to have it baby. You are free to live your life. I ain't trying to be a burden to you."

"Stop, ma, you my boo. I want to stay here with you." He gave her a kiss, sat down on the couch, and fell asleep as soon as he laid his head back.

Chapter 9

Nadja got up and went to her bed. She got up at 6 a.m., woke Chance up, and told him to go in the bed so her children wouldn't see him sleeping on the couch when they got up to get ready for school. She got the kids ready, made breakfast, and sent them off to the bus stop. Tariyah waited for her friends who came to get her to walk to her middle school and she left.

Nadja woke Chance up and told him she had a lot of running around to do and that he had to leave and come back later.

"Why I can't stay?" Chance walked toward the bathroom and Nadja stopped him.

"Because I don't want you to. And I don't have time for you to take a shower. Where you want me to drop you off at?" She didn't care where he was going; he was getting out of there, though.

"Take me to my moms." He sensed that she was very intent on getting rid of him and not just for the day. He couldn't have that.

"Boo, I'm sorry about last night. I should have just stayed here with you. I ain't gonna mess up, you just let me bring my clothes here. I want to stay forever." He started putting his clothes over his underwear and he put his sneakers on.

I bet you do, she thought, but said, "Well, call me later and see if I'm back. I'm gonna be in the city all day. I got to check on my spots." She led him out of the house and to her car.

They got in the car and Nadja drove to Chance's apartment building. She gave him a dry kiss and pulled off.

Chance walked into the house and his mother was sitting on the couch, watching television with Jonny.

"Ma, tell Jonny he gotta go." Chance looked at his mother in disgust and shook his head. Chance did not even look at Jonny. He knew that if he looked at him, he might strike him.

"Jonny, come back a little later, okay? Let me talk to Chance for a little while." Jonny stood up and had to steady his ground. He bent down to pick up his cigarettes and almost fell onto the coffee table. Chance knew that he was nodding out from the heroin. Vonetta tried to keep her eyes wide open so Chance wouldn't detect the same thing in her.

Jonny took a moment to stand straight without falling back down from his drunken stupor. Chance's blood began to boil. Chance stood in Jonny's way so that he would have to say excuse me to get past him.

Jonny brushed past Chance and Chance dropped him. He punched him in his head and Jonny fell flat on his back. Chance lifted up his foot and began to stomp Jonny out, repeatedly. He kicked him in his face numerous times. Vonetta was in her zone and moved in slow motion as she tried to effortlessly grab Chance. It took nothing for him to push her on the couch where she sat, hollering and wailing, "Stop Chance! Stop!"

Chance saw nothing but red. The red from his anger, blinded him from seeing the red blood from Johnny's head squirting all over the place. He couldn't see what he was doing, he didn't know that he was killing Jonny.

Chance didn't hear Corey come running into the living room when he came in the house and saw what was going on. Corey grabbed Chance and tackled him from behind. He jumped on Chance's back, pulled him backwards onto the ground, and held him tight. Chance was lying on top of Corey and could not release himself because Corey had him around his neck.

"Ma, call the ambulance!" Sparks had to yell to get Vonetta out of her zone.

"Yo, Corey, let me go!" Corey let Chance go and he ran out of the door. He ran the two blocks between his house and Star's house. He ran through the park and through Star's backyard. He started banging on Star's back door.

Malcolm came to the back door and opened it. His mouth dropped when he saw the blood all over Chance's clothes and sneakers. Chance pushed past him.

"What the fuck happened?" Malcolm whispered, not wanting his mother to hear the commotion. He motioned for Chance to go into the basement. He ran upstairs, got Star, and brought a sweat suit back down for Chance to change into.

Star looked like he saw a ghost when he saw Chance. Chance went into the laundry room and changed. His boxer shorts had bloodstains on them, too. He took his clothes and socks off and put them in a plastic garbage bag that Star gave him. He walks out of the laundry room and sits down with Malcolm and Star.

"Yo, what happened, Chance?" Star asked, calmly.

"I just stomped Jonny out. I might have killed his ass." Chance took a deep breath and kept picturing the scenario over and over again. "Let me use the phone..." Chance dialed Nadja's number and she answered.

"Baby, I need you to come get me." Chance said, humbly.

"Oh, word, baby?" Nadja replied, sarcastically. "Well, you got a phone call earlier."

"A phone call? What you mean?" Chance couldn't even think straight.

"Yeah, some girl name Twinkie called on my house phone asking for you." Chance wanted to drop the phone.

"For me? Who is Twinkie?" He didn't know how much she knew and he wasn't going to give up any information.

"Yeah, she said, can I speak to Chance and I said who is calling and she said my name is Twinkie. And I asked her how she got my number and she said that she thought this was his mother's house because the other night when he was here and his cell phone rang, he said that it was his mother calling and that he had to go." Chance couldn't believe his ears. He didn't know what to say.

"I don't know what you're talking about." Chance was furious.

"Oh, you don't? Well, I can tell you. You played yourself. Call Twinkie. You can pick your clothes up from outside by the trash can." Nadja hung up the phone.

Chance shook his head in disbelief. He dialed another number. Twinkie answered.

"What's up? What you doin'?" Chance asked Twinkie.

"Waiting for you. You coming by?" Twinkie asked.

"You gotta come and get me," Chance said, nicely.

"Where you at?" Twinkie asked, eagerly.

"Come to Harrison Street in Teaneck and call this number back." Chance hung up.

"So, you think you killed him for real?" Star reiterated.

"I don't know. I couldn't help it. The nigga was in my fuckin' house, all doped up and shit. He couldn't even stand up straight, my moms noddin' out on the fuckin' couch. I just had to drop the nigga and then I couldn't stop myself. I split his fucking face open." Chance sat on the couch going over and over it in his mind.

About a half-hour later, Star's house phone rang. Star answered and then handed the phone to Chance.

"Come down to 139." Chance got up, picked up the garbage bag, and went outside. Twinkie pulled up in her Honda Accord and Chance got in, after putting the bag on the back seat.

Twinkie smiled at him. Chance grabbed her around her neck and pushed her against the car window.

"Fuck you call my girl for?" He said between clenched teeth. Twinkie kept calm and waited for him to let go of the grasp around her neck. He let go to let her speak.

"I don't know. I'm sorry. I was letting you come through, but you can't never stay and shit. I know you like me more than you want to admit. I know you and me can have something but you trying to fake the funk with her. Why?

You don't think we can make money? You scared? You just want her because she's stable, but I know you don't really want her." Chance couldn't fight with Twinkie. He had nowhere to go. He wanted to tell her that she was just a slut that he liked to slore. But, he needed her at that moment.

"Well, I guess I'm staying with you until she takes me back. Drive around the corner and park. I gotta go get my clothes." Twinkie drove and parked where Chance told her to and watched him walk through someone's backyard.

"Niggas is so dumb, like I can't figure out where she lives at. All I gotta do is drive in this area and look for a damned blue Montero". She shook her head.

Chance came back very quickly with two black trash bags. He put them in Twinkie's trunk and they drove off.

"Yeah, I figured you need to see what it's like to be with me." Twinkie was very arrogant and Chance didn't like it, as much as he liked it.

"Bitch, shut the fuck up. You think I wanna hear that shit you talkin'? You don't know shit about me or my girl. Make a left." Chance drove past his mother's house and saw the two police cars parked outside of his mother's building. There was no ambulance. He figured the ambulance had already came and taken Jonny to the hospital. Make a right at this corner. Turn in that driveway and go to the back and pull by the dumpster."

Twinkie followed his orders and pulled over. Chance took the first bag that he had brought out of his friends' house and threw it in the dumpster. He got back in the car and they drove to Twinkie's apartment.

They walked in and he put his bags down. No sooner than he could turn around, his dick was in Twinkie's mouth. She pulled his pants down and didn't notice the blood on his boxers because she pulled them down with his pants. His dick did taste funny for the first few slurps but she swallowed her saliva and kept on licking. He grabbed her head and shoved himself down her throat. She gagged and opened her throat wider. He pulled back and rammed his dick down her throat again. Her tongue wrapped around his dick to stay attached to the ride. Chance pulled her hair tighter and thrust hard into the back of her throat. He let Twinkie slob and slurp. She moved her head back massaging him with her mouth on the way up and then on the way back down. He moaned and leaned his head back. He bent his knees a bit and up stroked her. Twinkie rose up and took his action. Twinkie was doing her job. She was slobbing his knob into oblivion. He was back on the beach in paradise. He didn't see Twinkie, he just felt what was happening to his manhood, and it was just what he needed. He didn't want to let the nut go, so he held out to let her wet mouth stay on the playground. He stroked hard then slow. She swirled and twirled around his dick like a graceful ballerina.

Chance was not worried about the police or Nadja. He came in Twinkie's mouth and told her to go to the store and buy something to eat and to CVS to get him some boxers. He told her that she would be hanging up his clothes when she came back.

"Yeah? You must be givin' up some dick then. Don't think I haven't noticed you always getting your dick sucked and shit but you stingy with the fucking. I need it in my mouth, so it's whatever, but my pussy needs love, too." Twinkie was smiling on the inside even though she was trying to sound like she was bitching on the outside. She knew that if Chance let her call his girl and he still went with her, that she didn't have anything to worry about. She was going to turn that nigga out. Twinkie walked out and slammed the door behind her.

Chance called Nadja from Twinkie's house phone. Nadja answered.

"Hello."

"Yo, I need you right now." Chance was not trying to stay with Twinkie but he would if Nadja stood her ground.

"Chance, you need me? I think you'll be a'ight, homie." Nadja was not going to be played. Chance had gotten it confused.

"Yeah, Nadja. I need to talk to you. When can I come over?" Chance didn't know what to do, but he knew he'd better try. Plus, she had the Faberge eggs and that chain. He needed that.

"Well, I have company call me tomorrow." Nadja hung up.

Chance hung up. He called his mother's house.

"Hello?" Chance heard Corey's worried voice.

"What happened?" Chance asked, rushing him.

"Yo, that nigga was bleeding so much we had to call the ambulance. We couldn't let the nigga die on the floor. Me and Ma didn't give any information, so they locked Ma up. They said she might have done it. They just trying to scare her into talking. They gave her an under the influence charge and interfering with a police investigation. She said they can't question me. So they locked her up." Chance fought back the tears that were welling up in his eyes. He tried to hold back the cracking of his voice as he continued to speak to his little brother.

"Yo, where's Chante?" Tears rolled down his face and he wiped them away angrily. He was a man; he wasn't supposed to cry.

"She with that nigga. She always at that nigga's house." Chance started hollering.

"What nigga? Who the fuck Chante sleeping with?"

"Yo, big bro, you buggin'. Chante 20, muhfuckin' years old. Yo' ass is stuck in time. You been home and it ain't even like you home." Chance ignored his brother's truth.

"So what they ask about me? Could Jonny talk; did he say my name?" Chance knew the police were already looking for him.

"He didn't say anything in here but maybe he told them in the ambulance." Corey continued to tell Chance whatever he wanted to know.

"Call the hospital and ask about his progress. I'll call you back." Chance hung up.

Corey called and got the nurse's station where he was told that Jonny was still in intensive care. He told Chance when he called back and Chance told him to find out in the morning what his mother had to do to get out and let him know when he called. Corey agreed and hung up.

Chance hung up and went to sleep. He woke up at three in the morning when Twinkie was walking in. She had on clothes as if she was coming from the club.

"Damn, where you been?" Twinkie smirked and dropped a stack of bills on the bed. She gave Chance a kiss and went to sleep, after taking all of her clothes and underwear off.

Chance went back to sleep.

The next morning, Chance woke up to another dick suck. He let Twinkie suck on him while holding his cum. He wanted to have that feeling all day if he could. He didn't want that feeling to go away. It was like a drug, a high that you didn't want to come down from.

Twinkie made sure that Chance got the release that he needed and she got up and took a shower. She came back into the room and got dressed. Chance counted the money that Twinkie had dropped on the bed that he had moved from the bed to the dresser. It was $500.

Twinkie asked Chance if he wanted to come with her to the grocery store. He said no. She left and Chance called his mother's house. He spoke to Corey who was going with Chance's uncle to post a thousand dollars for his mother's bail. He said that Jonny was still in the intensive care unit.

When Chance got off the phone, Twinkie's roommate knocked on the door. Chance told her to come in. Peaches came in the room with a tiny one piece on, see-through and crotch-less. Her body was banging. Twinkie was cute with a cute shape, but Peaches' body was rounder and plumper and every part was bigger. Chance instantly got hard. He didn't know if it was a setup, if Twinkie had put Peaches up to it and he cared more about fucking Peaches than knowing the answer, but he gave the inquiry a shot.

"Oh, you just come in here showin' yo' ass and tits and shit, huh? What? Twinkie tell you to see if I'm a grimy muh-fucka? Well, Twinkie ain't my fuckin' girl. She ain't got no ownership on me. I can fuck who I want to fuck." Peaches started laughing as she sat on the bed and opened her legs.

"Fuck Twinkie. She's my roommate. She ain't my friend. I don't fuck with her like that. She a grimy bitch and I know how to be grimy back. I stopped being friends with her when she fucked my man. I won't tell her shit if you don't." Chance felt like a kid in a candy store, *Two pieces of in-house pussy? Damn, can it get any better than this*, he thought.

"Now, you want some of this fat, juicy pussy or what?" Peaches lay back on her elbows and opened her legs wide. She started playing with her pussy with one hand and then she held up a condom in her other hand.

Chance took the condom out of Peaches' hand, dropped his boxers to the floor, and put it on his already aroused dick. He climbed in between her legs and put himself inside of her. The moment he did, her pussy wraps itself around his dick and started to caress and jerk it better than any pussy he'd ever felt. She felt like she had a thousand muscles that were each squeezing and letting go of his dick for another muscle to take over another piece of him.

"Damn, your pussy is alive. Your shit is pulling me in. I gotta come right now!" Chance hollered and let it all out. He kept pumping until all of his cum was in the condom.

"I'm cumming right now, too! I'm cumming! I want this dick again! That was too fast."

Chance pulled out of her and told her to go and get another condom. He was trying to hurry before Twinkie came back, but he had to get another piece of Peaches while the opportunity was there.

Peaches came back in the room and she asked Chance to fuck her in the ass.

He entered her from the back and smacked her ass as he fucked it. Her ass was jiggling and he grabbed it and squeezed it as he quickly came again.

"Damn, I gotta have that pussy again. You gonna give it to me whenever Twinkie ain't here," Chance whispered into her ear, although he couldn't believe he was open on Peaches like that, that fast.

"Yeah, I will. I'm a kinky bitch. I'm gonna want it nasty." She pulled herself off him and turned around. He lay on her stomach.

"I got that nasty nasty for you. Your pussy is the bomb. I'm gonna be thinking about you when I'm in here with Twinkie."

"I know," Peaches said, getting up and walking out of the room.

Chance took the condom off his dick and picked up the other used on off of the floor and flushed them down the toilet. He lay in the bed, flipping the channels with the remote.

Chapter 10

Chance woke up when he felt Twinkie sucking on his dick. He put his head up to make sure it was Twinkie and not Peaches back for Round 3. When he saw the top of Twinkie's head, he pushed her off him.

"What the fuck is wrong with you?" She sat up and on his legs. He moved her legs off him so that she would move, which she did.

"Nothin', damn. I know what you trying to do." Chance had too much on his mind.

"Oh yeah? And what is that? Let yo' ass stay here just like that? Wanna to try and rock wit' you? You met me for nothing? You came over with your girl in the store, just to fuck? Well, we did that and you came back. You ain't supposed to come back if it's just a fuck and when you do, it means you ain't gonna stop. You just wanna keep fuckin' me behind your girl's back or do the damned thing with me?" Chance wanted to tell the bitch that he was only there for a minute. Instead, he told her what she wanted to hear.

"Let's do the damn thing then. Fuck it, I'm down. Let's see if you can handle it."

"Handle it? Nigga, you about to get handled and you don't even know it. I'm gon' shut yo' ass down!" Twinkie started laughing and Chance was not the least bit amused. She talked too much shit as far as he was concerned and didn't even realize that she was a pigeon.

"Shut the fuck up and go make something to eat. I need you to take me somewhere tonight, too." Twinkie went to the kitchen to make Chance something to eat.

Chance picked up the phone and called Star.

"Yo, what up, nigga, you wanna do a B&E tonight?" Chance asked Star.

"Yeah, I need some money and I ain't fuckin' with Roderick, he shiesty as hell, even though he's my brother. And Malcolm, don't say shit. We can do it ourself." Star was ready.

"I got this bitch to drive, we straight. I'll pick you up when the sun drops." Chance hung up the phone. He went out in the living room and sat on the couch. Peaches came in the living room from her room and sat on the love seat across from Chance. She lifted one leg up and put it on the arm of the loveseat so that he could look over and see her crotch peeking out of her cutoff Daisy Duke jean shorts. She looked like she didn't have any underwear on. She gazed at Chance with a bold stare. He looked directly back at her.

Twinkie came in the room holding a fork in her hand.

"Damn, Peaches, put your fuckin' leg down. Everybody don't wanna see your fuckin' pussy." She looked at Chance who was still looking at Peaches. "Well, I don't. And Chance, don't think this bitch ain't gonna try to get some dick and all I gotta do is find out, and you can step. I'm just letting you know." Twinkie walked back in the kitchen to continue cooking.

"Fuck you, Twinkie, don't nobody want yo' shit. I ain't like you. I gots my own shit." Peaches winked at Chance. Chance looked away and at the T.V. He knew that that's all bitches did, argue and try to compete with each other. He was going to fuck Peaches if she was down to give up the pussy. He wasn't going to deprive her or him from a good fuck. He didn't owe Twinkie shit…but some dick too.

They started watching videos on BET. LL Cool J's "Around the way girl" video came on. Chance started singing, "I want a girl with extensions in her hair, bamboo earrings, at least two pair…" Twinkie came out and started dancing in front of Chance. When she turned around to dance with her butt in his face, he grabbed his crotch, looked over at Peaches, and then back at Twinkie when she turned around. Chance was in pimp mode. He just knew he was the man, with two bad slutty bitches at his disposal. He was in Playa Heaven.

The next video was Naughty by Nature, and Chance sang, "You down with OPP, yeah, you know me." He nodded his head, looked from Twinkie to Peaches, and told Twinkie, "Yo, go roll a blunt. And lace that shit and pour me some Hen-dog."

Twinkie poured the glass of Hennessy, rolled up the blunt with rocks in it, lit, and passed it to Chance. He leaned back on the couch, with his Mecca sweatpants pulled up to the knees and his wife beater tank top, and put one leg up on the couch and toked on the blunt like he was in Jamaica on a private island. That's how Boss he felt.

Twinkie bought in the fried chicken wings, macaroni, and cheese and collard greens. He stopped smoking and drinking to eat.

"Hold up. Everything on pause, let me stop this shit and eat, cuz after I eat, I'm gon' get fucked up and then I'ma wanna fuck." Twinkie sat down on a recliner that was next to the couch and replied, "Oh boy, we'll see."

"Yeah. What if I wanna fuck you and Peaches, Twink? You gon' let me?" Twinkie stared at the television set and ate her food without answering. "Well, since you don't wanna say nothing, eat and get ready to fuck me and Peaches."

Twinkie contemplated if she should do what Chance said he wanted her to do. Chance was arrogant, outspoken, and a good fuck. She liked him and his attitude. It wasn't like she was a prude and had never had a ménage-trios, it was the fact that she knew with him staying there and Peaches living there, she would just be condoning them fucking around whenever she wasn't there. If she started that right then it could turn ugly, like him starting to sleep in both rooms, and to the extreme. It was too early to let him get that off and plus she liked him too much. She knew that if she played it like she wouldn't have it, at least they would have to sneak and do it and then she'd probably end up busting them. She was not going to out and out agree with them fucking. That was not a good move to make. Twinkie finished eating her food and answered Chance's question.

"I ain't fuckin' you and Peaches and you can fuck with me or you can fuck with her. You ain't doin' both. And she can front all she want, she know she ain't bout it like me." Twinkie walked in the kitchen with her empty plate.

"Whatever, Twinkie. I ain't gonna do that to you, even though you did it to me." Peaches said and winked at Chance.

Chance didn't care what Twinkie said he was going to get it done. He was going to have a threesome with them.

He started smoking and checked the time. It was 5:30; he had until 8:00. He figured he'd spend two hours being fucked up and getting pussy and then he would get ready to hit a house.

Chance was feeling mellow and subdued. The Hennessy had him bent too. He felt like the couch was a cloud. He was floating deeper and deeper into the couch. He saw Twinkie walk over, grab his hand, and pull him up. He felt like he was floating to the bed.

Twinkie laid him on his back and took all of her clothes off. She had a DKNY sweat suit on and she stripped to her birthday suit. Chance kept his eyes on her. Even though she seemed to be blurry, he could see her body. Her body was tight; she looked like a Playboy bunny.

Twinkie straddled Chance and took his sweats off along with his boxers. He lifted himself up to help her. She put her pussy on top of his pole and immediately looked like she was riding a bull. Chance just laid back and enjoyed the show.

Twinkie hopped up and down, spun around on Chance's hardness, and started panting and yelling, "Yeah, muhfucka! How this pussy feel slidin' up and down this dick?"

"It feels da bomb, Twink. Fuck me, girl. Keep slidin' that pussy." Chance grabbed her waist, lifted her up, and pulled her down hard. He did pushups with her body as she bounced.

"You better stop tryin' to front on me, too. I feel your fucked up vibe, like you ain't really pressed. You frontin'," Twinkie assured him.

"I hear you," Chance said unconcerned. He grabbed her one hard time and came right inside of her. She relaxed and stayed on him as he dropped his arms to the side. He put his hands behind his head and playfully pumped her up and down.

"You like me, I know. You ain't gotta admit it." She leaned over to the ashtray, grabbed the blunt, and lit it. She smoked and passed it to Chance.

"I do like you. You trouble like me though. Two troublemakers cause too much trouble. But, fuck it, enjoy the ride." He pulled on the blunt and blew the smoke toward her face.

"I just did." Twinkie leaned forward and kissed Chance. He didn't kiss her back. He didn't want her to get it confused. She was going to be his ho, not his girl. "Let me guess, you're not into kissing?"

"Nah, I'm not." He pushed her off him and took the last swig of his glass. "Okay, we got two hours to sleep. Let's take a nap. We gotta pick my man up at 8:30 and you gotta drive us to handle something."

"Okay. I bet you will sleep with me, though, but you won't kiss me, huh? Nigga, you is full of shit, but it's okay. I dealt with niggas like you before."

"Shut the fuck up, Twinkie, before I bus' you in your muthafuckin' mouth." Chance grabbed her, laid her down in front of him, and put his arm around her stomach; and they slept.

At 8:15, Chance jumped up and woke Twinkie up.

"Let's go. Put on some dark shit. Like a black sweat suit or sweatshirt." Twinkie looked in her closet for some clothes like those that he had described. She didn't ask any questions because she had all ready been given the run down on Chance, and knew that he did B & Es. She was down to drive and get some of that burglary C.R.E.A.M.

Chance put a black long sleeve Nike t-shirt on and was getting ready to "Just Do It!" and some Black F.U.B.U. sweats with his black Timberlands. He got his black wool gloves out of the trash bag that Nadja left outside of her house and a black ski mask.

 133

They got in Twinkie's car and she went to Star's house. Star came around from the back of his parent's house, in all black and a black hoodie looking like a straight robber. He got in the back seat and leaned up to give Chance a pound. They dapped and Star leaned back.

"Where we goin'? I need some paper and no errors." Star looked out of the window.

"Nigga, we going to Paramus. You know that's where the money is at. Or Saddle River?" Chance rubbed his hands together and contemplated which town they should hit.

"Y'all should go to Saddle River. That's where the real money is at," Twinkie interjected.

Chance got ready to tell her to shut the fuck up, which was becoming a habit due to her never being able to shut the fuck up; but he wanted to hear about Saddle River.

"Yeah, I heard about Saddle River before. Where's that at?"

"It's North up Route 17. You wanna go there?" Chance looked back into Star's eyes, to catch his vibe.

"What up Star? You the vibe man, you feelin' that how that sound? Saddle River? I'm with you whatever you say Partner." Chance was ready to go wherever. His hand was itching and he knew that meant money.

"Yeah, Let's Do It, you got that shirt on, no need for thinking, we out!"

Twinkie jumped on Route 4 West and turned the music up. Black Sheep's "The Choice is Yours" came on and Chance recited, "You can get with this or you can get with that. You can get with this or you can get with that." He nodded his head and put the thought of what he had done to Jonnie further from his mind. He knew he had to get some money in case he had to leave town for a minute. He had a feeling that Jonny had given up his name to the police. He started going over the fact that he would have to use precision when he got in the house. He had to think fast and smell the money. It was like a craft, a gift to go into a large space that you are a stranger to and be able to find the hidden treasures. It took practice and Chance felt like he would get better and better at it.

"You ready man?" Chance asked Star who was also in deep meditation and as Twinkie pulled off the highway where the sign read "Saddle Brook".

"Hell yeah, I'm ready."

They pulled down a dark, quiet block that was lined with gigantic houses. Chance and Star both leaned close to their windows and gazed at the nice monuments.

"I like that one right there." Star pointed to a house that looked like it belonged in California. It had nice, red and cream-colored clay bricks and stones. It was far off of the street with a long winding driveway and massive amount of windows. Chance gazed at it as Twinkie slowly pulled over and shut off her lights. The block was quiet. All the houses were so big and far apart that it was easy not to know what was going on right next door. Right next door was like two houses down in one. The house looked empty and they both knew it was. Chance went into overdrive.

Twinkie ride around the block and park on the next street. We'll be back." They both jumped out of the car and Twinkie watched as they ran straight to the door and through it. One of them put the door back in place. Twinkie drove around to the next block. They would have quite a ways to run.

Chance ran to the bedroom and straight into the closet, which had a safe in it.

Star was in the room checking for jewelry.

"Fuck that, we got a safe. We in and out. Let's go." Chance waited as Star came in the closet and they lifted the safe up. It was about fifty pounds but they both had to carry it. They took careful steps going down the stairs with it so they didn't drop it on either one of their toes.

They got to the back door, it opened in, and it needed a key to be unlocked. They had to carry the safe through the living room and the large foyer to get it out of the front door. They started out of the door and around the large lawn to the back yard. They hopped in unison with the safe. They moved sideways, holding it and taking the same wide steps, almost jogging. They made it to the end of the yard and into the back neighbor's yard when they saw two police cars lights flashing from the house they had just robbed. They heard the officers slam their car doors and yell to each other as they approach the front of the house.

Chance and Star made it down a grassy hill, which blocked the officers who were running to the back of the burglarized home. They made it to the sidewalk and opened the door. Twinkie automatically popped the trunk. They loaded the safe in the trunk and jumped in the back seat. They both lay down on the seat.

"Drive Twinkie, like you're in the car by yourself," Chance said calmly from the back seat.

Twinkie drove the street parallel to the street that the police were on. She took it straight out and gave them a play by play of what was going on.

"Well, I don't see any cops going in that direction." Twinkie made a right turn onto the main street that would take them to the highway.

"Well, two cop cars pulled up in the front when we were in that other person's backyard. Two more minutes and they would have been pulling up as we came out the house. Yo, that shit was official. That was perfect timing," Chance cheered his and Star's good work.

"Yeah, because if they had a silent alarm, we would have five minutes, probably. I mean we got lucky that no cops were right in the area, but we were in and out. We were in and out in like probably four minutes. I been thinking we gotta stick to a set time and be in and out," Star divulged to Chance.

"Hold up, I see a cop car along the side of the road, he must be looking at the cars who pass to see if a suspicious group are driving past. I'm glad y'all are laying down. I just passed him and he's not coming out behind me so it looks like we good fellas. I'm about to jump on the highway. There's another cop ahead but I'm in the far left lane. I'm passing him too."

"All right, just drive like you got some sense and we straight." Chance pulled his hat off his head without sitting up. He took his wool gloves off and stuffed them in his hat and under Twinkie's seat. He was lying behind Star who was taller and whose head was resting on Chance's calves. They were laying still and breathing steady, staying calm and listening to Twinkie's play by play.

"Well, he just took the U-turn exit I guess to go back around."

"Like that night they all got popped. They ride the highway to see if they see thug-lookin' niggas driving and shit. He ain't see the culprits 'cause we laying right the fuck down in this here car," Chance joked.

Twinkie and Star both laughed.

"You a funny nigga," Star joked.

"I know I'm gonna be a rich nigga. Chance was tired of lying down. "Yo, can I raise up? We in the clear?" He wanted to sit up.

"Just stay down until I get off of Route 4 and then I'll tell you to get up."

"A'ight, Twink. You did your thing tonight. All calm and cool and shit," Chance said finally being nice to Twinkie for one second.

"Yup, cause I'm cool and shit. I hope I get a good reward when we get back."

"Yeah, you got that coming."

They rode, hiding in the back seat until Twinkie turned off Route 4 and onto Teaneck Rd.

"Okay, we're back in Teaneck. We are chillin'!" Twinkie exclaimed feeling a sigh of relief. She was nervous the whole time but she had to keep her composure.

"Damn, I feel like my neck is broke. My shit is stiff as hell from lying like that. But, we got this damn safe. Pull straight back in my driveway and we going in the garage to pop that shit open," Star instructed.

They got out of the car and carried the trunk into Star's garage, which was at the end of the driveway on the side of his house.

They dropped it to the floor and took a crowbar to pry it open. Chance and Star took turns and took about twenty minutes before they could bust the lock. Star put the crowbar in the bent up safe one last time and put his foot on it and put the whole weight of his body on the crowbar and hopped down on it, one last time, and "Pop!" the lock bust almost sending Star to the floor. He fell up against the wall and threw the crowbar down.

"Yeah!" He and Chance gave each other five.

They picked the safe up off its side and onto its legs. They pulled the door back and stood in awe at the stacks of money that were inside. There were ten stacks of hundreds. They began counting it and found that each stack that was paper clipped had a thousand dollars. Whoever was saving it seemed to be saving a thousand dollars at a time. They had saved ten thousand dollars.

"Damn, I thought it would be more than that." Chance was disappointed. "How a nigga like that in a big ass house only got ten thousand stashed? That's bullshit."

"Well, his bills must be out of this world. He probably barely can save that shit." Twinkie lit a cigarette and wondered how much she was getting.

"Well, why live in a house like that if you can't afford it?" Chance complained.

"We ain't get to look anywhere else, you never know. We be having to beat the burglar alarm. We should try to see if we can tell if the alarm is on or not, and go to only houses where the alarm is off. We need more time to search." Star was happy. Five thousand was fine with him. It was five thousand more than what he had."

"Nah, they would have all the money in this safe. Why would they have more than one safe with this little ass bit of money in it? Fuck it. Let's split. I gotta get high now, I thought it was gonna be a big payday."

Chance and Star took the five thousand each and they put the safe back in the car and drove to Paterson. They dumped the safe behind a factory and Twinkie dropped Star back off at home.

"We gotta go back out tomorrow," Chance warned Star.

"A'ight nigga, I'm down." Star said bye to Twinkie and went inside his parent's house.

"Go by my house, I gotta check on my mother." Chance directed Twinkie the way to get to his mother's house. Chance told her to park and he went around the back of the building. He wanted to go and make sure his mother was home and see what was up with Corey. He didn't want to go there but he figured that the cops wouldn't care about a junkie like Jonny to keep surveillance at his house. It wasn't like he beat up the mayor.

He walked in the door and his mother was on the couch. She smiled wide when she saw Chance come through the door. She stood up and stretched her arms out. He walked over and gave her a big hug.

"Mommy you Ok?" Chance wanted her to be better. He didn't know what else he could do for her.

"I'm okay. I was worried about you. I came home earlier; your uncle got me out. I still didn't tell them nothing. I'm going to the hospital to see Jonny tomorrow." He didn't understand how his mother could still love Jonny. He was a piece of shit, in Chance's eyes.

"Mommy, why you don't let Jonny go? You two are not good for each other." Chance looked intently into his mother's eyes.

"How aren't we? We understand each other's pains and struggles. At least I am not going through it alone. Chance, I'm sure there are mothers out there who would rather you not be loved by their daughters. But, I'm your mother and I love you and I know you are worthy. But, just think how some girl's mother looks at you and sees a loser. But, you are my son, and I love you. I love Jonny because Jonny loves me. Everybody needs someone to love. He' mine though. I don't have to worry about fighting over him. He may have some shit with him, but he puts a smile on my face. He makes me feel like I'm important and I am, to him."

"To me and Corey, and Chante, too, Ma. We need you to know how important you are so that you could see that you can do better."

"Yeah, that's my point, Jonny loves me just the way I am. My kids love me, because they have to. I haven't been that good of a mother to be proud of myself." Chance's mother started crying and he wiped her tears.

"Ma, you have to get yourself together. I can't do it for you. Jonny can't help you."

"Well, I don't want you to keep worrying about me. Now because of me, you might go back to prison. I want you to live for you. You have to have dreams of your own." Chance's mother stroked her son's short fro.

"Ma, my dreams died when my father did. I dreamed to be just like him and he died. I just want to have money. That is all that will change my life. I have nothing without paper. I am nothing without a knot in my pocket."

"Chance, I named you that name so you would feel hopeful. So that every time you came across an obstacle in your life, you would know that you have what it takes to turn a hopeless situation into a possible triumph. Your name should be a part of your drive and motivation to always give yourself another Chance to win."

"Ma, the only chance I have is to get money. I have to get it on my own. No one is going to get it for me or give it to me."

"But baby, you live by the sword, you die by the sword. You will reap whatever you sow, I am living proof. What I did in my youth is still a noose tied around my neck. I know that I am better than this but I have traveled down such a winding road that I am so far from myself that I don't know if I'll ever make it back. You need to take up a trade or something."

"Ma, it's too late for me."

"Chance, whatever you do bad, will come back and you will pay for it. Just don't say I never said it. I cannot pretend that you will not suffer for your wrongdoings. I have to tell you the truth. Please change your life."

Chance gave his mother a kiss and a hug and walked to the door.

"I love you, Mommy," Chance said.

"I love you, Chance."

Chance walked out the door and out the back door of the building. He looked before he walked down the street. As he was approaching Twinkie's car he did not see the detectives who were driving by his mother's block. They spotted him and made a U-turn.

Chance got in the car after wiping the tears that had fallen down his cheeks. He refused to let Twinkie see that he was crying.

He got in the car and didn't say a word.

"You okay? Your mom okay?" Twinkie looked at him with concern in her eyes.

"Yeah, I beat her boyfriend's ass and almost killed the nigga. The cops are looking for me."

As soon as Chance said that, the detective patrol car put their siren on behind Twinkie. Chance turned around and took a long sigh.

"Damn. Here take this money and use it to get me out."

Twinkie pulled over, the detectives jumped out, and each got on both sides of the car. Chance rolled down his window and Twinkie did too.

"Mr. Major. We have been looking for you. You're mother's boyfriend died just a few minutes ago. We are here to take you in."

Chance opened the car door and stepped out. He stood up and turned around, with no feeling. He was numb. Nevertheless, he was not without contemplation. He immediately began thinking of his case. He knew that if Jonny told them he beat him up, but if his mother and Corey said someone else did it, that would be a reasonable doubt. He also knew that they would try to set his bail extra high since Jonny died so he would probably not get to make the bail.

"Can I just give my girl a kiss?" he asked the detective. "I'm cuffed already let me just go to her side and give her a kiss.

The detectives stood close by in case Chance tried to run but far enough to give him a moment of privacy with Twinkie. He leaned in her window like he was about to kiss her and whispered in her ear.

"Look, don't waste that money on bail. Take the money I have in the closet in my jacket and get me a good lawyer. Go to my mom's right now, it's apartment 3B. Tell her to tell Corey that they both have to say that Jonny stole some drugs and his dealer came from New York and beat him up. I'll call you. Do that now."

Chance gave Twinkie the first real kiss since messing around with her. He stuck his tongue in her mouth and gently stroked her tongue with it. He gave her a kiss and then one with his lips before saying, "You proved that you are my *Around the Way Girl*, you're the one for me."

Chance walked with his head up and was helped into the back seat of the detective car. A few of his neighbors were standing outside but they didn't know him and he didn't know them. It seemed that the homeowners on the block were all friendly with each other but that hospitality didn't extend to the end of the block, where his lone apartment building stood.

Chance didn't feel shame or remorse. He just plotted his release. He knew that a murder charge wouldn't stick, because it wasn't premeditated murder. He knew that manslaughter would keep him from going to jail for life, but he wasn't willing to do a lot of time for a burnt out junkie. He was not going to give in and plead guilty. He was going to have a good lawyer use the fact that it was Jonny's word, which could not be trusted because he wouldn't want to tell on a drug dealer who would kill him later. He was going to force the state to lessen the charge and offer him a low sentence that he would eventually take if he and his lawyer didn't see him getting off scot-free. He already knew what to do; he just needed a cooperative lawyer who could put it in motion.

Chapter 11

T winkie drove back up the block to Chance's building, parked, and went to 3B. She knocked on the door and Chance's mother opened the door after seeing her in the peephole.

"Yes?" Vonetta opened the door slightly, coming from Brooklyn, she always stayed on point.

"I'm Twinkie. Hi. Chance just got arrested. He was in the car with me.

"Oh, my God, dammit. My baby!" The phone rang and Vonetta waved Twinkie in and signaled for her to close the door as she ran to get the phone.

"Hello? What! Noooooooo! Jonny!" Vonetta dropped the phone and fell to the floor. Twinkie ran over to her, picked her up, and helped her to the couch. "Tell them I'll call them back!

Twinkie picked up the phone and told the person on the other line that Vonetta said she would call them back.

Twinkie hung up, sat on the couch, and waited for Vonetta to get herself together. She went in the kitchen, got a paper towel, and passed it to her. Vonetta took it and wiped away her tears before asking all of her questions.

"What happened? They were waiting for him outside?" Vonetta kept shaking her head. "I'm sorry, I need a drink. You want a drink?" Vonetta got up, went into the kitchen, and poured her and Twinkie a drink. She had gin and put some

 143

Kool-Aid in it, being out of juice. She passed Twinkie a glass and sat back down.

"I didn't see them waiting for him. No cars were even parked in the street from the corner to the first stop sign, so I don't see how they would have seen him. I think they pulled down the block when he was walking to my car. They must have turned off Teaneck Rd when they saw him. So, they told him that your boyfriend died and they arrested him."

"Please say he didn't give them a hard time?" Vonetta took a swig of her drink and shook her head.

Twinkie looked over Chance's mother. She was glad to meet the woman who gave birth to the *Bad Boy* that she was open on. Vonetta was pretty in the face. She looked almost like Phylicia Rashad, the actress; but had the look of years of stress. She looked like she had been on drugs or had had a hard life. Twinkie didn't see that her casual use of crack would turn into a monster and take over her life as well. Twinkie realized that she knew nothing about Chance, but wanted to know all there was to know. Twinkie was going to be Vonetta's friend because she wanted to be in Chance's family.

"He didn't give them a hard time at all. He gave me money for a lawyer and he has some money at my house. I am going to put some money together and we are going to get him a good lawyer. I have an old boss that I can call who can probably direct me to a good attorney and maybe even get us a better price than what he will normally charge." Vonetta listened intently.

"So you're the girl whose been keeping my son away from me?" Vonetta joked. Twinkie laughed and shook her head. Her asking Twinkie that made her think that Chance must not have introduced Nadja to his mom. She smiled on the inside.

"Yeah, we met a couple of weeks ago now." Twinkie couldn't help or hide her wide-faced smile.

"Well, damn, girl, my son is that good? You all cheesin' from ear to ear and shit." They both laughed. "Girl, I know 'cause his father was the shit, too."

"Oh, is he still living?" Twinkie pried, skillfully.

 144

"No girl, he died in prison. And I don't want my son to die the same way. There's just nothing I can do for him. Chance is stubborn and head strong. Nobody can tell him anything. Not a damned thing. I can't believe my son beat my man to death. I just can't believe it." Just then Vonetta started crying as a girl came walking in the door.

The girl was a younger, prettier version of Vonetta. She looked healthy and fresh. She looked fly.

"Mommy, why you crying? Hi." Chante spoke to her mother and the stranger in her house.

"Jonny died." Chante fell on the couch and put her hands over her mouth. She sat in silence with her eyes wide open and her hands covering her mouth. She looked like she couldn't breathe.

"What about Chanc,e Mommy? Oh my God, what is going to happen to Chance?" Chante said, slowly and shockingly.

"They took him down. He is probably getting processed. Nothing is going to happen until tomorrow. Can you take us tomorrow, Twinkie? Twinkie, this is Chance's baby sister, Chante, and the only one who loves Chance maybe more than me."

Chante put her hands down and tears started falling down her face. She looked at her mother and hid the disgust that she had for her. She knew that it wasn't her mother's fault but she felt like it was.

Chante got up, went in her room, and closed the door. Vonetta got ready to go and knock on her door but she turned around and sat on the couch, defeated.

"I know she ain't gonna say it, but she is gonna feel like this is my fault. It *is* my fault," Vonetta continued.

Twinkie didn't know what to say. She was startled when the door opened yet again, to a young boy coming through it. Vonetta got up, ran to the boy, and wrapped her arms around him, burying her face in his chest. He stood there still without embracing Vonetta back.

"Corey! Jonny died and Chance got arrested." The boy shook his head and looked up to the ceiling. Twinkie could see the tears welling up and his fight to keep them from falling out of his eyes and down his face. He focused hard on the ceiling, looking hardly at it, like there was something there.

"Did you hear me?" Vonetta asked holding his arms and pulling herself away from him to look at him face to face.

"Yeah, Ma, I heard you. I knew this shit was gonna happen. We can't get no fuckin' breaks in this house. We must be cursed or some shit. Only bad shit happens to us while everything good happens to everyone else. Who is this?" Corey said pointing at Twinkie.

"Oh that's Chance's girlfriend. She was with him just now when he got arrested." Corey said hello to Twinkie when Vonetta introduced them. Twinkie liked to hear her title, but Corey knew better. He could tell from the looks of her that she was just a trick Chance was fucking and using for something. He knew how his brother got down.

Corey went and sat on the couch in the same desperate way that Chante had. He stared blankly at the wall, trying to guess the amount of years it would be before his brother would make it back out to the streets.

"Corey, tell Chante to come out here." Vonetta got up and went into the bathroom. She washed the tears off her face and brushed her teeth. She had to get herself together.

Corey and Chante went into the living room and sat on the couch. Vonetta stood in front of them.

"Now, listen to me. I am not perfect, but I love you guys. I have had hard knocks in my life that I have had to bear. The things that happened to me growing up and the choices that I made began before you two, or Chance, was even thought of. And they have influenced the path that my life has taken because I let it. And because I had no one there to help me or love me past it. I could have loved myself more but believe me you kids are my only hope. Corey, look at Chance. He is great in our eyes but he has to be great in his own eyes to do great things. It's the same for everyone. I can't make your life; you have got to make it."

"Yeah, but Mommy, other people have parents that bring them up in a way that they have a better chance of a better life." Chante took a deep breath.

"Chante, we all come in this world and have different circumstances and we don't choose them. We have made the best of them. There are kids whose parents give them everything and they still fuck their life up. There are plenty of people in the world who beat out all kinds of odds, who had no parents and succeeded in life. I always directed you guys to do good and do right. I always taught you right from wrong."

"And showed us wrong. Ma, you were supposed to be a leader, some fuckin' type of example," Corey yelled.

"What the fuck about your father? You and Chance dying to be like him! For what? You got a fuckin' death wish or something? I guess I did too! But, guess what? You are smart enough and old enough not to make excuses. Chante didn't let the shit stop her. She's in college because she looked at me and said 'Uh-uh" I'm not going to be like that. Why the men and boys gotta be so lost and weak?"

"No fucking Fathers! Fuck you think? At least girls see their mother's struggling and being strong no matter what! Where are the fuckin' men who ain't run or die? Or get strung the fuck out and leave? How many of them stayed and showed strength?" Corey got up and stormed off to his room, slamming the door.

"Twinkie, I am going to spend some time with my kids, at this horrible time in our lives. Can I have your number and can you take me to the courthouse for Chance's arraignment tomorrow morning?" Twinkie wrote her number down and told Vonetta that she would be there in the morning.

Chance was taken to the Bergen County Jail. He was processed and charged with Manslaughter. He was taken to a holding pen.

The jail was like a hang out with all the street thugs meeting up for a same sex, confined, "vacation" from bills, responsibility and progress.

Chance saw one of his old high school friends in there. He sat down next to Junior. He was half-black and half-white but he looked Puerto Rican.

"What up, dude?" Junior gave Chance a pound.

"My nigga. Where you been? I heard you was sendin' them birds down south, nigga, heavy-like."

"Yeah, nigga, I was makin' that DC, VA, and Maryland paper and fucked up and went to North Carolina and got popped. I'm off a three-year bid. I got six months and I'm out! I had some minor shit up here to finish up. It ain't nothin'. I got my stash waitin'. Y'all niggas up here kickin' in doors, I heard. That might be a new occupation for me. Easy money." Junior laughed.

"Easy money? Nigga, you think it's easy to run up in a crib, not knowing if someone is there and where to find some shit? You gotta be like a robot, like a laser beam zeroing in on the kill, with only minutes to win, muhfucka. Don't get it twisted."

"Yeah, but you know that's some grimy shit, robbing a nigga while his back is turned. You ain't stickin' up nothin'."

"Nigga, this is Jersey. You do what is conducive to the environment. A real hustler knows how to change the game when a new board or playing field is in place. You want me to go stick a gun up in some Jew muhfuckas face out here in this Garden State? Oh, you want me to just go out in a blaze with these redneck police shit, they might wanna tie my ass to a tree and lynch me in the park or some shit." Chance shook his head.

"Yeah, that's true. Word is Bond, that's true. It is the perfect crime though because as long as you make it out of the house, you good."

"Nah, you gotta make it home. Then, you gotta be able to get rid of the shit. Or not get caught with the shit in your car. It ain't easy at all. But it pays," Chance joked.

"Yeah," Junior laughed and said, "You still a funny nigga Chance, I see." They gave each other a pound.

Chance was arraigned the next morning in court. He was brought into the courtroom in the orange jumper that was the uniform. He was brought in through a side door and saw his mother, Twinkie, Corey, and Chante sitting in the chairs for the courtroom audience. He winked at them and looked ahead.

"Chance Major, you are hereby charged with Manslaughter for your part in the death of Jonathan Rivera Rodriguez...." The judge continued to talk but Chance tuned him out. He wondered if Twinkie had gotten a lawyer. He was not planning to do a lot of time for a heroin addict. He stood there until the judge asked him to speak. Chance said that he would be getting a lawyer and the bail was set at $500,000. Chance knew they were going to fuck with him so he wasn't surprised. When the arraignment was done and as they were leading him out, he said to his mother, "Come visit me tomorrow. Twinkie get a lawyer, don't post bail."

Chance had to wait in the holding cell until all of the detainees were charged. They were taken by van back from the courthouse. The only thing he could do was wait for his visit the next day. He was not going to worry. He was going to eat, shoot the gab, and watch TV. He knew what the routine was.

There were two towns surrounding Teaneck. They were Englewood and Hackensack and they were one collective 'hood of three small ones and they intertwined. Everyone from each knew, each other, hung out in all three areas, and dated and hated on each other.

Chance ran into one of his 'hood rivals, from Hackensack, named Mack. Mack and Chance had dated the same girl in high school. The girl was actually Mack's girl who was messing with Chance, so he and Mack had run-ins whenever they saw each other, even though years had passed.

Mack saw Chance coming and stood in the way. Chance went the other way.

Mack said, "Yeah you know you in Hackensack, you ain't got a chance."

"I don't need a chance. You still beat about your high school ho? Man, ain't we men now? You stuck on one pussy? I got a murder charge, you don't want to see me right now Mack, just fall back. Word is Bond," Chance said calmly and went over to the television and sat down by Junior.

"Yo, that nigga ain't a threat. You good for not even wastin' your time, bruh." Junior shot Mack a grill to let him know that he was rolling with Chance if anything went down. Mack stared right back to let him know that he was ready, whenever they were. "He can look mean all he wants, if he was gonna clip you, he would have."

"I ain't thinkin' 'bout that, nigga. He mad at me over a bitch. That's a bitch move right there. Shit, I ain't rob him. I don't owe that nigga no money. I'm fightin' a grown man over some pigeon that's not even his wifey now?"

"You funny, I forgot." Junior clapped his hands.

"And I forgot, you repeat yourself a million times, nigga, remember what you be saying so you ain't gotta keep repeatin' it." They both laughed.

They passed the time cracking jokes and talking about the streets. Chance filled Junior in on what was going on out there. Junior listened while twirling his long braid in his hand. He had two long cornrows that stopped in the middle of his chest.

The next day, Chance was called for his visit at two in the afternoon. It was only his mother and Twinkie. He picked up the phone and asked, "Where's Corey and Chante?"

"Corey went to school. We all decided to do better for ourselves and for you. This time when you come home, we will be doing good. Chante had to work. She got a job at the hospital part-time to help her with school and she's trying to get her own apartment."

"So what about my lawyer?" Chance asked anxiously. Vonetta passed Twinkie the phone.

"I got a lawyer coming to see you for a consultation. From what he heard, he said $7,000 to start. I want to see if you feel him. You gotta feel like you can trust him," Twinkie replied. He will be here today or tomorrow the latest he said.

"He had a death in his family. Just give it a chance, Chance, damn. Calm down." Twinkie hated his quick temper.

"Well, what did he sound like over the phone?"

"He sounded cool. He's Italian. I believe they are like black people so I called him. You don't want no prejudiced prick." Twinkie was going to be patient because she knew that Chance was in a bad situation.

"They don't like black people; they call us moolies and junk. And dumb ass rappers name themselves after the mafia. That's some dumb as shit, but that ain't the point." Twinkie and Chance laughed.

"Chance just call me and tell me if you want me to retain him or not. Then we will take it from there. How you feelin'?" Twinkie licked her lips to remind him of what he was missing. He caught her hint and nodded his head yes. He told her to pass the phone to his mother.

"Ma, she tellin' you she my girl?" He asked making sure Twinkie wasn't reading his lips. She stood back to give Vonetta and Chance some privacy. Vonetta nodded her head yes.

"Look Ma, that's my ho. Make sure she do whatever you need her to do. Take you to the store, whatever. If you need something let me know and I will make sure she gives it to you."

"Okay," his mother said like she was his daughter.

"Okay. So, what's this, y'all are gonna do right? You gonna do right, too?" Vonetta nodded and Chance said, "Why? Why you? Why now, Mommy?"

"Because I want to live. I don't want to be the walking dead. And we want to do it for you because, just like we always leaned on you to take care of the family and head the household, you needed us, too. You need us to be strong so you can be too. I'm sorry I put such a weight on your shoulders from a young age. You just wore the responsibility so well. You would make sure the kids were up and dressed for school when I was out of it. You would cook them breakfast and dinner. I love you Chance. You are gonna be okay, my son."

"I know Ma. I have to."

"It ain't no guarantee. You gotta watch what you do." She mouthed to him "Jonnie had a knife and did the motion like she was stabbing the air. Chance got it. She was telling him to tell the lawyer that Jonnie had a knife. She was telling him to claim self-defense. He smiled. Damn, his mother was

 151

the truth. She had given him a better strategy than his idea to say someone else did it.

"Ma, don't start this shit right now. Are they having a memorial for Jonny? Oh yeah, but I guess they won't want you there since your son...." Chance stopped talking. He knew he was being recorded. "Well, shit he might have had an overdose or a heart attack or some shit. You don't know what those drugs have done to his body." Chance looked in his mother's eyes and she knew that her son was a Bull and he was going to fight. He was not going to go down easy.

They finished talking and Chance went back to his unit. He didn't do anything but wave at Twinkie when she left and she blew him a kiss. He blew a fake one at the last minute knowing he needed her and if he had to play along and make her think he was her man, he was going to have to do that for his own benefit.

Chance went to talk with Junior and then was called out into a private visiting room for attorneys and their clients.

The lawyer was young and sharp. He had a bit of a long hairstyle, not too much like a hippy but he didn't look like a prick. Chance liked him.

"Chance Major," he held his hand out and Chance shook it. "My name in Sebastian Corvo. I talked to your girlfriend and she told me what happened but I would like to hear it from you."

"I was tired of my mother's heroin addicted loser boy-friend putting his hands on her. I came home, they were arguing, I tried to break it up, he pulled out a knife on me, and I stomped him. Them drugs probably took him out. I fought him, man to a man. I didn't try to kill him. You can have an autopsy done on him before they cremate him? Can you stop them from doing it?"

"Well, when anyone dies like that there is an autopsy done so we do have to see what condition his body was in at the time. So, you felt that your life was in danger? Was he a threat?"

"Well he wasn't a threat by himself but he was a threat with that knife in his hand." Chance couldn't help but to crack a joke. That was his personality. The lawyer chuckled, not wanting to laugh and have Chance get offended.

"Okay, so had he hit your mother?"

"Yes, he was hitting her when I walked in the house. We started fighting and my brother came in as I was kickin' Jonny."

"So Jonny was alive in the hospital from what I understand. How long had he been in your mom's life?"

"For years. Since I was little. I never liked him." Chance said then second guessing if he should have said that.

"Well in any case, we would say that you did. We don't want built up animosity. Okay, so is there anything else you want me to know?"

"How does it look?"

"Well, I will get the autopsy and I have to talk to your mom and brother. We just have to put together a strong case and that takes time." Chance knew that he meant money when he said time.

"Well, tell me something to make me know you are they guy I need." Chance wanted to be sure.

"I can win. That's what I can tell you. Worst case scenario, you will do some time because he died but you won't get a lot of time. We have to use his drug problem, the domestic violence against your mother, and the self-defense. You can take a day or so to decide if you'd like to put me on retainer so I can get to work."

"Well, how much do you think it will cost over all?" Chance knew he couldn't afford this man.

"I'm not seeing this as too complicated. I would say maybe like twelve thousand to fifteen thousand."

"I need you to say ten thousand." Chance would have to call Nadja and ask her to cash in those two Faberge eggs and that diamond necklace that he left there.

"Let's say twelve thousand for now. I'm trying to be generous." Chance knew he was full of shit. Like he cared.

"Deal." Chance knew he had ten thousand and he knew Twinkie was good for two thousand if Nadja fronted. He was going to have a problem with Nadja if she did some dirty shit and kept his money.

Chance called Nadja and she answered.

"Hey, Nadja. I got locked up for beating up my mother's boyfriend. I'm gonna need that money, you know." He couldn't say the eggs and jewels over the phone.

"Money? Oh, I don't even know where that money is Sweetie. I'm sorry, you must have lost it, it ain't here." Click.

Chance looked at the phone. She had basically told him "Fuck you, I'm keeping your money you lost."

He slammed the phone down. "That bitch gon' see me when this shit is over," he said and went to his bunk to rest his head.

Chapter 12

C hance spent what went from weeks to months waiting for his case to come up. No one visited him but his family, Twinkie, who was claiming to be pregnant with his baby, and his other chicks. His so-called friends were nowhere to be found. It was the way it was because co-defendants could not communicate or visit with each other, even after time served.

His case started a year after the arrest. He had pleaded not guilty and the case took forever to come up. He was ready for trial because he just knew that he would get off on the self-defense defense.

Chante was required by Mr. Corvo to have at least two suits, which Chante bought for him. Chance had gained about ten pounds so was looking more stocky and grown. Chance looked sharp. He had a fresh shave and his hair was low-cut and lined up.

He sat through all of the usual protocol of court, this time it being a little different because he did not plead guilty. So, there was a jury and he was surprised that there was a considerable amount of people in the courtroom.

His mother, Twinkie, the baby girl that was supposed to be his, Corey, Chante, and some dude with Chante that Chance guessed was her boyfriend were on one side.

Jonny's daughters and son, his mother, and sisters were there on the other side. They were all sitting with hate in their eyes and their expressions. "Cut it out, that nigga would have ODed sooner or later," Chance thought.

The trial lasted for a month. Chance was not found guilty of murder but of criminally negligent homicide, which is involuntary manslaughter. He was furious. He was facing ten years. When he came back two weeks later for sentencing, he was scared for the first time in a long time. He couldn't imagine spending ten years in prison.

The judge when he sentenced Chance said, "Young man, it must be an awful thing to grow up with the unfortunate things that have come out about your life, in this trial. I did believe that you were angry toward Mr. Rodriquez. I believe that you probably have anger issues. I believe that you did a little more than just beat Mr. Rodriquez like a regular fight. You stomped him in his head continuously, he was no longer a threat to you and you continued. I grew up very similar to you. My mother raised me alone. I had to help raise my younger siblings. But, I wanted to make it easier on her, not harder. I am sentencing you to five years, with one year already served. Mr. Rodriquez' drug use is what helped his demise. The doctor testified that Jonny's body was so damaged by the drugs, so you are not fully responsible for his death, but I believe that beating quickened it. The jury obviously didn't believe that you killed him on purpose. Get your life on track when you get home."

Chance walked away not responding. That was the second judge to try to give him a lecture. "Shit, if they cared about me, they'd let me go," Chance thought ignorantly not realizing that the more he got away with, the more he was going to get into.

Chance remained at the Bergen County Jail for another six months before being sent to Trenton State Prison. It was in South Jersey and out of his element. Every 'hood is different and has its own swag. Most of the inmates there were from South Jersey or Philly. Trenton State was a real prison, not like Lewisburg, where he spent almost two years.

Trenton State was for grown men who were hardened criminals. For the first two weeks, Chance stayed in the receiving area and then he was moved to his cell. He was put in the cell with a man named Victor, who was serving a 15-year sentence for armed robbery. Victor was twenty-nine and had been in Trenton State for five years. He greeted Chance when he moved into his new home.

"How you doing, Brother, my name is Victor," he said and extended his hand. Chance shook Victor's hand and took his seat on his bottom bunk. "What's your name?"

"Oh, I thought my name was Brother. Isn't that what you called me?" Chance said sarcastically.

"Oh, I see you have jokes. I guess it's better to laugh then cry." Victor climbed on his bunk and opened his Bible to read. Chance didn't know that Victor was reading so he began talking.

"My bad, my name is Chance. I'm just aggravated, that's all. I got a long way ahead of me."

"How long is long, and for what?" Victor asked.

"I got four years and I killed my mother's boyfriend in a fight. I didn't mean to kill him I just kicked his face in and he died days later. I shouldn't be in here wasting my life for somebody that didn't even care about his. He was a junkie."

"Well, think of it this way. You could be doing way more time than that. So be thankful." Victor said expecting that he would get a negative response for it.

"Oh, word? I should be happy, huh? I guess you're right. I could be out in the world making some paper too. I could be living my life." Chance was angry and bitter.

"Well, what was your life like? What were you doing for a living?"

"Hold up. What are you a reporter? What you here for?" Chance was being defensive.

"Armed robbery. I used to get paper, too. But, I'm not a reporter, just a messenger. I will give you a message; let me find something for you. Hold on. Okay, got it. *My son, if sinners entice thee, Consent thou not. If they say come with us, let us swallow them up alive as Sheol, We shall find all precious substance; Though shalt cast thy lot among us; My son, walk not thou in the way with them. For their feet run to evil, for in vain is the net spread. And these lay in wait for their own blood; so are the ways of every one that is greedy of gain.*"

"Oh, Lawd, have mussy," Chance ridiculed. "You one of *those*? I'm gonna tell you right now. I don't believe in that shit. And I don't want to hear it."

"*For that they hated knowledge, they would none of my counsel; Therefore shall they eat of the fruit of their own way, for the backsliding of the simple shall slay them.* Those were from Proverbs Chapter 1. And you don't have to listen, but I will be reading out loud sometimes, so you can just ignore The Word if you want to, but it won't make The Truth go away." Victor closed his Bible and went to sleep.

Chance lay looking at the bunk above him. He kept asking himself how he was wrong but the fact that he had taken another human being's life was not clear to him. It wasn't clear to him that just as he had devalued Jonny's importance and right to be treated like a human being, the judicial and prison system would do the same thing to him.

Chance knew that he and Victor were not going to get along. He did not believe in any mystery God. If there was a God, his life would have been better and the world would be a better place to live in. His mother wouldn't have a drug problem and his father would be alive. He was angry that he was sharing a cell with a self-righteous religious fanatic. Chance slept until dinner.

When it was time for dinner, he searched for someone to get acquainted with. He got his tray and food, sat alone, and observed his surroundings. He could tell that there were some dangerous gangs and cliques in Trenton State Prison. It was scary but he would show no fear. He got plenty of looks and jeers and he returned the stares. He knew that a man who looked away from another man's eye, would be considered a punk. However, his look could also not be inviting or friendly because he was not looking for sex. He had to be careful to give a mean enough mug to show his machismo without inciting a fight. He ate his food without catching too many eyes. He just needed one person who could tell him the ins and outs, until he could learn them on his own.

When Chance was done eating, he went to the rec room. He sat by the television and knew that someone would come to try to put him on or recruit him into one of their "groups". He could not have been more right. A tall, burly, dread wearing muscular thug looking cat noisily dragged a chair over and extended his hand to Chance.

"Peace", he said, "My name is Soldier." Chance told Soldier his name.

"Where are you from my dude?" Soldier asked Chance.

"I'm from Brooklyn, but I live in North Jersey. What it be like down here? These niggas look real official. I'm trying to get the word on what the haps are." Chance didn't know what angle that Soldier was coming from, but he was the first one to talk to Chance and Chance was going to get as much information as he could.

"It's bad here. It's bad like Rahway. Well, not as bad as Rahway, but this is a jungle too. This is hard time man. You must keep your eyes open in the back of your head, at all times. You can't sleep on no one. I am used to it now, I been down for fifteen years, but when I first came man, I wanted to kill myself. I was eighteen and had no idea I was not a man, until I got here."

"So, you a Blood or Crip, what?" Chance asked getting straight to the point.

"I'm a Disciple. I'm not in a gang. I am a Soldier in the Army of the Lord. I don't kill my brothers. I don't seek their blood to destroy my own kind." Chance wanted to dis Soldier like he had Victor but he wasn't sure if being a disciple meant that Soldier wouldn't fight and since he was about 6'5" and almost 300 pounds, Chance decided to be wise and just listen.

"Oh, so do you know my celly? His name is Victor."

"Yes, the church people all know each other here. We are outnumbered greatly by the gangs. The funny thing is that they respect our faith because they keep the gang stuff between the gangs. They don't really bother us. Probably because, although they claim not to believe, deep down no one can deny the power of God and his light. So they know we have something special."

"And what is that?" Chance asked looking around hoping to see someone else more like him to relate to.

"We have the Armor of God. Someone can stab me and even if I die, they will be punished and not by my hands. God will deliver his punishment later. Many people know not to mess with children of God." Chance thought Soldier was mentally touched. He figured he probably had been there so long that he was out of touch with reality or that he had been so medicated that he began to believe crazy things.

"I hear you man. Well, I'm going to go back to my cell. It was nice meeting you. God bless you." Chance was being sarcastic but he said it to sound sincere.

"God bless you to my brother. I hope to see you in church on Sunday." Chance walked away shaking his head. *They're worse than a gang trying to get me to join some group that thinks they can walk on water and shit*, he thought.

As Chance was walking to his unit, he saw three cats walking toward him. They were walking next to each other and would run into him if none of them, or he, didn't move. Chance stopped walking and stood still. He stopped dead in his tracks. They men walked up to him and stopped.

"Yo, you from up North?" one of them asked him.

"I'm from New York. I live in Teaneck." Chance didn't know that Teaneck, because it was a suburb and interracial was not considered the "ghetto". It was considered a rich neighborhood where the thugs that came from there were wannabes.

"Oh word," they laughed. "You from Soft Town, huh?" one of them taunted. Everyone from there claims to be from New York. Y'all niggas from the suburbs play that hard role, but you ain't from the projects." The three of them surrounded Chance.

"No, I'm from Brooklyn, I just said that." Chance knew they were trying him.

"So, y'all about to run me for something? I ain't got shit. I got my balls though, and I'll take a beating and I will get back up. But one of y'all will be going down with me, trust and believe that homeys." Chance knew it was risky to challenge three men of which, probably all, had a shank or some sort of weapon on them.

"Word is Bond? Don't be so sure about that. We can run you or we can protect you."

Chance sized the three men up. He hauled his arm back and punched the biggest one in the side of his head, on his temple. The dude dropped. He took the plastic fork from dinner out of his pocket and held it up eye length to the other two. He started walking backwards. They knew that a plastic fork in their eye would be no less painful than a metal one and could take an eye out, just the same.

As he was walking backward, the two men tried to wake up the other. Chance bumped in to another dude who he didn't see behind him, as he rounded the corridor.

"Oh pardon," he said and made sure that his back was not to anyone.

"You all right Partner?" A light-skinned, stocky man, a little taller than Chance, asked.

"Man, I feel like I'm in a war zone with good and evil. Everywhere I turn someone is either trying to get me to worship God or kill me. Is there anything in between? I just want to do my time in peace and go the fuck home." Chance stood far enough away just in case this was a friend of the three men around the corner and a plan to sabotage him.

"You have everything in here that the world has, except real women, but just the worst of everything. This is hell without heaven; at least out there, you have both. This is the belly of the beast. This your first bid?"

"In adult prison," Chance answered and realized at the same time that this would be the first real fight of his life. Yes, he had seen gunfights in Brooklyn and had gotten into shit; but, he was stuck in this shit. He was confined to this animal house. He was like a caged animal, but a zoo would be 10 times better because those animals are treated very well.

"So, what do you do? How do you cope?" Chance asked not wanting to sound soft and desperate, although he felt both. The dude laughed.

"Listen. When you are drowning, you can grab onto water or you can grab onto a paddle. You cannot stand on something that is not solid. I told them from the beginning that my brother was killed by a gang. There is no place for me with a group of people who are against the truth and the truth is the light. I'm not here to preach to you. You have to choose the path that is best for you. You want to go work out and talk?" Chance hoped this cat wasn't on any freaky shit. *He better not try no homo shit.*

Chance and Tyrone went to the roof to the weights. They had a half-hour before it would close. It was six-thirty. They continued to talk and bond.

Tyrone was twenty-seven and in Trenton State Prison for grand larceny. He had been in for five years and had two more years to go.

"I was twenty-two and ruthless. I thought nothing could stop me. No matter how many fallen soldiers I had seen before me, take the wrong path and fail; I still had to learn the hard way. How can I continue the same way? It didn't get me anywhere but in here."

"Nigga, you gotta handle that. That's all." Chance said.

"Nigga, you sound crazy. You sound institutionalized already. It ain't all right. We are like cattle. This is modern-day slavery. Do you know that this has been the plan since slavery? We are not able to understand that what we choose to do wrong affects our friends, family, children, women, communities, and society. It keeps us in a place of bondage, mentally and physically. We cannot progress and succeed with ignorant thinking. I committed crimes before I got caught. I got away for a long time. I made money, chased bitches and hos, and was 'the man' and all in an instant that meant nothing. I had fifty thousand dollars saved. That money went to a lawyer. So, had I worked a regular job and saved my money, I'd be free and I'd have much more. Fifty thousand divided by five years, is ten thousand dollars a year. A job would have paid more than that. Divide two more years into that 50,000 and that means that I risked my freedom for a bullshit 7,000 dollars a year."

"Listen, I'm gonna make my money and then start my own business. It's not like I'm Chinese or Jewish. A bank won't give me a loan to start a business." Chance did not

want to hear it. He was going to score big on a house and reap
the benefits. He knew that all he needed was one big score.

"That's another cop out. How are Spanish people doing
it? Don't think that all Chinese or Jewish people get all the
breaks. All three of those nationalities rely on themselves to
be disciplined, unified, and sacrificial. They work together.
They struggle by living together and not living the life of
'Rock Stars' to accomplish their goals. It's about knowing
how to suffer so that you can prosper. Niggas want to floss
and shine and spend every penny they get to have materialis-
tic things. Why have a BMW and you live with your mother
or in the projects. We have to learn how to be smart, not
flashy."

"I ain't working for no white man for scraps. That's
modern-day slavery." Chance put the weights down and stood
up.

"A'ight man, I'm done with this class for now. You
should have been a history teacher or some shit." Tyrone
shook his head. "Damn, lighten up. It's all copasetic. I'm a
criminal. That's what I am. I accept who and what I am. I'm a
loser in society's eyes, but I am gonna have my time to
shine."

Chance and Tyrone walked back to their units and gave
each other a dap.

Chance's cellmate was on his bunk reading the Bible.
Chance quickly put his Walkman on his ears so that he didn't
have to hear more rhetoric that was nothing but propaganda as
far as he was concerned.

The next day while on the yard, Chance sat on the side
watching a basketball game when one of the dudes that had
tried to jump him sat next to him. Chance braced himself for a
fight. The dude felt the tension and spoke.

"Yo, we was just testing you to see if you was a tho-
rough nigga. Now that we see that you are, I'm here to give
you an invitation to be down with the Affiliates."

"I'm not into gangs. I ain't got no beef with you, but
that's just not my thing. I'm just doing my bid so I can get
back out there and finish what I started. No disrespect, but no

thanks, man. Tell your leader or boss or whatever the fuck you wanna call it." Chance stood up.

"I ain't got no boss," he replied.

"Well to me the shit is corny. I don't do nothing with a whole bunch of people. I don't follow nobody else's rules and I don't need to belong to a clique. I like to shoot the shit with niggas and do me. I'm my own muhfuckin' man, you dig?" Chance walked away, sat, and watched a chess game.

The two men who were playing were discussing politics, got into an altercation, and one got up, took a shank out, and slashed the other across the face. Chance looked around to the other people who were standing there. No one was fazed. He expected a guard to come running over, not one did. The man, with blood running down his face, neck, and shirt held his face and slowly stood up.

"Fuck you Leonard. You can slash my neck, it won't change the fact that ain't no ain't no black man that can get elected president. Al Sharpton, if he was smart, he'd take them damned curls out of his head. You think white people gonna vote for a damn nigga with Jheri curls?" The man slapped the chess pieces off the table and walked away. "You better hope I don't need stitches for this shit, muthafucka."

The men that were standing around started laughing.

"That nigga Clarence is crazy," another onlooker said, shaking his head.

"We all going fucking crazy in here. But, don't let them give you any medicine, that will make you a fucking zombie. Did you see Mike from B-More? That nigga is walking around like a dope fiend."

"That is dope. He ain't on no medication. I wouldn't trust none of the drugs these gangs are smuggling in here."

Chance walked away and sat on a bench by himself. He looked around at all of the men that were outside. He started to feel the pressure of his confinement. He started to realize that he had 51 months to go. He was sentenced to five years but with state convictions you usually only had to do 85% of your time, if you had good behavior. 51 months was about 1,530   days. He had to figure out a way to stay out of trouble and stay alive for that long. He figured that a gang might be his only option because he wasn't going to church.

As he was walking to the shower room Chance passed the dude who had approached him on the basketball court about being down with them. He caught a bad vibe from the look that he got and continued with caution. As he was showering, two extra-grimy looking niggas started showering. Chance knew that they were in a gang and probably Chance looked at both of them in the eyes and neither of them looked at him directly. His mind told him that they were about to be on some bullshit. Chance turned off the water and before he could turn around, one of the guys grabbed him from behind and had him in a chokehold. He pushed Chance up against the wall and Chance saw the other about to kneel down and grabbed his ankles. Chance did a back kick and caught him in his chin and he put his weight and leaned back. He was able to shift the dude that was holding him around to the side of him and he lifted his foot, put it down on the other cat's cheek, and stepped on his head. The one holding him was unstable on his feet. Chance elbowed him, broke free and ran out of the shower without his towel. He knew that he would not win in there. He knew that if they needed the lookout at the door, whoever had set Chance up to be raped, then branded, and embarrassed, would have joined in if he had to. As he ran past the dude, he clocked him in his chin and kept it moving. The dude was caught off guard and fell to the ground. Chance was butt-naked and he made it to his cell. His roommate gave him a weird look and said, "You all right man?"

"I'm a warrior, hell-yeah, I'm muthafuckin' all right. But thanks for asking though G." Chance laughed at his own sarcasm as he grabbed his boxers and his stiff sleeping pants. They were more like scrubs and he didn't like the facility issued pair, but he had to wait for his commissary money that he made sure Twinkie would supply to his mother, to clear.

"Well, when pride cometh, then cometh shame; the integrity of the upright shall guide them; Riches profit not in the day of wrath; the righteousness of the upright shall deliver them. That's Proverbs11:1-6."

 165

"Vic man, I hear you. I am glad that you were delivered, man. I'm still in the trenches 'Oh righteous One'," Chance said sarcastically. "And shut that shit down right now. No reading out loud tonight man, can you respect my wishes 'Prince of Peace'?"

"Good night sir, I will give you peace tonight. *He that diligently seeketh good seeketh favor; He that trusteth in his riches shall fail.*"

Chance went to bed and decided that he would get a job. Tyrone had told him that the best way to do the bid was to work most of the day away. That way you stay out of the gang activity, violent activity, and getting more time for bullshit. He started out working in the kitchen and then he got friendly with someone who told him that if he worked maintenance, he would have the run of the jail and the cells, which meant knowing about the different crews, cliques, and their locations. He said that all Chance had to do was find out who the leaders in certain areas were and do "favors" for them in terms of stashing weapons for them or moving weapons for them, or drugs, or stolen property that he would take from people's cells.

Chance was a natural born thief so that job was right up his alley. Chance became cool with many different crews because one didn't know what he might do for the other, but he would do for them all. That got him free weed when he needed it. Chance knew not to mess with cocaine while he was behind bars. He had to keep his mind right and strong. He was not going to be anybody's "flunky junky" because then he would not have the respect that he needed from the different groups. He worked with the people in the kitchen and was able to get knives, forks, and spoons into the hands of people that would be able to make weapons.

The five years turned into four and a quarter years and he spent it doing what he did best, robbing and stealing. The bid was a hard one but thanks to his survival ability, he was good. He saw a few people killed while he was there. He saw a lot of fights and blood. He got used to it. However, the one thing he could never get used to or stomach was the homos. There were men who looked just like women in there. There were men who paid for their lovers and they would sell fags to someone else when they were done. Some of the men who had life or double digit numbers had been taken over by the desire to have sex and resorted to being sexual with men, since they wouldn't be seeing women on the street for a very long time, if ever. The correction officers were slime. They would sometimes let a newcomer be raped if they got smart or seemed to have a bad attitude. The CO would let a known rapist out in the vicinity of the fresh inmate and they would look the other why while his sex was taken. There were a few female correction officers who would sell their bodies to inmates but they were choosy with who they would do it to. The thing that he would never forget was walking into the showers when the two Bloods that tried to rape him had just finished raping a newcomer who must have refused the gang affiliation. The kid ran from the bathroom with blood dripping out of his ass. Chance stood still and looked at the two homo thugs that he had fought off. He stood his ground and they walked out. Chance took his shower with no incident. The boy killed himself shortly after the rape.

Chance knew that he had spent the last four and a quarter years in hell and he was glad to have come out with breath still in his body and no scars. Chance was 26.

1995
Chapter 13

C hance was released on June 25, 1995. It was prime time summertime and he was ready for drama, money, and fun. Twinkie picked him up with their three-year old daughter that Chance had only seen pictures of. He had forbid Twinkie to bring the baby to see him in prison. Chance never thought the baby was his anyway. He had only allowed his family to come see him twice a year because seeing them regularly would have made it harder, because of the pain of seeing them go, and being left where he was. Twinkie came once a month so that he can get a forbidden dick suck when a cool C.O. would allow him a few minutes to turn his head and not see Twinkie with her head under the table. Some COs were cool like that, if you paid them.

Chance had planned to force Twinkie to take a blood test, once he got on his feet and was able to move from her. He had no intention on being with Twinkie. He just needed to stay with her initially until he found another woman to move in with. In the meantime, he would have the use of her car, her money, and her submission.

Twinkie was waiting outside of the gate for Chance. When he walked out with his belongings in one bag, she jumped in his arms, making him drop the bag. He wanted to black out and was already annoyed with her within the first ten minutes but he had to keep his cool. Once she was far enough away from the prison, he told her to pull over on a residential street, before getting on the highway. Twinkie pulled over and Chance unzipped his pants and took his dick out.

"You know I been dreaming about this all night." She took his penis in her mouth and worked her magic. Chance grabbed her head and held it down so that she would take all of him into her mouth, he pumped up and down and his hands suddenly grabbed onto his window and her headrest while he enjoyed the explosion of his cum up into the top of her throat. He turned up the Biggie, laid his head back, and sang Big Poppa...

To all the ladies in the place with style and grace
Allow me to lace these lyrical douches in your bushes
Who rock grooves and make moves
with all the mommies?
The back of the club, sippin' Moet,
is where you'll find me
The back of the club, mackin' hos, my crew's behind me
Mad question askin', blunt passin', music blastin'
But I just can't quit
Because one of these honies Biggie gots ta creep with
Sleep with, keep the ep a secret why not
Why blow up my spot cause we both got hot
Now check it, I got more Mack than Craig
and in the bed
Believe me sweetie I got enough to feed the needy
No need to be greedy I got mad friends with Benz's
C-notes by the layers, true fuckin players
Jump in the Rover and come over
tell your friends jump in the GS3, I got the chronic by the tree
(I love it when you call me Big Pop-pa)
Throw your hands in the air, if youse a true player
(I love it when you call me Big Pop-pa)
To the honies gettin' money playin' niggas like dummies
(I love it when you call me Big Pop-pa)
If you got a gun up in your waist,

please don't shoot up the place
'Cause I see some ladies tonight
who should be havin' my baby
Bay-bee

"Yeah, that's what I been dreaming about, too. Now, let's go. Did you get in contact with Star and tell him that I'm coming home today?"

Twinkie nodded her head yes and then asked, "Aren't you going to spend some time getting to know your daughter, spending some time with her? Chanel keeps your picture in her hand and walks around the apartment with it, telling everybody 'That's Daddy' all the time."

"A'ight, well, I'm going to be staying there, I'll get to know her."

"What's up, Chance, you never used to ask about her much when you called or I would come see you. You don't think Chanel is yours do you?"

"Look Twinkie, if you say she's mine, she's mine. I gotta take care of shit, I just touched down, I gotta see my mom's and Chante too."

Twinkie was already disappointed in Chance's lack of concern. She turned up the radio and Biggie's song *Unbelievable* came on. Chance sang along and added his own words. "It's Unbelievable…That my bid is up! It's unbelievable!" he clapped his hands and smiled. Twinkie was happy to see him home and flashing that charismatic smile of his. The one that always made her melt. Chance wondered what was up with Nadja and if she still hated him and if she still had his shit or at least his money. He would definitely get in touch with her.

"So where is the girl, I mean Chanel? With Peaches?" Chance had never asked about Peaches because he knew Twinkie wouldn't like it but he was hoping that she was still living with Twinkie because he wanted to pick up where they had left off.

"I never told you, but that bitch, Peaches, got that HIV shit. She went back home to live with her mother. She was getting sick all the time and shit. She couldn't hold her shit from coming out all over her and shit; that shit was nasty and I wasn't 'bout to clean up no chick's doo doo and shit." Chance wasn't worried about that because he had used a condom with Peaches and, when he was released from Trenton State, his HIV test was negative.

"My cousin lives here with me for now, with her two-year old daughter. I moved to a different apartment anyway."

Damn, Chance thought, *an apartment full of kids. How shit changes.*

They drove for the nearly two hours that it took to get back to Northern Jersey. Chance was ecstatic when he started seeing familiar locations. They got off the New Jersey Turnpike and were in Englewood, where Twinkie had moved. Chance walked in and saw Chanel. She was the prettiest thing in the world to him. He knew that she was his, from the look in her eye. It was instant love. He dropped his bag and the pretty, little black princess ran straight to his arms.

"Hi, Daddy. That's you," Chanel said showing Chance a picture of him. He took it and looked at himself in khakis and slip on skips. He had the usual jail picture pose. Head back, hands to his side in fists, and mean grill on his face.

"Daddy's home now. What's your name pretty little princess?"

"My names is Chanel, Daddy." She hugged him and leaned back on one of his arms to get the view of her daddy again.

"You mean your name is Chanel, not names. Well, Chanel, Daddy loves you."

"I love you too Daddy, I missed you. I'm so glad you're here." Chanel hugged Chance again and he carried her, hugging her back, to the couch where he sat and put her on his knee.

"How old are you?" Chance was in awe. When Chanel looked up at him, he saw a glimpse of his mother in her face. Then she smiled and he saw himself. His little girl had his eyes and his mouth. He looked in her eyes and saw like a mirror of himself. *Wow, this is my little girl*, he thought, and *I love her forever.*

"Daddy, I have to take a nap now. I waited a long time for you and Mommy to come. I'm tired." Chance cracked up laughing and Twinkie who was admiring this from the kitchen started laughing along with her cousin.

"I told you she was smart Chance," Twinkie said and then introduced him to her cousin Nelly, who was watching his meeting with his daughter quietly from the time he walked in and Chanel had ran over to him. They exchanged hellos.

"Let's go Mommy." Chanel walked, picked her teddy bear up off the floor, and continued into her room.

"Girl, you better watch your mouth. Here Chance, take the car and my cell. Call me on this number; it's the last number in the phone. I will call you from here so you'll have it."

"Wait, you gotta show me how to use this shit, I been down damn near five years."

Twinkie showed Chance how to work the phone and she told him to go inside the bathroom and put on his new clothes. He smiled and grabbed her and gave her a peck on her lips.

"Thanks, Twink." Chance started walking to see what new outfit she had set aside for his first day home. He turned around and said, "Oh and my daughter is beautiful."

There was a Dada sweat suit that was green with white strips down the leg. The tee shirt was the same brand and he had matching white Dada sneakers. It looked slick and clean. It was grown and mature looking he liked it. Chance had a fresh low-cut, a fresh sweat suit and kicks. He was so ready for the streets. He looked at himself in the mirror and said, "Let's go get it Nigga." He walked out leaving the basic jeans and button down shirt that he left the prison in.

Chance got in the car and put the radio on full blast. He pulled out of the parking space in Forest Gardens complex. He still knew his way around his stomping grounds; Teaneck, Englewood, Hackensack, and Paterson...on this side of the George Washington Bridge anyway.

Da Brat's song "Give it to Ya" was playing and he started singing "Word up, Hey, Word up, Hey" at the end of the song.

"I'm gonna give it to ya." Chance drove to a gambling spot, which was in the basement of one of his friend's house. Twinkie had already found out the location before Chance came home and she gave him all of the places to find who and what he needed to find since people who are criminals have to move around a lot. She also told him where Star and his girl were staying.

Chance drove up Tryon Ave., turned onto Teaneck Road, and made the left onto his mother's block. He wanted to run out of the car and up the steps to his apartment. He missed his mother and wanted to see her looking like she was on the visits that she made to him. She kept saying that she had been clean since Jonny's death and Chance believed her.

Chance rang the doorbell and as soon as the door cracked, he pushed it in and grabbed his mother.

"My baby. My baby is home. Thank you Jesus." Vonetta held Chance tight for a good five minutes.

He pulled her back from him and looked her over. He twirled her around and smacked her on her ass.

"Damn, Ma, you must really be doing good. You got fat and shit. You look beautiful Ma."

"Chance, I really had to work on myself. I'm so sorry Jonny died but it's like his death made me really get myself together, because I knew I was gonna die. And I thought about that day you asked me about that dream you had about me and Daddy. I had pushed a lot of my hurt away and I never dealt with it. I will tell you the truth about why I started using drugs. One of your father's friends raped me while your father was away and I couldn't deal with the pain of knowing that if your father had only been the man that I needed him to be, he would have been home for his family and not behind bars. I lost everything when your father got locked up. My family, my strength, my protection. A woman needs her man and children need their father. I was so angry with your father that I wanted to hurt him and I just started using because I couldn't do anything else. I couldn't bring him back. And then when he died, all hope was really lost." Chance was starting to get upset and he felt the same anger his mother described, *Fuck my father, he let us all down and made our lives end up like this,* Chance thought.

"So, that dream that I had was true, wasn't it? I really saw him after he stuck somebody up that night. Or, it wasn't a dream. I must just remember that night." Vonetta looked into her son's eyes. She saw a hopeless, angry, and lost young man. She wished that she could go back and raise him all over again. But, she hadn't been able to raise Chance since he was nine. He became a man when his father died and would never listen to her.

"Chance, you saw it and I couldn't do anything about it. Your father resorted to what he thought was his only option. But, look at what his option got us."

"That's all right Mommy. I will make sure we rise to the top. We gonna be fine. My baby is so beautiful Ma." They went to sit on the couch.

"Boy, I have my granddaughter all the time. Who do you think keeps her when Twinkie goes to work?"

"I know Ma. But, boy, she is so beautiful. So what's going on? I haven't spoken to you in a month. Why you ain't make Twinkie pay the bill, you let the phone get cut off."

"Do you know how damn much you was calling collect to talk about nothing?" Chance opened his eyes wide.

"Oh, that's foul, Ma, you was tired of me calling?"

"Boy, shut up. Corey is locked up." Vonetta knew that she should have written Chance and told him but she didn't want him to be upset and worrying about Corey while he was in prison.

"What, Ma? Why?" Chance got up, picked up a lamp, and threw it against the wall.

"Hey! Don't be in here fucking my house up. Your stupid brother thought he could be a drug dealer and he got caught in New York buying a bunch of crack so now he's on Riker's Island for the next three years."

"Corey is on Riker's? Damn, Ma. Where's Chante? I want to go see my sister right now."

"She should be getting off of work. Let me call her job….Chante Major, please...Hi, Channy, Chance is home. You going straight home? Okay, we will meet you there."

Chance and Vonetta drove to Chante's apartment in Lodi, New Jersey. She was pulling in at the same time, driving a brand new Nissan Maxima that was fully loaded. Chance watched his baby sister get out of her car and he parked and beeped his horn. Chante looked and ran over to the car when she noticed her brother who she loved so much.

Chance jumped out and grabbed his sister, kissed her, and grabbed her again. He picked her up and swung her around.

All three of them walked into Chante's apartment, which was a modest first-floor garden apartment that was decorated like it was a house. When Chante opened her door and they stepped in Chance looked around at the all brand new furniture and suspected that her boyfriend was a drug dealer, since Chante was only working in a school as a teacher's assistant.

"Hold up, I know you ain't messin' with no drug dealer?" Chance said and grabbed Chante so that she could look him in the eye.

"Boy, I don't like boys that get in trouble. I miss you too much, I can't be with somebody I love and then they get snatched away from me. No, my boyfriend Travis is an electrician. He works for his father's company. He is a good guy."

"Oh yeah, well you're 23. How old is he?" Chance would never stop being overprotective of his family.

"He's 24. We've been liking each other since high school."

Travis came walking through the door and smiled. He said hello, walked over, kissed Chante, and said hi to Vonetta. He reached his hand out and Chance shook it. Travis was tall and light-skinned with a medium build. He was clean-shaven and good-looking. He did not look like a thug. He looked, to Chance, like a hardworking, good guy. He kind of reminded Chance, of LL Cool J.

"I'm Travis. Welcome home man. Excuse me while I change into something more comfortable." Travis went in the back room to take his electrician's uniform off. He went back into the living room and continued his meeting with Chance.

"So it must feel good to be home. I had a cousin who just came home from doing ten years and he doesn't even know what to do with himself. He's trying to make up for every second he lost." Chance and Travis laughed. As men, they knew all the many things that he was trying to catch up on. Women.

"Man, that bid was hard, but I kept disciplined. This cat named Tyrone pretty much schooled me when I got there on what to do, which was basically work and I worked so I could get money. Real money on the side, you know, I was good with all the gangs because I would get paid for doing shit for all of them. So, I was good. I stayed neutral and strictly business. I'm a businessman. I see you are too."

"Yeah, I been working with my dad since I was like 13. I am about to inherit at least one of his companies soon. I run his electrician business now though."

Chance spent time with his family for about an hour. He liked Travis for his sister. He dropped his mother off and then went to handle his business.

Chance pulled up in front of Marquise's house that he shared with his wife and three kids. He had a gambling hole in the basement of his house on a nice residential block in Hackensack. He got out of Twinkie's Intrepid that she had recently bought used. Chance only got from her that she was working as a home health aide so she had a flexible schedule.

Marquise was coming out of the house at the same time and was ecstatic to see Chance walking up.

"Yo, my nigga! Damn, you out and you fresh to death, huh? What up, dude? You ready to make this money?" They gave a clap and a hug and patted each other's backs.

"You asking the wrong question. Where's the money at?"

"There's a meeting downstairs right now. Yo, I'll be back; I'm going to get my daughter and drop her off at my wife job. Go down from that side entrance right there."

Chance walked down to see four of his boys sitting around a table with a bottle of Cristal on the table. They all got up and took their daps and hugs. The last two to hug were Chance and Star. In attendance where four guys who had gone to Teaneck High School at corresponding times, if not the same, who had known each other and grown up together since childhood. It was Chance, 27, Star, 25, and Tricky, 26, and they were in Marquise's house. He was the oldest, 30, and closer to Roderick but they were all boys. Roderick and Malcolm had been extradited out of the country back to Brazil where they were believed to have shot an official there as a contract killing. They told Chance that Roderick had hooked up with a Columbian drug lord while in prison and started working for him when they both got out, and of course, Malcolm was his right hand man, so they were both in a Brazilian jail.

They filled Chance in on the fact that they had a good run going. They had been working together, Star, Tricky, and Marquise. They all didn't go out together every time and but they didn't like to do much dealing with other people. About three different crews were doing the same thing. They all were affiliated but different people would link up due to the recurring and constant incarceration of others.

The local authorities in Englewood, Teaneck, and Hackensack had enlisted the Bergen County police department. They were able to figure that there were local men from Teaneck and Englewood who were robbing houses in the surrounding towns within and outside of those three adjoining towns. The net spread West into Paramus and those towns more so than other places but they were noticing that they crew was beginning to branch out and they had to come together to be able to see the bigger picture. They had pretty much exhausted houses in Teaneck and Englewood. They had to stay out of those towns because the local police knew them.

"So, how much money y'all been makin'?" Chance asked as he sipped on the champagne that the friends were drinking.

"Nigga, we try to keep the crews to three. Four is too many in the car; it's too suspicious. When two people pull that shit off, it's real sweet. But we ain't been cashing in with less than like ten thousand, at least every house!" Marquise said, hearing the conversation as he was walking down the steps.

"10,000, at least, every job? That shit is what's up." Chance was ready.

"Yeah, there's your bad nights when you can't find a house or shit just seems off, or you just don't find shit, but it's like if you score at all, it's a nice score. And, of course, it ain't always straight cash. You got jewels, electronics, and shit. Whatever can be carried easily. You know light shit costs more." They all started laughing.

"So what y'all do with the jewels?" Chance asked.

"Jason got some Jewish bitch that he fuckin' so he got the hook up. That nigga wasn't even always goin' out he would get his cut from us for trading the shit in. But, he just went out with some Englewood niggas last night and they got knocked, so now we gotta find another fucking Jewish nigga." Chance instantly thought of Nadja.

"Yo, I'll go see Nadja, she was doing that shit for us before. That bitch may not even open the door up when she sees me at her door. She gotta man? I gotta make sure I go when that nigga ain't there."

"Yeah, she fuck back with Dip. You good if you don't see his black Suburban in front of the house, you good."

"Dip? What's that nigga's hustle?"

"That nigga do stickups around the country. He running with Junior."

"Junior? Junior Mackay? I was in the county with him before I got shipped to Trenton State. Yeah, that's a real dude."

"Yeah, nigga be goin' out with us, too." Star said.

"So where are y'all doing it now?" Chance was serious about catching up.

"Well, we doing Ringwood tonight. It's Me, Star, and Chance in one car and Tricky gonna be the decoy. If worse comes to worse we have another car to use to leave in. Chance I will drive my Audi 5000 and Tricky will be driving his Tahoe. The cops expect to see niggas in broke down hoopties, so they don't even notice you because you're driving in a car that fits in the area. We don't stick out as much in an expensive car."

"True, true. So that's how y'all have been able to get in and out without getting fucked with huh?"

"Yessir. Now we got two hours to get it rich, y'all niggas go home and go to bed." Marquise lead everyone up the stairs and out onto the street. Star and Tricky were in Star's Pathfinder and Chance got in Twinkie's car and pulled off. He stopped at Sears to get gloves, a hat, and black sweatpants and a long-sleeve t-shirt. He went to Englewood and when he walked in, the house was empty. Twinkie left a note that read that she, her cousin, and the kids would be back.

Chance got undressed and got in the bed. He jerked off as he looked around the room noticing that Twinkie didn't have a setup like it was a brothel anymore. There was no lingerie hanging all over the room. The room was violet instead of red and the veils and feathers were gone from the bed. *Aw, shit, Twinkie done gone and fooled herself into thinking that she ain't a whore no more.* Chance laughed. At least, having a daughter had a positive impact on her, but Chance knew that things with her just seemed too neat and clean. He was waiting for another gunman to come through the door, or some drama to transpire so that he could take his daughter, give her to his mother, and move out and on to something better. He drifted off to sleep and jumped up when he heard Twinkie coming through the door. At the same time, Twinkie's Motorola flip phone went off.

"Hello." Chance answered.

"Yo, nigga, we outside, let's go!"

"A'ight."

Chance threw his black gear on and kissed Chanel on his way out. He closed the door behind him before Chanel could jump in his arms. He would not have been able to put her down. He was so happy about his daughter. He made a vow that he was going to be a good father, regardless to what else he did in his life.

He got in the car with Marquise and sat in the back. It was dark and they jumped on Route 4 West to Route 208 to Route 287. They were going up in the mountains and Chance didn't like going that far.

"Yo, we can get trapped off up here. We going too far in. It's a long highway; they can put cops all along the route back if they know a house has been robbed."

"That's why we have to be gone before anybody even knows there's been a robbery in the first place. Tricky is in the truck. If we gotta park this and come back and get it, that's what we gonna have to do. You gotta ask Twinkie about some of her clients that she don't service anymore. The rich ones. She could tell us the breakdown of the house," Star said.

"Yeah, I'll get her to work on that. This shit right here looks crazy."

"Listen, this one is gonna be cake. The maid's daughter is a Spanish chick from Harlem. I brought her mother out here from New York one day, with her daughter and her daughter ran down the information about the house. The family is on vacation until next week and my slutty Spanish girl went to work with her mother today to 'help' out and made sure she turned the alarm off, before leaving. The family left today. The neighbors will start paying attention tomorrow. We straight." Marquise explained.

"Oh, well. Why you ain't just say that," Chance asked.

"Come on nigga, you gotta be on point at all times. You can never get comfortable and let your guards down," Star answered for Marquise.

They approached the house and parked around the corner. They walked through the back yard and Star bust through the back door. The basement was where the back door led into. The basement was a game room.

"Yo, let's play some fuckin' games for a little while. Whoever beats me in Pac Man can get 50% of my cut." Marquise was very arrogant and competitive.

"Word? I got yo' ass right now!" Chance was player one. He got out after 50,000 points. Marquise took his turn. He got out at 40,000. Chance went again, totaling 65,000 points.

Tricky came walking in the back door and blacked out, "Yo, y'all got me out in the car waiting and you in here playing video games and shit. Y'all off your fucking game, fuck y'all, I'm going to get some riches."

Tricky started running up the stairs and Star, Marquise, and Chance were right on his tail. They all went in different directions. Star went into the garage and found a gun collection. The guns were in a wooden box, two mac 10s and two 9 mms. He took the box and put it by the back door.

Marquise was in the living room in a china cabinet taking a coin collection.

Chance was in a teenager's room, taking laptops, and gaming consoles.

Tricky was in the master bedroom searching for jewels, safes, and money. He found a small safe in the bottom cabinet of the bed frame. There was a female Rolex and diamond studs in a Tiffany's box on the dresser. When Tricky opened a drawer there were five other boxes from Tiffany's. He put everything in the pillowcase that he snatched off the pillow. He looked around the room to see where someone might hide money. He saw a loveseat in the far corner of the room. It sat by the window. The cushion looked funny to him. Tricky's nose twitched. He knew that meant money. He walked over to the small couch like he was about to beat it up and he snatched the cushion off. Money came flying out of the unzipped side. He stuffed his hand in and started pulling it out. He held the hundreds and thought about putting some in his pocket. Chance snuck in the room and startled Tricky.

"Yo, nigga, don't even think about it. Put it right in that there pillowcase. Or you want me to hold it in *my* pockets for you?" They both started laughing and Chance walked over, lay back on the people's bed, and put his hands behind his head.

"Man, people got it made." He looked around the large Roman-inspired decorated bedroom. "Look at this shit here. Everything looks like a damn column or scroll." Chance and Tricky started laughing.

"Yo, check this cushion for dough instead of laying yo' lazy ass down. Get up nigga." Tricky threw the other cushion from the love seat at Chance's head. Chance moved and

 181

caught the cushion unzipped it and started pulling the rest of it out.

"See now, you ain't got no business having money if you gotta stuff it in a damn couch. That's having too fucking much money," Chance complained.

"Well, when you got niggas breaking into your house, you got to think smart. I looked at it and the damn cushions weren't smooth so I knew something was in there."

"Yeah well I bet there's some shit in the shoeboxes in that closet, Chance challenged Tricky.

"Nah, I say there's some shit under the bed," Tricky said competitively.

"A'ight, you check mine and I'll check yours."

Chance looked under the bed after stuffing the last bit of money that he got from the cushion, into the pillowcase. He saw nothing.

Tricky came out of the closet that belonged to the woman of the house and had about four different containers of pills.

"I told you. These rich people ain't even happy to be rich. They got every fucking thing and they still ain't satisfied. If I had money, that would be my high. Shit." Chance got up and went through a cabinet that Tricky said he hadn't touched. He didn't find anything.

"Let's go downstairs. What you got in there?"

"I got the money, some jewels and shit…" he was cut off by Chance, as they approached Star and Marquise who were in the kitchen eating sandwiches. They all took seats around the kitchen table.

"Okay, so I got a coin collection and some silverware and some stamps. Star got guns in a box. What y'all got?"

"We got pills, money, and jewels. Damn, they ain't got no real food to eat, I'm hungry as hell."

"They out of town, you ain't supposed to leave food in the refrigerator and you going away for two weeks," Tricky instructed. Tricky was the paranoid, calculating mastermind of the group. He was always thinking or thinking negative. He had an answer for everything and was always wanting to debate about something. Tricky was slim and yellow. He kept a short fro and was a neat dresser, a neat person like Oscar Madison. He was not a dirty dude. He was meticulous and usually argumentative and a pain-in-the-ass. But, he was also very smart and being a perfectionist had helped him be very successful at finding lots of money. He and Chance had been friends since high school although there personalities matched the characters in the classic television show, *The Odd Couple.* The two rarely saw eye to eye. Travis always warned Chance about his loyalty to cut throat niggas in the street. He always tried to give Chance good advice, which fell on deaf ears, but they both had love and respect for each other. In addition, they both worked very well together.

"No shit, Sherlock. You got it," Marquise joked on Tricky. "I gotta go take a shit, Mr. Sherlock Holmes. Marquise went to use the bathroom and came back minutes later and said, "Yo, is that wrong if I shitted on their bed?"

"Yo, nigga! You a crazy nigga? That's disgusting man," Tricky said agitated by Marquise's ignorant behavior. "Why you gotta be so fucking ignorant, man? Just because we are criminals, that doesn't mean that we have to be animals. We can still be civilized. We can still be men of honor and integrity." They all laughed at Tricky.

"Fuck it, they some white racist muhfuckas, probably. We shittin' on them because they don't try to help the fuckin' poor people. Shit, we doing this for all the fucked up poor people out here who can't get a break in life, while these people have pounds and pounds of shit to just waste."

"All right, all jokes aside. What's the plan for leaving? We need to do two in each car and split the weight." Star was his usual serious self. He was always on edge or agitated about something. He was one of few words; he listened and observed people more than talk, as much as Tricky was known to. Star kept the joking for after work. He didn't like when they relaxed and played around. He felt that they should have been out of the house already.

"You know we should have been out of here already. We been in here 25 minutes. I know the people are away but let's stop this dumb shit. Everybody grab what they found and book to the cars."

They all got up, leaving their mess and went to the basement. Chance picked up three laptops and the PlayStation and Nintendo unit he was taking. Marquise picked up the coin, stamp, and silverware collections that he *found* and Star picked up the wooden box of guns. They were all dressed in black with their black skullies pulled down low, just above their eyes. They all ran crouching low and holding their loot through the backyard to the one behind it. As they entered, they heard the people in the driveway as they were approaching. They all stopped in their tracks and kneeled down with precision. They heard the voices fade and heard their front door close.

They took off running and stopped again so that Marquise could look up and down the street. They were on the side of the house where the people had just entered. The coast was clear and Marquise took off first. The car was unlocked. He quickly dropped the collections, popped the trunk and put the stuff in, Star then put in the box of guns and they jumped in the car.

Chance and Tricky had made it to his truck and was already driving off. They had parked on opposite sides of the street and in the opposite directions. They were going to meet up at Marquise's house.

Chance felt more comfortable driving back with Tricky. Tricky looked more straight and narrow than Marquise. Marquise looked like a criminal. He looked like the bad guy that he was because he was the type of guy who wouldn't look you in your eye. He would always cut his eyes when he talked and he was the knucklehead of the group. He wanted trouble and liked conflict. Marquise had always been in trouble. He started robbing houses in Teaneck at fifteen years old. He had been in and out of jail since then. Marquise was dark-skinned and suspicious looking. However, all the girls loved his grimy ass.

"Yo, I don't trust Marquise," Tricky said.

"Listen, Marquise is just grimy naturally. You just gotta stay on top of him, that's all. He always been shiesty. "

As Marquise was getting on the highway, a police car was riding next to him. He was stopped at a light, looked over at the officer, and nodded his head. The officer nodded back. When they pulled off Marquise got on the highway and the cop did as well. He made sure that he drove slowly. He got ahead of the officer and said to Star, "It's a good thing you decided to lay in the back. There's a coppie behind us. I'm cool though. I gave him a nod. He nodded back. He's behind us, but he ain't pullin' me, so I guess we good. Nah, fuck that, we good."

"He's still behind you?" Star asked, looking into the back of Marquise's seat, putting all his mental energy to not allow them to be pulled over. "It don't matter, he's about to turn off."

Marquise started laughing. "What are you psychic nigga, or you a prophet? He just turned off the exit. You a bad man, Star."

"I'm on point. Now stop talking to me and focus on getting to your fuckin' house. I don't feel like talking. I'm all crunched the fuck up back here and shit." They both started laughing.

They all met up at Marquise's within minutes of each other. They started unloading and taking the stuff into Marquise's basement, so they could tally and count everything.

They ended up down in Marquise's basement drinking, sniffing coke, and looking over and counting the money repeatedly. Tricky left entrusting his cut or number that he might expect to come to him through Chance. Tricky did not use drugs and he did not like to be around people when they were using them. He knew that Chance was a man of his word and wouldn't try to cheat him.

They counted a total of $75,000.00 in cash. They called someone in the city about taking the guns who was on his way to come and check them out. They were going to give the collection to Star's aunt who owned a real estate agency and could get rid of them quickly before they were reported stolen. The jewelry they were holding for Chance to take to Nadja. He decided he would give it a shot when he left from Marquise's house.

About an hour later, there was a knock on the door. It was Chico, the gun dealer from Spanish Harlem. He walked in with Junior.

"Yo, Chance! My nigga, you home and eating already I see!" Junior gave everyone a dap and Chance a clap and a hug.

"Yo, Chance, this my man, Chico. I been dealin' with him for years and just found out he's Junior's cousin." Chance and Chico gave each other a pound and nodded heads.

"Yeah, who you think I be getting my ratchets from for my stick-ups?"

"So what you got? Okay you got two macs and two nines. I'll give you $5,000. For this mac, it's an Ingram Mac 10 9MM Subgun with a matching suppressor. These two 9 MMs are old, especially this glock. So, I'll give you a thousand for both and this other mac is a good one but it's not in the best condition, so $500 for this. You good with that?"

"Yeah, we okay with it. I just want to get rid of them. I didn't do my research or nothing and you my man Chico; I know you will not try to play me."

Chico gave them $6,500 and him and Junior left. Junior gave Chance his number and told him they should hang out.

Marquise, Star, and Chance were high and ready to go outside and spend some money. They had made $81,000 in cash so far, from one hit. They were ready to paint the town and the city green.

Their first stop was the local bar, Ray's. It was a Thursday night and the bar was packed. Chance had just came home that day and had already become a Daddy, saw his mother clean off of Heroin, found out that his brother was serving three years for selling crack, and had made $22,000. *Not bad*, he thought to himself.

The first ass he saw mesmerized him and, as he was passing by the girl and the crowd, a familiar face that belonged to the ass, turned around. It was Kelly. She was clearly drunk and looking like a whore. He wasn't surprised. She had been a whore since high school. All he ever heard about her over the years in the mail that different women had written to him was that Kelly was a straight whore who went to the bar every weekend and took a different victim home when the bar closed.

"Oh, my God! It's Chance!" Everybody turned around and started hollering and shouting Chance out. Kelly grabbed Chance around his neck and he hugged her around her waist and then palmed her ass with his hands. He gave her a kiss on the cheek and whispered in her ear, "I'm leaving with you tonight." She nodded her head yes and let go of him so he could continue to the back to sit at a table.

He made it to the back where he got street love showered over him. All the niggas wanted to buy him drinks and all of the women wanted to give him some pussy. He had switched back into his Dada Supreme outfit. He was looking *fresh, fresh like a million bucks.*

The deejay was B-Doggs and he was playing all the latest hip-hop. The hot albums were Raekwon, Only Built 4Cuban Linx, The Pharcyde, Smif-N-Wessun, Dah Shining, Mobb Deep, The Infamous, and 2Pac, All Eyes on Me and Nas Illmatic and Biggie, Ready to Die.

All eyes were on Marquise, Star, and Chance. They started ordering Moet bottles and stealing all of the attention. Everyone knew that they were doing B&Es (breaking and entering) but no one cared because they knew that they robbed from the rich to take care of their families and friends, while splurging or "flossing". They had to be flashy; it was only right. They believed that if they risked their freedom to live, then they would "live it up with their earnings".

When Mobb Deep, Shook Ones Pt. 2 came on, everyone went to the dance floor. Chance walked over to the floor and walked up on Kelly's ass while she was dancing with her girls. She turned around and started reciting the lyrics along with the song…

We got you stuck off the realness, we be the infamous, you heard of us
Official Queensbridge murderers

The mob comes equipped with warfare, beware, of my crime family who got nuff shots to share for all those who wanna profile and pose,

Rock you in your face, stab your brain wit your nose bone....you ain't a crook son, you're just a shook one.

Kelly leaned in and yelled in Chance's ear, "I know you ain' t a shook one, you gonna beat this pussy up tonight?"

"Hell yeah."

B-Doggs then mixed Raekwon's Incarcerated Scarfaces in and the dance floor got even more packed with people just vibing, nodding their heads and signing the lyrics...

Now yo, yo, what up, yo' time is runnin' out
It's for real though let's connect politic-ditto!
We could trade places, get lifted in the staircases
Word up, peace incarcerated scarfaces

Chance was feeling like he was on top of the world. Although he heard these songs when he was in Trenton State Prison, it was nothing like being on the street and hearing it, and living it. He had seen many incarcerated scarfaces during his bid and he was glad that he wasn't going to see them again. *Shit, they'll send me to another prison next time*, he thought to himself.

Chance was not really a dancer but he was celebrating. Janet came up behind him and wrapped her arms around his stomach. He turned around and she leaned up to kiss him. He kissed her on her lips. He turned to Kelly and said in her ear, "I want to bring Janet too, okay?"

Kelly shrugged her shoulders although she really didn't want to have a threesome. She wanted Chance to herself, but she would rather agree then risk him choosing Janet over her. Janet was prettier than her, and she knew Janet and Chance had a *thing* that was tighter than what she'd had with Chance, since high school.

Chance told Janet to meet him and Kelly outside, once the bar was closing. He walked around and got about four more phone numbers of girls he knew and didn't know. When

Chance walked back upstairs to their table, Marquise had the Spanish girl who set the robbery up, sitting on his lap. He introduced her to Chance and gave him the signal as to who she was.

Star was in the corner with his girl, who showed up without him knowing that she was coming. He was lucky that when she walked in, he was not in any broad's face. Star left shortly thereafter with his girl.

Marquise got up and told Chance he was leaving. "Unless you want to go to the city. I can take her to the hotel and drop her off and go back later."

Chance wanted to have his ménage trios. He wasn't thinking about New York.

"Nah, kid, go 'head with mamacita. I got two black chicks that's about to be swinging from my nuts. I'll get up with you tomorrow. Yo, give me some coke. I know you got some." Chance waited for Marquise to go in the bathroom and dish him some cocaine into a dollar bill for his "after party".

The bar was shutting down. The interior lights came on. Everyone was making their plans on where and who they were going to link up with. Chance was all ready secured. He walked outside, met Kelly and Janet, and had the best time of his life in four and a half years.

1996
Chapter 14

The next afternoon, when Chance came home, he went into Twinkie's apartment, which was a mess. He walked in the room and found his daughter playing with the crack pipe that Twinkie had dropped on the floor when she passed out in the early morning hours. Chanel was putting it to her mouth and pretending to smoke on it.

"What the fuck is my daughter doing with this!" Chance snatched the pipe out of Chanel's hand and walked her out of the room.

"Don't worry; I gotta talk to Mommy for a few minutes. Go in your room and play." Chance walked a hesitant Chanel to her room. He put a movie in for her and turned up the volume so she wouldn't hear the commotion that was about to start.

When he walked back in Twinkie's room, she had not budged.

"Bitch! What the fuck you smoking crack in front of my daughter for?" Twinkie raised her head, looked at Chance, and her head dropped back on the pillow without her saying a word.

Chance jumped on top of Twinkie and started choking her. Her eyes were bulging out of her eye sockets while she was gasping for air and trying to pull his arms from her throat.

Chance was calling her all types of whores, bitches, and sluts and her eyes began to roll in the back of her head. Jonny's bloody face flashed into his memory and he jumped off Twinkie. She sat up coughing and rubbing her neck. She had tears in her eyes but she still didn't say a word.

Chance didn't say another word either. He started pulling his clothes out of the closets and the drawers. Twinkie lay back down and fell back to sleep while rubbing her neck.

Chance packed his belongings in a black trash bag and went to Chanel's room. He pulled all of her clothes out of the closets and drawers as well. He had three garbage bags worth of their clothes and all of Chanel's toys. He packed them in Twinkie's car and drove to his mother's house. When his mother answered the front door, he walked in with Chanel and her toys and clothes. He put the bag down, pushed Chanel in the door and went back to the car to get the other two bags.

"What happened Chance?" his mother asked when he came back in.

"That bitch Twinkie is a crack head, full force now. She's doing the shit in front of my daughter. Ma, Chanel gotta stay with you until I find a place for us to stay. The first person who popped into Chance's mind was Janet. He picked up the phone and called her.

"Yo, can I stay with you for a while, until I get my own place?" Janet said yes, without any hesitation. He returned Twinkie's car the next day and gathered the belongings that he had left behind; Janet was waiting outside and they left in her Nissan Maxima.

"Chance moved in with Janet in her apartment in Ridgefield Park, a white town next to Teaneck. Within a month, Janet had agreed to take Chanel in too. She would become Chanel's stepmother and caretaker.

Chance spent the next six months of 1995 making and spending money. He, Marquise, Star, Tricky, and Junior were the main crew. The night they robbed the house in Ringwood, things changed a bit. When the owners of the house came back, they reported their house robbed and the Ringwood police showed up at Marquise's house to ask him questions. They told him that someone had jotted down the license plate because they car was strange but Marquise believed that the cop who he was riding next to had probably ran his plate. They really didn't have enough to get a search warrant, so they didn't bother him again. They knew that the cop had just missed out on a score, since he didn't pull them over.

They began renting cars in girls' names instead of using cars that were registered to them. Most of their cars were registered in friends' or relatives' names as well.

One day Chance paid a visit to Nadja. When he got down the street, he didn't see Dip's truck, but he did see a new Benz that he knew was Nadja's.

Chance rang the bell and Nadja came to the door with a denim one-piece miniskirt dress. She had gained weight but still had all of her curves intact. When she opened the door, she looked Chance up and down before saying anything. She stepped out on the porch, wrapped her arms around his neck, and planted a juicy peck on his lips.

"Damn Chance, you looking good baby." Nadja held his hands and backed up. "Nigga, come on and just beat this pussy up real fast 'for my man get back. Shit. I heard you was home. I can't pass this shit up." Nadja walked in and Chance followed. He was licking his lips as her ass cheeks went up and down with her walk. *Damn this bitch ass is juicy*, Chance thought. *Fuck it, me and Dip will have to share this pussy here and scrap if the nigga walks in.*

Nadja lifted up her mini dress over her head as she walked up the second flight to her bedroom. Her fat ass swallowed up her thong. Chance smacked her ass and she turned around, stuck her finger in her mouth, and then put it in her pussy. She then sucked on her finger.

"Damn, you missed me huh?" Chance was pulling off his t-shirt.

They got to her bed and were already undressed. There was no need for foreplay he wanted to get in that pussy, like he had never left. As soon as Nadja lay on her back Chance crawled on the bed taking her legs up into the inside of his elbows and entering right into her, with no hands. He was already sticking straight and he opened her right up and shot right in. Nadja took him in, arched her back, and moved her hips and pussy in rotation so she could feel Chance on every side of her pussy. She arched her back and he plunged forward. She pulled up on her elbows so she could look at her *long lost baby.*

She had been mad with him but she knew he was a fucked up nigga when she got with him. She knew he would end up doing some dumb shit eventually. That didn't mean shit to her seeing him at the door. That anger was out of the window and he was filling her up with his good ass dick. She smiled and he looked up and saw her.

He took a slow stroke while talking to her, looking in her eyes, "You happy to see me Mommy?"

"Yes baby," Nadja pulled his head to her breast and watched him start to suck on them. He ran his tongue gently across her nipples and then took them gently in his mouth. He stopped sucking and was feeling the rush about to come. He didn't want to hold his cum, he wanted to nut all in her. He wasn't worried about her getting pregnant; she told him that her tubes were tied.

Chance told her and she came with him. Right after she quickly got dressed and was like, "Listen let's take a ride and talk. Go wait in the car, let me wash up and change real fast. Dip ain't too far from here."

"A'ight, unlock the door." Chance didn't give a fuck about Dip. They knew each other and respected each other's hustle and positions, had the same friends, but had never really fucked with each other. They had been in the same circles and surroundings for years but never said many words to each other. Whatever happened, Chance would deal with it. A shook one, he wasn't.

Nadja came out in terry cloth short shorts set with a matching jacket by DKNY. She had on canary yellow with yellow Nike's.

Chance asked her about the money she had for him from the jewels that were left with her. She said she kept the diamond necklace and pendant as a reminder of him and that he wasn't getting that back. She still had the two Faberge eggs. He asked her if she could still go to the same Jewish guy in the diamond district and she said she would. That was what started their business and pleasure all over again. Nadja was the one who would sell the jewelry for them.

By the time 1996 came in, Chance had made and spent about 100,000 dollars by himself. He spent most of his time, with different girls. He stayed with Janet more than anyone else because his daughter was there. He used condoms with the random girls, most of the time. The only girl he didn't use condoms with was Nadja. Since Dip would go out of town frequently to do stickups, Chance was able to stay with Nadja when Dip was gone.

Chance was generous with his money. Everybody loved to be around Chance because he was a person to try to help people. He was not tight with his money. He was doing for others. All he bought for himself was a used Q45 Infiniti. Chance had a good heart, under all of his armor.

One day Chance was over Chante's house and when Chante left to go to an appointment, Travis finally asked him about what he was into.

"Yo, I see you got a good hustle going, man." Travis had seen Chance splurging a couple of times that Chance was able to drag him out. Travis was not a street guy. He was very much in love with Chante and had no intention of neglecting her or cheating. He knew that it was what you surround yourself with in life that you become. If you hang in the slop, you become a pig. He was content with being a smart businessman at his young age.

"Yeah, but you know what's funny, the more money you have, the more money you lose. I can't keep money for shit. I been out here six months and I ain't doing bad, though."

"I see. What you into man, I might need to get down with some action with you temporarily. I want to buy your sister a extra phat engagement ring." Chance thought for a second. "I can put some money in if you can flip that shit." Travis assumed that Chance was selling drugs.

"Yo, I am gonna tell you this shit, but let me just tell you. I take my freedom very seriously. So, you better keep your ears open and your mouth shut. You feel where I'm coming from?" Travis nodded his head and waited for the story.

"I run up in houses with my crew. We get like $50,000 to $100,000 a night usually."

Travis' eyebrows rose. "Damn, but people got alarm systems, nowadays. How do you know if there alarm is off or on?"

"We don't. If the alarm system goes off, we bounce. Shit we get lucky more than we don't. If the alarm goes off, the cops gotta get there. By the time they do, we already out." Travis thought for a few moments.

"Why don't you just cut the alarm system?" Travis looked Chance dead in the eye, with an interest in really being a part of that enterprise.

"Oh shit! You a fucking electrician! Damn, am I that muhfuckin' slow? I should have been talked to you. Nah, but I had to feel you out. You know criminals and hard-working men are not the same type of guys you know." Chance joked.

"Yeah, you cut the phone wires and the alarm can't go off. The police department can't be notified."

"Yo, nigga, you just took the game to the next fucking level! Oh, shit, jackpot! Let's go take a ride." Travis put his sneakers on, they got in Chance's Q45, and Chance jumped on the New Jersey Turnpike south.

"I had met this girl who was visiting her brother, when my mom had came to see me. She was beautiful. Her brother wouldn't let me holler at her. We was cool down there, but he wasn't havin' it and I would be the same way, but she was from Somerset. I just want to see what it's like. I heard it's a lot of nice homes there."

"Oh yeah, they definitely do. I travel all over Jersey, Rockland County, and Westchester County. I know my way every which way from New Jersey to New York State. There's a lot of rich towns. White people are living."

"Nigga, you ain't lying. They got money coming out the seams in the walls. Shit, and they don't give a fuck about people that's starving and poor and shit."

"A lot of them inherit money. It's old money. Money that just keeps growing and growing, non-stop." Travis was eager to get involved with Chance's operation.

"So you don't case the homes first? You just go on a whim?" Travis asked.

"We don't want to look suspicious driving around a rich white neighborhood in the daytime. So we case them before we do them."

"So either rent a van and look like a landscaper or a worker or rent expensive foreign cars so that the car at least fits in the neighborhood."

"Yo, let's use your work van." Chance pulled off the exit and into Somerset. He remembered the exit when he was going home with Twinkie from Trenton State Prison.

"Well, it can only be you and me. I'm not putting a bunch of niggas in my father's company van and then get his name mixed up in some burglary shit." Travis had always been his own person. He was never a follower or one to give in to peer pressure. He didn't have anything to prove to anybody. He and Tricky were a lot alike in that regard. Tricky was looking into businesses that he could open once he had saved a sufficient amount of money. He was very practical and frugal, never splurging his money to impress anybody.

"Nah, I wouldn't expect you to. But, you right, we need to make sure the cars are luxury, not just regular rental joints like we been doing. It's time to change the game. I been wanting to take this shit to the next level and you just made that shit happen. Fuck it; let's do a job right now. It's two in the afternoon. Everyone is at work. You might as well show me how to cut a wire right now." Chance drove slowly down an immaculate block with mansions that looked like they belonged in Beverly Hills California.

"How do you know that I brought my snippers," Travis said, jokingly, holding up his wire cutters from work.

"Because you are a smart man. I'll let you pick the house." Travis looked from each side of the street and back and forth.

"That one. I love stone brick houses. That shit looks crazy. It looks like money, you know why?" Travis was starting to feel like an expert and he hadn't robbed one home.

"Why, Mr. Boss Man? You own your own company and shit," Chance teased Travis.

"Not yet. You have to look at the lawns. You have to look in the driveways, and in the windows. From here, without even getting out of the car, I can tell you that they pay for landscaping. There flowers and bushes are freshly planted and cut. There is no old or broken down car in the driveway, and look inside, paintings on the wall. Paintings are expensive. So they have money to burn."

"Shit, everyone on this block has money to burn. Look at the houses." Chance was not going to let Travis tell him about *his* business.

"That's not true. There have to be people living here that are barely holding on to their house. It could be a woman who just got separated or divorced. Or, someone who just lost his job. Having a house doesn't mean that you have a lot of disposable income. So if they lawn is shabby, they are probably struggling." Chance started laughing.

"I can tell you gonna be a pro at this, a hot boy. You might end up being a sniffer."

"Nah, I don't sniff no coke." Travis shook his head.

"Nah man, some niggas just have good noses to sniff out money. My whole crew, we are all keen niggas who smell that paper right on out. We all different types, we think differently, so we all try different hiding spots. And, we gets it! I like the daytime better so we don't have to be walking around a house with small flashlights trying to find shit in the dark. But, we still gets it done!"

"Okay, I'm ready. The alarm box is on the side of the house."

"A'ight, we gotta park around the corner."

"Just pull up on the other side of the street and enough houses down that whoever's house we pull in front of they can't see where we are going. What, are they gonna call the cops because two black men are walking down the street?"

"Shit, you never know, but let's make it."

 197

They both got out of the car and walked along the sidewalk across the street from the house they were about to rob. They crossed over and to the side of the house and Travis took out his cutters. He showed Chance the box and snipped the wires and pulled the box, snipped the bottom wires and pulled the box from the house. He carried it with them to the back of the house where they put their gloves (that Chance had in his car) on.

Chance demonstrated how to break the door off its hinges with a kick. Sometimes, he would use his shoulder, but if his kick worked, he wouldn't have to worry about possibly throwing his arm out of socket. One kick was all it took and the wooden back door cracked. The deadbolt busted through the door panel and the door was hanging off the bottom hinge. They ran in.

Travis went with Chance into the bedroom where there was jewelry lying on the dresser and in a jewelry box.

"See, one thing is true for most people. They may put on an alarm, but they don't secure their house in case someone breaks in anyway. They still keep the inside of the house unprotected because most people are not going to lock up and secure everything, every time they go out of the house. They are used to having the comfort of leaving things out, in their own home. The only thing people hid really is money."

"Well, they didn't hide this good." Travis had been kneeling down looking under the bed and he stood up and signaled for Chance to pull the bed from the wall. There was something bulky under the carpet in the corner under the bed. Chance put the leg of the bed down and lifted up the carpet. There was a plastic bag that was for a comforter, but it was packed with money. Chance threw it to Travis.

"Yeah, see I guess black people aren't the only ones who don't trust banks." Chance declared.

"I see. Damn, this looks like a good amount of money." Travis said.

"Well, hurry up and go through the drawers real fast and I'll do this cabinet and the closet. We been in here for four minutes. It's time to go."

They ransacked the bedroom finding more jewelry. Chance put all of the jewelry and money in the pillowcase and then put the pillowcase in the clear comforter carrying bag. They went into the garage, got a black trash bag, and put the comforter bag in the trash bag. Travis went to the kitchen and took a piece of mail from the house. They exited the house and walked calmly back to the car. Chance carried the trash bag over his shoulder inconspicuously. Someone driving past them would probably think that he had clothes in the bag. He popped the trunk and put the bag in the trunk, closed it and got in the car.

They drove slowly back to the highway. They didn't see any cop cars until they got on the Turnpike and they were there with their radar guns checking for speeders.

Travis was quiet. Chance turned up the radio on full blast.

Jay Z's Politics As Usual came on and Chance got hyped up. He started rapping as if he was the artist of the song…

You can catch me skatin' through your town, putting it down y'all relatin'
No waitin', I'll make your block infrared hot I'm like Satan
Y'all feel a nigga's struggle; y'all think a nigga love to hustle behind the wheel, tryin' to escape my trouble…
Politics as usual
I took my Frito to Tito in the district, blessed me with some
VS and something I can live with, stop frontin'
And for the dough I raise, gotta get shit appraised
No disrespect to you, make sure your word is true…
Politics as Usual

"Yo, what we gonna do with the jewelry?" Travis wanted to know how much money they had made.

"I got a girl that sells it to this Jew at the diamond district for me. It's time for me to meet the nigga, though, 'cause she got a man and I be having to wait for the nigga to go out of town and shit for her to be able to move and shit. I gotta talk to her about that. We can go to your house and count this money. This bitch, Janet, telling me she pregnant. She saying she's three months. I ain't been home but six months and I already got another baby on the way. "

"You better cover up, nigga, that HIV shit is starting to show up in niggas and shit. It's starting to be a big thing," Travis warned.

"Yeah, I know. But, it's still strictly homos and drug users, but I feel you. They keep talking about that shit more and more." Chance contemplated. "I don't wanna think about that shit, we got some thousands to play with."

"I ain't playing with nothing. I'm going to the jewelry store if it's more than ten thousand." Travis wanted to buy Chante the biggest rock she had ever seen.

"Yo, tell the truth. You never cheated on my sister? I know you like 'Nigga I ain't dumb enough to tell you' but I know how the shit is. Bitches want to own your dick and balls and shit. As long as you take good care of her and don't disrespect her and keep that shit to a minimum and meaningless." Chance knew that he had never been faithful and he didn't see himself ever being with only one woman.

"No. I don't think it's worth it to hurt my girl for some temporary instant gratification. It's too much work trying to keep more than one woman happy. Eventually the girl on the side wants you to leave your girl and then if you don't, she'll tell on you to ruin your relationship. I love my girl. I don't see nothing that any other bitch has that's better than what my girl has. I know I sound like an alien talking like that, but all men don't cheat. I know some men like the rush they get and the pursuit and the *Pussy Chase* but when the shit hits the fan and your girl don't want yo' ass no more, then thinking of that piece of pussy you got that ruined it all, will make you sick." Chance laughed, while Travis remained straight face. "I'm serious, that shit is too much of a headache. When you make a woman happy, she will do everything in her power to make sure she keeps you happy. She will do anything for you, the more you treat her right."

"I want to be like you when I grow up, Nigga, damn, you just made me feel like a piece of shit. I just ain't find that woman that can keep me paying attention to her like that. I get bored fast."

"You probably don't take the time to get to know the woman, but do what works for you, to each his own."

They pulled into Travis and Chante's apartment complex and Chance took the bag out of the trunk and brought it into the house.

Chante was sitting on the ottoman relaxed with her feet up. When her two favorite men in the world walked through the door, she started cheering and clapping.

hance bowed in front of her. "Thank you, thank you. I know I'm a stud. I'm a hot boy." Chance bowed again and put the bag down.

"I'm clapping for that *other* hot boy right there. The one who is now my baby daddy and not just my boyfriend." It took a few seconds for it to register with Chance and Travis. Chance gave Travis a big hug and patted him on his back while Travis looked at Chante with her ear-to-ear smile. He moved from Chance and lifted Chante up from the one-seater couch and into the air.

"You serious? You sure? We having a baby?" Travis had tears in his eyes.

"Yes, and I love you so much. You are gonna be such a good daddy." Travis and Chante kissed while Chance began to empty the contents of the bag on the dining room table. He separated all of the jewelry to check it out.

"What is all this? Ooh, I need some diamond studs." Chante started picking up the different diamond pieces of jewelry. "Wait, what are you doing with Chance with this stuff? Chance, I know you are not having Travis get involved with your *jobs*!"

"Relax Lil Mommy, I got him. I ain't gonna let nothin' happen. He just helped me out in a major way."

"Chance!" Chante did not want her brother corrupting her man.

"Chante, I promise, he will be okay. How am I gonna bring harm to my niece or nephew's father?"

Chance laid out all of the jewelry and then he and Travis started counting the money. It came to $65,000." Chante was going to end up with a hell-of-a-ring!

1997
Chapter 15

Chance and Travis robbed 45 homes throughout 1996. Thanks to Travis' knowledge of directions throughout all of New Jersey and New York, they were able to hit many different areas. They never continued to hit homes in one area, which would make that area hot. Therefore, they would shift around both states so that there was no pattern. All of the individual areas were so spread apart that they did not realize the connection. They were going to five or six different counties in New Jersey and New York State. Some of them had been caught with stolen property or burglary tools. Marquise had charges pending from three different arrests. He would continue robbing houses until it was time to do some time, so that he would have money to come home to. Junior had been arrested twice with Marquise and Chance and Star were arrested together twice for burglary tools and stolen property from one home. He was also arrested with Marquise for having stolen property. They made sure they took the stolen property out of the car right away, so that items from different places could not be found together, giving them more charges. They would always make bail right away and the court cases didn't usually come up before at least six months. Tricky and Travis, the two smartest ones of the gang, had yet to have been even stopped by the police.

The Teaneck, Englewood, Hackensack and the Bergen County police departments had been able to catch some of them, not for a string of burglaries, but individual ones. In addition, they couldn't be charged with burglary if not found in the house. They could only be charged with the possession of the stolen property. The local authorities knew who they were and what they were doing; they just couldn't catch or stop them.

Travis had gone out with Chance, Tricky, Star, and Junior on different occasions. He didn't like Marquise and stayed away from him. Marquise had acquired a worsening crack habit, so he was volatile and frustrated many times. He was irritable and fidgety, a loose cannon.

Chance had been home for a year and six months, and had three charges related to burglaries. He knew that they would not proceed with the trials right away. The authorities liked to give them enough rope to hang themselves by continuing to let them out on low bails so that they would accumulate more and more charges over time and then get them all added up. That way they could be given a lot of time, but it would never compare to the amount of houses that they got away with. They got away far more than they were popped, by a wide margin. So, the money was stacking and they were in the 'hood, splurging.

Chance also had a brand new son, by Janet. She had their son, Jayvon, in July of 1996. He was six months old. Chance was a good father. He knew that Chanel was not going to go back to her mother. Twinkie kept being locked up and DYFS became involved. Chance was not about to let his daughter go into social services. He made sure that Janet treated Chanel like she was her own. Chanel was five.

Nadja finally took Chance to meet the fence, Sherim, when he threatened to leave her alone if she didn't. He was doing a lot of business with him. The only other person that would go with Chance would be Tricky. Tricky was a good mouthpiece because he could negotiate without blowing his stack like Chance would sometimes.

One day in March, Chance and Tricky were at Sherim's counter. They were escorted to the office across the street.

Tricky put a leather bag on the desk and opened it to reveal about sixty different pieces of diamond and gold jewelry. There were plenty of heirlooms and rare, antique and expensive pieces. Tricky told Sherim that he needed an even split for five.

The fence took out a scale and weighed the gold as his brother walks in. Sherim examines the diamonds as well. Chance didn't like the vibe that he got from Sherim's brother. They did not speak although he had seen him three times at that point, so he knew that meant not to trust him. Harum walked back out. Travis and Tricky should their heads.

"I can tell your brother's a real dick," Chance said.

"Yeah, he is," Sherim confessed, laughing.

"So I have $150,000.00 for you guys. That was quite some stuff there. You know, I may have to let you know of a few places that you should visit, you know what I mean," Sherim laughed, and was joined by Tricky and Chance.

"Hey, just let us know. You got our numbers." Sherim said he would have some addresses for them the next time they came.

They left with their bag of money. Tricky took his $50,000 and went his own way. Tricky was still pretty much a loner. He didn't do too much socializing. He was very disciplined and regimented ever since doing his first three-year bid at 19 for burglaries. Tricky was very savvy with his money. He invested his money in various places. He had stocks, mutual funds, and CDs. He lived in a townhouse by himself and owned two luxury vehicles. A Porsche 928 and a Range Rover truck. Tricky had five hundred thousand in cash assets and $50,000.00 worth of investments.

Chance met up with Marquise, Star, and Junior and gave them $50,000 each. Chance and Junior left and went their own ways. Marquise and Star decide to go case some homes.

Chance left to go to the house he was renting with Janet. Chance was not nearly as practical or organized with his money. He was taking care of his mother, Janet, who was not working, and his two children. He had an aunt that had lost her job, and her and her kids were very much dependent on

Chance. Then Chance was generous in the street. People would come to him all the time with a sob story and he would try to help them. Add that to his overall fast life of overconsumption and he was spending more than 10,000 dollars a month. Chance did have a nice Ford Expedition. He was not into spending an astronomical amount of money on a vehicle.

Junior, the youngest of the crew, was more of a splurge than Chance or any of the rest of them. Junior owned three very expensive vehicles and was paying bookoo money on rent in a Manhattan high-rise. Junior owned a Lamborghini, an 850 BMW and a Lexus truck. Junior could not live in Jersey because the police were always harassing him, angry because they couldn't catch him. He spent all of his money on cars, expensive vacations, expensive jewels, and buying everything he saw that he wanted.

Marquise was spending all of his money on drugs and trying to keep his house and his marriage together. Marquise and Star had started to branch off and do their own thing, separate from the rest of the group. Oftentimes, it was Chance, Junior, Tricky, and Travis, when Travis decided to go out. Travis had controlled himself to only go out once, every two weeks, so that he wouldn't get addicted. He had managed to put $200,000 up in stash. Travis was only interested in saving money for a rainy day for his family. Chante was four months pregnant.

Star was also caught up in a strengthening addiction, which would keep him from going out as frequently as the others, like Marquise. Star didn't have a lot of money because he was always nowhere to be found. None of them knew that Star's girlfriend was messed up on drugs along with Star, which was making his problem only worse.

Marquise and Star remained at Marquise's house and decided to go out on a job. They decided to go to Westchester County. It would be a move that would take the local police departments to another level, and closer to their goal of bringing the "gang" down.

Marquise drove around Westchester County in New York State They did not notice that they were being followed by a New York detective who had run Marquise's plate. He did not want to waste time or money renting a car. When Marquise's criminal history came across the officer's screen, he immediately knew that the occupants of Marquise's car were casing homes.

Marquise boldly pulls into a driveway of a home with no cars in the front. The detectives pull over far enough down the street to go undetected by the men, but not too far to not be able to see them get out and approach the home.

Marquise got out, rang the doorbell, and then peeked into the window on the front door. No one came to the door to see who was visiting. He gave the nod to Star who got out and went around the back. Boom!

Star bust through the back door and opened the front so they could quickly leave out of the front door and into their car in the driveway. Marquise ran into the bedroom and was shocked to see an old woman laying down watching television. The woman began to wail at the top of her lungs when she saw him. Marquise dove on top of the woman and smacked his palm over her mouth. Star came running in when he heard the commotion.

When Star saw the woman being muzzled and restrained by Marquise, he grabbed her bathrobe belt. He wrapped the belt around her wrists, with her arms squeezed together and tied her to the bedpost. He didn't mean to hurt her; he was making sure that she wouldn't make it to a phone to call the police. He then snatched her pantyhose off her, that she was wearing and tied them around the woman's mouth so that Marquise could move his hand. He wrapped the stocking around and around her mouth and tied them behind her head.

They jumped up and began to search the drawers while the woman moaned in fear. They heard footsteps running up the stairs. Someone yelled, "Police!" and Star opened the window and jumped out, landing on Marquise's car. He got in the passenger side as Marquise jumped out the window, rolled off the car and jumped in the car.

As he was backing out, he saw the detective looking out of the window, while the other one came running out of the front door. Marquise was down the street when he saw three police cars with sirens blaring quickly approaching behind him.

"Yo, don't stop! Take this shit as far as you can. Maybe we can jump out once we get farther from them! Let's go Marquise gun it Nigga!" Star yelled. They ran a red light and almost crashed into a family of four that was passing through the intersection. They were able to gain some leeway because the officers had to cautiously go around cars.

Busta Rhyme's "Dangerous" came on the radio and was blasting while they ran from the police. They made it to the highway with what had now become five police cars in high pursuit.

Marquise hit the ramp to the highway doing 100 mph and lost control of the car on the turn. The car skidded and smacked into a divider, almost falling off the ramp and avoiding a drop of 1,000 feet. They were both injured. Marquise had a gash on his head and a broken wrist. Star had a broken rib and knee. They had to be cut out of Marquise's car. They were arrested and taken to a local hospital where they were treated while handcuffed to their hospital beds.

Chance was awakened at 10 pm by a loud knock on his door. He had fallen asleep to do a job, but never woke up to go out. Janet told him that Junior was downstairs saying that it was urgent for him to speak to Chance.

Chance went down to the living room in his boxer shorts.

"Yo, I been calling your cell like crazy! Marquise and Star got busted in Westchester. They was just on the news."

"Word?" Chance grabbed the remote and turned to the news to wait for the story to come on. There was a press conference. The chief expressed to the news cameras that the two men that were caught red-handed trying to rob a woman's house after tying her up, were from New Jersey and were known house burglars. "They tied a woman up! They know we don't fuck with people. If someone is home, we are supposed to leave! Now they are bringing heat from New York; they are going to put two and two together. Chance's prediction was right.

The chief explained that they were going to start working with the New Jersey authorities to see if they could find similarities or comparisons between their recent rash of burglaries. "It seems that we had a large amount of homes where the alarm systems lines have been cut, and that is a signature in plenty of robberies in Northern New Jersey, where these guys have been robbing homes for years, since they were in high school.

"Damn! We gotta get them out before they get questioned about the other robberies." Chance paced the floor. He ran up to his room to get dressed so that he and Junior could go get a girl to post bail and sign for them to get out.

Chance and Junior go to the apartment of one of the many girls that Junior is seeing. They get her to call and inquire about the charges. She was told the arraignment would be held the next day. They start to call the rest of the crew to gather up money toward bail, that Marquise and Star will have to repay. They also go to both of their families and relatives to collect money.

A few days later Marquise and Star are bailed out with bails that were $100,000 each. The girl bails them out and they gather five people to sign to cover the amount of bail, in terms of proof of income.

Marquise had been released to the Westchester County jail where his wife picked him up. Star was still in the hospital. He was bailed out from there and signed himself out before the doctor wanted to release him.

Travis and Chante were married in June. They moved into a large three-bedroom townhouse in Edgewater, overlooking the Hudson River and the New York Skyline. They could see the Twin Towers from their window. Chante was six months pregnant and had a beautiful white gown that was satin and so complementary to her baby bump. The dress was simple and classy. It was a V-neck with pearls adorning the collar and sleeves and trim of the bottom of the dress. Vonetta was her maid of honor and she looked beautiful and healthy in a silk violet colored dress. With all of the madness that was going on in Chance's life, the wedding of his sister and the closest thing that he had to brother, Travis, was a happy and stress-free day for him. He was proud of his baby sister, Chante.

1998
Chapter 16

Tavis and Chance met up one day after he and Chante came back from their honeymoon. It was July of 1997. They had been going out every other night. Travis had picked up his amount of participation because the family business was suffering and business was very slow. He only dealt with Chance, Tricky, and Junior. Chance had three cases pending for receiving stolen property that were coming up at the end of 1997.

It was Travis' birthday and he wanted to treat himself to something nice. He had taken good care of Chante. Her engagement ring was 4-karat and cost $12,000 and her matching wedding band was a diamond band that had diamonds encrusted around the whole band. It looked like a ring of crushed ice and it cost $17,000. Travis was never flashy but he wanted Chante's whole hand to shine.

He spent $75,000 on their wedding and honeymoon, but he also had $500,000 dollars stashed by that point.

Travis drove his Pathfinder to a BMW dealer. They went inside and Travis saw exactly what he wanted. He wanted a 750, fully loaded. He saw the all-white, with white leather interior that he wanted. It had red piping on the seats and red Pirelli rims. The car shined like a star in the sky. It was whiter than the clouds.

Travis was so excited when he saw that car that he decided to buy Chante a matching convertible BMW 5-series.

Travis traded his truck and Chante's car in. Travis was not greedy. He was business savvy and knew that they did not need four cars, even if they could afford it.

The next day Travis and Chance went to pick up both cars. Travis had told Chante that he needed her had put both of their cars in the shop to get work done to them. They drove Chante's car to her job and Travis went in and brought her outside. Chante was so happy to get her brand new convertible BMW.

Travis and Chance left Chante's job and went straight to Franklin Lakes. Travis was not concerned with renting a car. He knew his brand new car would fit in. It was them in the car in that neighborhood, that didn't.

Just as Chance and Travis parked and were ready to get out and approach a house that Sherim had given him to go to, a police officer pulled up alongside the car.

Chance let go of the door handle when he looked into the cop's eyes. The officer, whose window was down like Travis' asked them what they were doing there.

Chance said that they liked the area and were looking at the houses. The officer put his car in park and got out. He requested back up and asked for Travis and Chance's identification. He ran their names in the computer.

"Why'd you say that? That shit sounded suspicious."

"Fuck you wanted me to say? Ain't a crime to look at nice houses." Chance was agitated, but glad they had nothing in the car.

A few minutes later the officer approached them.

"Mr. Major, you are a known house burglar. What are you doing in this neighborhood?"

"My brother-in-law here is looking to move my sister and their baby to a new home. We were here looking at houses." Chance was exhibiting attitude and the officer did not like it.

"Well, who is to say that you are not here, casing homes to rob them?" the officer asked while his backup showed up.

"I am to say, as a matter of fact, I already said," Chance answered sarcastically.

"Okay, smart ass, step out of the car. You too, Mr. Johnson, please step out of the car."

The approaching officer stood by Chance and Travis while the other officer searched the car. When he saw the wire cutters and gloves on the back seat, he brought them out to question the two. They were glad that it was daytime. If it had been nighttime, they would have also had their ski masks, flashlights, and walkie-talkies. They were glad that they were not in possession of those things or an arrest would have been definite.

"Mr. Johnson, can you tell me why you have wire cutters and gloves in your vehicle?"

"Yes, because I am an electrician. I can get you my license and show you my badge." The officer let Travis get his electrician's license.

They looked everything over and stepped to the side to decide whether to let the two go. The officer returned.

"Mr. Johnson, I'm gonna let you guys go now, but just know you can get yourself into trouble driving around with burglary tools with a known burglar."

"Thank you, sir. That is my work tools. Have a good day Officer." Travis and Chance got in the car and drove off.

"Yo, it's a good thing we traveled light today." Travis was calm. He never let anything excite him.

"Yeah, you're right. And it's a great thing that they didn't catch us coming *out* of the house."

"Word. You know what? I got something for this problem." Travis got on the highway to go back home.

"What now? I trust you're thinking. Can it get better than your idea to clip the phone wires?"

"Hell, yeah. I can show you better than I can tell you. Just sit back and enjoy the ride." Travis smiled and turned up the radio.

Big Pun's "Still Not a Player came on and Chance and Travis sang the words…

I don't wanna be a player no more
I'm not a player I just fuck a lot
But Big Punisher, still got what you're lookin' for
For my thug niggas, for my thug niggas
Uptown baby, uptown
Don't wanna be, don't wanna be - I don't wanna be a player
no more
I'm not a player I just fuck a lot
But you know Big Punisher still down by law
Who's down to crush a lot
Hey yo, I'm still not a player but you still a hater
Elevator to the top hah, see you later, I'm gone
Penthouse suite, Penthouse freaks
In house beach, French countess, ten thou piece
Rent-out lease, with a option to buy
Coppin a five-oh Benz for when I'm not,
far up in the sky
Puffin the lye, from my Twinzito
Up in the Benzito with my kiko from Queens, nicknamed Peri-
co
We go back like PA's and wearing PJ's
Now we reach the peakage,
running trains for three days
Who wanna ride it won't cost you a dollar
whether soft or harder of course you still gonna holla
My my, I'm big huh,
I rip my (prick) through your hooters
I'm sick, you couldn't measure my (dick) with six rulers
Hold up, chula, I'm all about gettin' loot
But I knock that boot, if you out to get HOOF
I don't wanna be a player no more
I'm not a player I just fuck a lot
But Big Punisher, still got what you're lookin' for

They pulled into the driveway of an auto body shop on Route 46 East. Travis and Chance got out of the car. Travis approached one of his old friends from high school who had opened up his own auto body shop.

The guy, Jose, was surprised and happy to see Travis, who had been in his auto shop class.

"Hey guy, long time no see," Jose said.

"I know I heard you had this shop, this is my brother-in-law, Chance. But, I need you to do a big job for me." Travis looked Jose directly and seriously in the eye.

"Yeah, anything for you guy, que pasa?" Travis led Jose and Chance over to his car.

"I need some secret compartments in here. I need to make sure that if I get stopped, the coppers don't find what they're looking for comprende, amigo?" Travis continued with his request.

"I need you to go into the dashboard and build some drawers that will work electronically. If you can't make the drawers come out, I will do that part but I need you to rebuild the inside of my dashboard so that I can have drawers come out, when I push a button, or turn the key or whatever. Do you understand what I'm saying?"

"Sure, sure. I got you hombre."

"Okay, and I'm gonna need a fog light behind the license plate and I want to be able to release some oil out of a fuel pipe from the back, too."

"Wow. What do you want to be James Bond or something?" They all started laughing.

"Yeah, that's exactly what I want to be. Can you do it? And don't charge me too much."

"Hey, that's some work. I can do it but you have to pay *homeboy*." Jose rubbed his fingers together symbolizing money.

"Okay, okay, I got you Jose, you ain't changed a bit. Still robbing people I see." Travis and Jose used to steal radios out of cars when they were in high school.

Jose told Travis to bring his car back the next day and he would be able to give him an estimate by the end of the day, for everything. Travis dropped Chance home and went home.

Corey came home from jail that year and continued getting into a lot of trouble. Chance found out that Corey was running with his old friends from Brooklyn, doing stick ups.

He constantly fought with Corey about doing right but Corey would always say, "When I see you change, I'll change." Their relationship was strained and they did not get along any longer. Corey was a man and Chance was powerless to run his life, or keep him on the right track. He was not being a good example, but he didn't want to own up to that fact.

Then one day, Marquise was home when he received a phone call from a friend who worked in a number spot. His friend told Marquise that there was an old man in the city at the spot who had just hit the street number for a lot of money. The man is in Harlem waiting for them to pay him his money. He said that Marquise should come, follow the man home to New Jersey, and rob him.

Marquise called Star who lived in Harlem with his girl.

"Yo, I'm on my way. We got a job to do." Star said okay and hung up. Marquise picked Star up twenty minutes later. They drove to the block where the number spot was and spotted the man's red Cadillac that was described to Marquise.

They waited a half hour and went over their plan of how to strong arm the man when he gets home and force him to turn the money over. When they get to the man's home in Cresskill, they cannot run up on him outside of his car because a neighbor is standing outside when the man pulls in his driveway.

"Damn, we could have just stuck his ass up before he even got out the car. Now we are gonna have to break in or ring the doorbell and force our way in," Marquise decides.

"So fuck it, we gonna do what we gotta do. He got the bag in his hand right there. When that person goes inside you can go and ring the doorbell. If he doesn't come I'll be on the side and I'll run around back and you follow me."

"Let's wait another hour, it's almost dark. Shit, I got this crumb right here we can smoke until it's time." Marquise pulls out a stem and starts to smoke crack in the car. Star joins him. They begin to get paranoid and impatient. By the time the sun sets, they are overly anxious. Marquise puts his gun in the small of his back in his pants and checks to make sure no one in eye range is outside or in their window. He gets out and Star follows.

Marquise rings the doorbell and a woman in her sixties came to the door. As soon as she cracked the door, Marquise pushed past her and Star slid in and closed the door as Marquise grabbed the woman's mouth before she could begin to scream. Just as he grabbed her, the man came walking down the stairs and stopped in his tracks. Star pointed a gun at his head and told him to continue coming down.

"We are going to make this short and sweet old man. We want that money. We want it now." Marquise was shaking and sweating. The old man noticed Marquise's agitation and thought that he could take him. He knew that his wife could be in danger if he tried to take either one of the guys.

"What money? I ain't got no money. I'm retired. Y'all need to get on and go rob some young drug dealer that can afford to be robbed or something. Leave me and my wife alone."

"Old man, I think you need to listen and give it up," Star said wanting to keep Marquise calm.

"Yeah old man, you need to just listen." Marquise dragged the man's wife into the kitchen and began to tie her up with garbage bags that were visible from the open cabinet door.

"Please don't hurt my wife. Okay, I'll take you to the money. It's in the basement."

Marquise finished tying the woman's feet and arms to the kitchen chair. He and Star follow the man down to the cellar. He tells Star to open the cedar closet door, which he does. While his gun is down, the man pushed away from Marquise, grabs his pistol off a shelf, and shoots at Marquise. The man misses and Marquise shoots him on time, point blank, in the face. The man drops to the ground.

They begin searching the basement. Meanwhile the woman was able to move her hands and move the plastic bag through a crack in the wooden chair's post to allow her hands to reach her ankles. With her hands still tied, she was able to loosen the knot that was on one of her ankles, reach for a knife on the counter, and cut the other piece. The woman quietly ran to her neighbor's house for help.

Marquise and Star tore the basement apart. Star found the safe and lifted it up. They ran out the back door. They got to the car just as four police cars were turning the corner. They jumped in the car and took off. The officers followed them to the George Washington Bridge. Star jumped out of the car and took off running.

Marquise tried to drive through a police barricade. The police had been notified that the older gentleman, whose wife had called the police, had been murdered. When Marquise had no intention of stopping, the police who were outside of their vehicles opened fire on Marquise's car, riddling him with bullets and killing him.

1999
Chapter 17

C hance hears about Marquise in the street and watches
the story on the news. For the first time he begins to
fear for his life and his future. He looks at his friends
and they are mostly either dead or in jail. Roderick and Malcolm were charged with murder and sentenced to life in prison. Jason had cooperated with that investigation because he
was harboring fugitives and did not want to get into trouble,
so Chance did not mess with him anymore.

Chance was tired of his surroundings. He was tired of
the race against prison. He had managed to have his lawyer
postpone his cases but, in September of 1998, he was sentenced to six months in the county jail. He needed a break
from the street so that he could get his stamina back up for
what he was trying to do. Chance's goal was to be a millionaire before they really caught him. He knew that he wasn't
going to quit until he made that money and the authorities
weren't going to quit chasing his tail. If he could stash the
money, he would do the time and come home a rich man.
Then he would put this life behind him.

Chance was in the Bergen County Jail from September
of 1998 to February of 1999. A local bid at the local jail was a
piece of cake. It was like high school, but being on detention
and not being able to go home. He rested up, socialized with

all of the local criminals who went in and out of jail on the regular. There was no danger; Chance was the man in his 'hood.

Star was caught in South Carolina in December so he and Chance were together for the last time ever, from December to February when Chance was released. Star would be charged, found guilty, and sentenced by the end of 1998 with the murder of the man whose name was Robert Sterling. He was a husband and father of four. Star is sentenced to 25 years to life.

When Chance is released in February of 1999, he picks up with Travis, Junior, and Tricky who have kept the business going. As a coming home present, Travis gives Chance $50,000 and, three months later, they go on a trip to Aruba.

Chance took a girl that he had started seeing before he went in. Janet was having another baby by Chance. She was two months pregnant. The girl that he was seeing was Sabrina. She was independent and professional. She was a bank manager and Chance's criminal history meant nothing to her. She liked the way he made her feel. She had just lost her husband and she was tired of her boring life. The day Chance walked in to the bank, and wooed her, was the day that she felt beautiful again, thanks to him.

Travis, Chante, Chance, and Sabrina stayed at the Aruba Surfside Marina. It was a beautiful hotel. The Aruba Surfside Marina was a charming yet modern vacation retreat located on the peaceful white sand beach of Surfside, just minutes away from the bustling capitol of Oranjestad. The Marina had five deluxe beachfront suites with spectacular views of the ocean.

Chance felt a peace that he had never felt, on that beach. He was able to put all of his worries and stress to the side. He was able to breathe without the pressure that was on him every day. Living his life was full of pain and struggle. He always had to look over his shoulder. No sex, drug, or drink could take him away like the vacation did. Chasing money and opportunity was draining, especially when your means to support yourself was through illegal activity. He wanted out; he just didn't have enough money yet to be able to create a new life out of.

They were lying out on the beach when Chante and Sabrina decided to go in the water. Chance and Travis stayed behind.

"Yo, I needed this man. I'm glad you made me get up off them streets for this. I really was starting to feel like I was about to go crazy. After that shit with Marquise and Star, I really have to try and find another way to live." Chance was glad that he could confide in someone who didn't have the same street mentality as he did.

"Is this my man, *No Limit*, talking about changing his life? I'm glad to hear that man. I was getting caught up in this shit, too. I am about done. That car has saved us from disaster plenty of times. When you was locked up, me, Tricky, and Junior must have gotten stopped at least five times, with all types of money and jewels in the car. I told them they can't bring shit in the car that won't fit in the stash boxes. Shit, we got seven different hiding spots. And, the cops don't know how to turn the knobs and hit the switches to make the drawers come out. They search and search and if they find any tools at all, I say it's for my business. They can't find the loot so they can't do shit."

"Yeah, that was the best thing you ever thought of. These niggas be hating on you, man. They be trying to call you a punk because you don't hang out with us and shit. But, that street shit is bogus. Ain't no real love out there." Chance sipped his drink.

"Fuck them niggas. I'm a man, I don't play in the streets, I drive on them to my destination. My father always taught me that if you do the same as everyone else, you will get the same result and all I see niggas on the street doing is messing up their lives. I don't need to be in the same boat with them crabs in a barrel. I'm jumping that boat and swimming to my yacht. I'm gonna win, because I do the opposite of what everyone else does, it's called being a leader. We can open up a business, man. We gotta do something because the FEDS ain't gon' stop 'til we do. They aren't going to give up on bringing us down."

"Nigga, how much money you got? I need a million dollars to quit. I'm down about $700,000. I only have $300,000."

"Damn nigga. I got my million and a half already. That's because I don't play in those streets. The streets will spend you man. Between all them hos and all that trickin' and flossin' in front of everybody every weekend or every other night, that shit adds up, nigga. You gotta be done with that shit."

"You have a good point. Maybe Sabrina can be that woman to me, like Chante is to you. But, I didn't tell her about Janet. She knows about Chanel and Jayvon, but not the one on the way. When she finds out, she's probably gonna want to leave me. I know I ain't usin' coke no more. That shit is starting to affect me too much. It started out as fun, and it ain't fun no more. I'm done."

"That's what happens to players, man. Players usually end up playing themselves. You know, my father always told me, if a man wants to play the field, he gotta know that his bases will get loaded." Chance laughed.

"Well, that's not bad for homeruns."

"Well, when you pack the women around the bases, they are bound to all want homeruns with you. You will end up with a whole lot of drama on your hands. No woman really wants to be on the side, they just pretend they're okay with it 'til they get to third and then they wanna bring it home. They all want to end up being your girl, in the long run."

"Yeah, you ain't lyin' about that. But, you had a father to tell you stuff and lead you in the right direction. I didn't. I've been trying to figure this whole man thing out all my life, and all I know is that if you want something in life, you gotta take it."

"Or get it. Some people work hard to get it instead of taking it."

"Yeah, but if you mess up early on, it's too late. I can't go back to high school and start all over." Chance was starting to face the reality of his circumstance and he didn't like it.

"Listen, man, I'm gonna help you get that million and then we are going to have to hang up our hats. The purpose of committing crime is to benefit from it, and get out of it. What's the point of making all this money to lose it to jail time? The key is not *Do the Crime, Do the Time*, that's the authorities' motto. Our motto is, "*Do the Crime, Stay Outside. You got it?*" Chance nodded his head. "So, let's do it. Now, let's enjoy the rest of this vacation, you deserve it man.

Two girls in thongs walked past and Chance was about to stop them. Travis shook his head. "Nigga is you crazy, our girls are right there!" Chance laughed, "Man, it's like there's always girls everywhere. I can't help myself. He started singing Tupac's song with Nate Dogg on the hook, All About You...

Every other city we go, every other vi-de-o
(It's all about you)
No matter where I go, I see the same ho
(Yeah nigga, ha ha ha ha!)
Every other city we go, every other vi-de-o
(It's all about you)
No matter where I go, I see the same ho

Travis shook his head.

They spent the rest of the week, doing all types of activities, and excursions. Aruba had a nice nightlife. They went to different clubs each night and enjoyed the latest in songs that were parallel with their lives. The artists that were out in 1998 and 1999 were Biggie, of course, N.O.R.E., Juvenile, DMX, Big Pun, Black Star, Outkast, Lauren Hill, Nas, Mos Def, Tupac, Missy Elliot, Jay Z, Method Man & Redman, The Roots, and Dr. Dre.

Chance wished that he could be a successful businessman who could enjoy this type of living without the drama, but he was just a criminal, trying to survive.

2000
Chapter 18

The summer of 2000 proved to be the best year for the four business partners. What they didn't know was that their time was running out.

Travis began taking classes at the Community College for Business Management. He intended on opening a business of his own. Travis' father decided to move back South where he was raised and he sold his businesses when he started to get wind of Travis being involved. His father was very disappointed in the turn that Travis' life was taking. Travis planned to make his father proud of him again. In the meantime...

The authorities from New Jersey, New York, and Connecticut had come up with a list of 200 burglaries that had the signature of Chance and his crew. There were other crews doing the same thing and the cops wanted them all. The information they gathered was enough for the FBI to agree to pick up the cases and make them federal. The local arrests were not doing anything to deter the robbers, who the FBI had named, "The Robbin Hoods."

They knew who they wanted: Chance Major, Donovan Peterson (Tricky), Felipe Brown (Junior), and they suspected Travis Johnson to be involved because he had been stopped with the others on a few occasions, with no arrests being made. Not only were the burglary tools being hid in the stash so was the loot after the job was done. The Robbin' Hoods had their shit together.

All of the jurisdictions began to work together with the FBI to come up with an airtight way to bring "The Robbin Hoods" down.

They put a burglary task force together, with two detectives from each department that would meet up every week to compare notes to try to come up with a specific map of how the Robbin' Hoods were moving. To see if there was a pattern.

They also had their patrol and they knew to look for black men in expensive cars, especially a white BMW.

They had pictures of Chance, Junior, and Tricky from their mug shots.

"I know one thing we have got to do," said a young detective from Englewood, New Jersey. "We have got to get the stolen property. They have got to be taking it to the diamond district. We have to go and start looking for the jewels and roll on the fences who are buying the stuff. They will roll on these guys. They will point them out in a second if they think that they will lose their business and go to prison." The other officers clapped for Officer Melvin.

"We also have got to gather all of the DNA information from the different locations. We can place them in the home, if we can show their DNA was left there." This comment was made by an officer Lewis from Teaneck, New Jersey who also received applause.

Four FBI agents were working with each department. They put the robberies under the organized crime ring status. That way, the charges would be federal, the sentences stiffer, and the time would have to be done full term, not like the state sentences that are reduced over time.

"We will bring them down. We need to focus more on the loot, the fences, and science right now. If we gather the DNA from all of the robberies, we are bound to get something. And, if it turns out that up to this point the departments have slacked on taking proper DNA samples at the scene, then from now on, it must be gathered just like if it was a murder scene. Does everyone understand?" The head of the

FBI task force that was leading the other cities and counties in The Robbin Hoods investigation asked all of the officers involved. "We will also continue the surveillance of each of them. They are very slick because they all always know when they are being followed. So, they will spend an hour driving around in circles, so we have to abort for that time or day. They are very hard to follow."

They had their assignments. The two officers who made the commendable statements, Officer Melvin and Officer Lewis, both black, were instructed to visit the diamond district just to look before asking any questions. They had been given descriptions of some of the rare pieces. Another problem was that people rarely had pictures of their jewelry so that the police can look for it specifically. Only when the stolen goods are found on the perpetrator, can robbery victims come and claim their belonging, which also gets difficult when they don't have papers on the jewels.

Tricky and Chance had jewelry to take to Sherim. They went to New York in a rented car. They were being extra cautious. They were not driving their own cars around town. Moreover, there rental cars were standard and basic cars, not flashy. They knew that the detectives knew their M.O. from the press conference that was held about Marquise and Star's incident. They knew they would expect to find them in expensive cars, so they changed the game and started driving low-key ones. Tricky was driving the Ford Taurus and Chance was on the passenger side being the DJ. He put in a cd of M.O.P from Warrior 2. He put Ante Up on and started performing it in his seat like he was on stage. He was hopping up and down so hard he was bouncing the car. He was pumping his fist in the air. Tricky kept looking at him like he had lost his mind....

Take minks off! Take things off!
Take chains off! Take rings off!
Bracelets is yapped, Fame came off!
[Ante Up!] Everything off!
Fool what you want, we stiflin' fools
Fool what you want? Your life or your jewels?

The rules, (back 'em down), next thing (clap 'em down)
Respect mine we Brooklyn bound, (bound!) now, (now!)
Brownsville, home of the brave
Put in work in the street like a slave
Keep a rugged dress code, always in this stress mode
[That shit will send you to your grave] So?!
You think I don't know that? (BLOW!)
Nigga hold that! (BLOW!) Nigga hold that! (BLOW!) Nigga
hold that!
From the street cousin, you know the drill
I'm nine hundred and ninety nine thou short of a mil
Ante Up! Yap that fool!
Ante Up! Kidnap that fool!
It's the perfect timin', you see the man shinin'
Get up off them goddamn diamonds! Huh!
Ante Up! Oh! Yap that fool! Oh!
Ante Up! Oh! Kidnap that fool!
Get him (get him) get him! Hit him (hit him) hit him!
Yap him! (Zap him!) Yap him! (Zap him!)

Tricky turned the radio off abruptly and waved his hand for Chance to be quiet when his phone started ringing.

"Hello." Tricky listened intently to the person on the other line. He hung up and shared with Chance what he heard.

"Yo, there's a task force made of the FBI and they on us." Tricky paid the toll and proceeded across the bridge.

"So, we good. We just gonna put one more year in and then whatever is whatever. I'm good for one more year." Chance turned the music back up and Travis turned it down.

"We have to have a meeting about what we gotta do if we start getting pulled in for questioning and shit. We all have to meet, tonight." Tricky was always anxious about every-thing.

"Okay, we can do that but right now, I'm feeling the sun and New York. Let's pump this shit and forget about them fucking niggas. We are gonna have to stay three steps ahead of them. But, you right, we need to go over that shit tonight. We good, Inspector Gadget."

"Nah, that nigga Travis is Inspector Gadget. We need to get another car like that."

Chance was not interested in having a meeting with Tricky. He wanted to take his jewels and get his money. He turned up the music and Common, The Light came on...

> *I never knew a luh, luh-luh, a love like this*
> *Gotta be somethin' for me to write this*
> *Queen, I ain't seen you in a minute*
> *Wrote this letter, and finally decide to send it*
> *Signed sealed delivered for us to grow together*
> *Love has no limit, let's spend it slow forever*
> *I know your heart is weathered by*
> *what studs did to you*
> *I ain't gon' assault 'em 'cause I probably did it, too*
> *Because of you, feelings I handle with care*
> *Some niggas recognize the light*
> *but they can't handle the glare*
> *You know I ain't the type to walk around*
> *with matchin' shirts*
> *If relationship is effort I will match your work*
> *I wanna be the one to make you happiest,*
> *it hurts you the most*
> *They say the end is near,*
> *it's important that we close... to the most, high*
> *Regardless of what happen on him let's rely*
> *There are times...when you'll need someone..*
> *I will be by your side...*
> *There is a light, that shines,*
> *special for you, and me...*

They parked in a lot and walked around 5th Ave to 47th St. Harum gave them a dirty look when they walked up. Sherim walked over and they followed him across the street. As they walked in the building, the two detectives were walking down 47th Street. They did not see Tricky and Chance going in the other building.

The detectives inconspicuously began going to the different counters showing pictures of Chance, Tricky, Junior, and Travis. Most of the people just shook their heads without even looking at the pictures. They went to about ten counters. When they got to Harum, he looked and said that he wasn't sure. He asked for the detective's card and said that if he saw them he would call them. The detectives continued to ask through the gallery with no positive responses.

Chance had brought the jewels from a previous three nights' robberies. They had plenty of diamonds and gold. It seemed like there was never going to be an end to that life. There were millions of homes, everywhere. There were plenty of people living good and comfortably in their homes, which is only natural. Most people do not lock up things inside their houses; they just lock up their house. If there is something valuable, it should be secured somewhere hidden.

There was usually a safe, but it was usually open due to the laziness of the owner. Instead of wanting to have to use the combination, every time they wanted to put something in or take it out, they wouldn't lock it.

Sherim gave them $65,000 for the rare gems, brooches, pins, cufflinks, diamond studs, diamond and gold rings, earrings, diamond chokers, watches, and pinky rings.

"Well, as usual. It's nice doing business with you guys." Sherim stood up and shook both of their hands after they finished counting their money and secured it somewhere safe. This time it was a backpack. They were both dressed very casual, as not to stand out. Chance didn't have his jewels on and Tricky left his Presidential Rolex at home. They were dressed very plain, not flashy at all.

When they walked out of the building, they turned right and went to the lot. They didn't see the detectives sitting in the coffee shop watching them pass. They both tapped each other and pointed at Chance and Tricky as they walked by. One of them took out a camera, stood in the doorway, and took shots of Chance and Tricky crossing to the other side of the street. They figured they had money in the backpack. It was a jackpot. Although the two were walking away, they knew the vicinity in which they were selling the stolen goods. That was a major break.

They started walking far behind Chance and Tricky. They saw them go into a parking lot and get into a Gray Ford Taurus. They took down the license plate when Tricky pulled out. The two detectives who were known by Chance as well as Tricky were disguised with baseball caps and shades.

Tricky called Junior and told him that they had money for him. Travis wasn't in on that robbery so he didn't get anything. But they were going to Mahwah that night and Travis needed to be ready to meet them.

The way they were doing it since all the heat was on was to take two cars, every time. Travis would drive by himself with the tools stashed in his car. He kept the walkie-talkies, flashlights, ski masks, gloves, and wire cutters. He would give them to them and then drive somewhere close. He would wait for them to call him and tell them where he was and they would bring everything to him and he would stash it while they drove ahead home. Then, if their car is stopped because an eyewitness saw their car by the robbery, the cops wouldn't find anything and if Travis was stopped, he would be alone with nothing in his car.

Tricky dropped Chance off at the house he shared with Janet and their kids. Janet was miserable with Chance. He was never home and when he was, he only paid the kids attention. He spent no time with her and did nothing with her. He was emotionally unattached. Living with him was like living with a ghost. Someone who was there, but not really there. He was a good father, though, very hands on.

Chance was happy when he walked through the door and his kids were happy to see him.

Chanel was seven, Jayvon was two, and his new son, Trevor, was four months. He went inside and Jayvon was getting on Chanel's nerves trying to play her PlayStation 2 without knowing what he was doing.

"Daddy, he always messes up my game," Chanel complained as soon as Chance walked in the door.

"Is that the first thing you say when Daddy comes through the door? What about 'Hi Daddy, I love you. Are you okay?" Chanel repeated everything Chance had just said to her.

"Now, Daddy what are you going to do about this? Can you buy him his own PlayStation 2?" She put her hands together like she was pleading.

"So, let me get this straight, he doesn't know how to use it but you want me to go out there with my hard earned money and just throw away like $300 to get him a game he can't play?"

"Yes Daddy, that's what I want you to do." Chanel sat on Chance's lap.

"Well, Daddy is not going to do that. Now, let's watch a movie. Turn the game off and spend some time with your Daddy because I have to go to work later."

"Daddy I don't want you to go to work. I want you to stay with me forever. I don't ever want you to leave me Daddy." Chanel squeezed her father tight as he put 102 Dalmatians and they talked about how mean Cruella Deville was. They watched the whole movie and talked about the plot. Chance taught her life lessons throughout the storyline that would help her understand some of life's conflicts. He always tried to instill the right thinking and the right behavior into Chanel. He wished that his father had been there to instill it in him.

"Let me play with my little man. He's over there looking like he's neglected. Hey, Jay, you want Daddy to play with you?" Jayvon started smiling and laughing when Chance started talking to him. He got up, walked over to Chance, and stepped on him to get in his arms.

"All right man, you are heavy. You gonna be a fat boy." Chanel reprimanded Chance for calling her brother fat.

"Daddy, don't say that. That's not nice."

Janet fixed dinner and called them all in to eat. Chance sat down. Chance felt on Janet's ass as he sat down.

"What the fuck you touching my ass for; you want to get me pregnant again and then get mad because you don't want me or these babies?" Janet could not talk to Chance without arguing with him. She was tired of him coming and going as he pleased without any consideration of her feelings.

"Look, Janet, don't start this shit. I don't want to hear it." He started to eat his food.

"You know, what's sad is that you really don't care."

"It's sad that you really don't care. I risked my freedom for you and my kids to live comfortable and all you do is complain all the fucking time."

"Daddy, don't talk like that to Mommy; she's a lady," Chanel scolded.

"I'm sorry, Mommy; Chanel said I can't talk to you like that. I apologize. Can I have a kiss?" Chance puckered up.

"Mommy, give Daddy a kiss," Chanel said, calling Janet Mommy, as she always did. Janet gave Chance a kiss and Chanel started clapping, laughing, and jumping up and down.

Chanel hadn't seen her real mother in two years. Twinkie was a prostitute on the streets of New York, selling her body for crack. When Chance heard that Twinkie was doing that bad, he decided to go on a mission to find her.

For about a month, Chance went to different parts of New York City where prostitutes were known to "stroll". One night, he went to Hunts Point, in the Bronx. He searched for Twinkie but did not see her. He asked the girls who were out there and they knew her and told him that she was usually out there. A few days later, he returned to Hunts Point and saw Twinkie getting out of a car.

He pulled up and she walked right over, not even knowing it was him. When he rolled down his tinted window, she was startled but not deterred.

"Is this my Baby Daddy coming to get some head or some pussy? Your price is higher than the regular price." Twinkie started laughed and moving from side to side like she was anxious for a hit.

"Twinkie. Listen, I know I never treated you like a lady and believe me that is because you never carried yourself like one. But, you had my daughter; let me help you. Let me take you to a rehab or something." Twinkie leaned down in the car, as far as she could stick her head in through the window. She licked her lips.

"Chance. Do you want some head or some sex? It'll be 150 for either." Chance looked at

Twinkie and her raggedy body and clothing and started laughing.

"Twinkie, you must really be out of your mind to think that I would pay a penny for that stinkin' pussy. Now, do you want to get help for your daughter's sake or what?"

"Chance, suck my dick! Take care of my daughter, muthafucka! You ain't better than me; you was smoking that shit, too! Fuck you!"

Chance pulled off and watched Twinkie in the rearview mirror still waving her arms and ranting and raving. She threw a bottle at his car, which missed. He shook his head as she faded out of his sight. He didn't know that, within two months, Twinkie would be raped and brutally murdered.

Janet was home, with her high school friend, Nina, one day. Her friend was concerned about the bad things she was hearing about Chance in the street. She didn't know how to bring the issue up to Janet, but she had made the visit for that particular reason. They were sitting on the couch, watching television, while their children were playing in the playroom. When a commercial came on, Nina carefully picked her words.

"So, girl, you think you and Chance are gonna get married?" Janet took a moment to try to read Nina's face to see if she was being sarcastic or facetious.

"What makes you ask?" Janet chose her words just as carefully.

"Well, for one, you have two kids by him. But, I'm just asking. I know you've always been into Chance since high school. Remember that day we went to Supreme's house to meet him, Chance and Star? Girl, you've been in love with him ever since." Janet shook her head and they both started laughing.

"I don't know about that, but I love him now; I can't front. I do. People think so bad of Chance but he has a kind heart. He is a good provider. He is always trying to do for everyone and all people have is bad things to say about him." Janet leaned back and waited for the ammunition that she knew was about to be shot back at her. She could just feel that it was coming.

"Yeah, but Janet, he is running around here with all types of chicks and that ain't right. He be in the bar with this

one and here and there with that one, while you're home raising his kids. And then, if he gets locked up, you will be the
one having to hold him down. Men like him don't appreciate
what they have and they take advantage of and use women."
Once Nina started, she couldn't stop herself from saying what
she really meant to say. The look on Janet's face told her that
Janet was offended.

"Nina, most men do that." Janet said, humbly and inse-
curely.

"Janet, that's a cop out. A man will do to you what you
allow him to do. Don't you know that you deserve better than
that?" Nina was on a roll.

"I know that he is a black man, with the world against
him, and all he has is his woman and his children. And all we
have is him." Janet started cleaning up to give Nina the hint
that her welcome was about to be worn out.

"And everyone knows that he is out here robbing houses. How come men can't make it their business to stay out of
prison, to raise their children, and take care of their women?
He may be taking care of you now, but if he goes to prison,
you will suffer and so will the children. Men should think
about that."

"And so will he, Nina."

"And that is his choice Janet." Janet was about to give
Nina another rebuttal when Chance walked through the door.

Chance said hello to Nina and gave Janet a kiss. He
went to the playroom, picked up his kids, gave them hugs and
kisses, and then went to his room to get rest for his night's
work. He walked back past the living room toward the bedroom.

"Can you meet Daddy in the room when your company
leaves?" Chance winked at Janet, making her blush.

"Yes, Mommy will meet you," she said, smiling and
looking directly in Nina's eyes thinking, *I don't give a fuck
what you think, this is Black Love.*

Nina thought, *That's some dysfunctional love if I've ever seen it.*

Janet let Nina out after Nina made her daughter help
Chance's daughter clean up the playroom.

She then went into her and Chance's bedroom. Their whole house was nice and Janet took good care of it. She kept it neat and clean.

Chance was laying on his California king bed and felt an attitude from the look that Janet gave him.

"What's the problem, Janet?" Chance was only going to give her a short amount of time.

"I'm raising three kids and I don't get any type of time with you. You are always out in the street. What are you with me for?"

"We have a child together. Well, two kids now."

"So, that's it, you are only with me because you have two kids with me?" Tears formed in Janet's eyes.

"I was with you before the kids, remember, that's how you got pregnant. But, me and you never became nothing. We were just fuckin' Janet. You was never my girl, and now you my baby mama."

"So what are you saying. Chance?" she wiped her tears.

"I'm saying be glad I'm here. There's a lot of bitches that ain't seen their baby fathers. You should respect that I'm here with you with the kids. I'm gon' do me. I can do me, with you or do me, without you." Chance got up to go back in the kitchen with the kids. They were being too quiet and he wanted to check on them.

"I hear that, Chance. You are a great man." Janet lay on the bed to take a nap.

"I never claimed to be." Chance went in the kitchen to see Chanel making a mess with her food along with Jayvon.

"Look at y'all, Messy Marvins," Chance teased.

"My name is not Marvin, Daddy." Chanel continued eating her food with her hand, while Jayvon copied from his high chair.

Chance took a nap with Janet after he made the kids lie down and go to sleep. He held her in his arms. He loved Janet in his own way. He was not planning to settle down and get married any time soon, but he respected her as the mother of his children. He just never imagined it going much further with them. He did appreciate her for the good woman that she was to him and his kids.

He never had one girl. He didn't think that he could ever be conquered by one woman. He never intended to be.

When they woke up, he looked Janet in the eyes and said, "I love you, Janet. Love me for who I am."

Janet looked at Chance in the eyes and said, "I love you, Chance, and I love you for who you are."

For the next year, the saga continued.

2001
Chapter 19

Corey was arrested in February for sticking up a gas station. He would ultimately be sentenced to eight years in prison because one of his friends shot and critically wounded the gas station attendant. The robbery occurred in New York so Corey would be doing time in New York. Had he been in New Jersey, he probably would have been given more years, but New York prisons made New Jersey prisons. Most of them anyway, look like camps.

Chance, Junior, Tricky, and Travis were doing jobs twice a week and they rotated days every week, so as not to have a pattern. They had to be extra cautious if they intended to stay on the streets. They had had a very serious meeting led by Tricky, which discussed what they would do when they started being brought in for questioning. They knew that just because they weren't being arrested that didn't mean that the investigation was not ongoing. Their first rule was not to talk at all, before being bailed out. There was no reason to. They could refuse to speak without a lawyer and they could keep their mouth shut until they were all out and able to corroborate their stories. Rule #1 Do not speak before getting bailed Rule #2 was do not speak without a lawyer Rule #3 was never to believe that the detectives are there to help you or cut you a deal when they don't even have a case. Do not fall for the

"You help us and we'll help you" lie. Rule #4 always know that your guilt has to be proven. Never tell on yourself.

The two detectives that took pictures of Chance and Tricky were in the same coffee shop for the next week every day waiting for Chance and Tricky to show up. They did and they were able to see them approach the booth and then follow a man into a building across the street. They took pictures of the two with the fence. They would use the pictures to obtain a search warrant of the fence's office. They also walked to the fence's public counter and snapped pictures of the jewelry that was in their cases to see if there was anything that can be identified by the robbery victims. There were just so many robbery victims and so much stolen property to try to keep up with. They were gathering DNA on all new burglaries.

For The Robbin' Hoods, it was like Jay Z Said in 1996, *Politics as Usual*.... But the arrests started to pile up.

September 2000

Chance and Junior travel to Long Island and rob a house. They rob three houses in one night. On the way back, they are stopped and the stolen property is found from all three homes. They bailed out for $50,000

They continue to make large scores in Long Island and then move to Rockland County. They do ten successful robberies where they find safes, jewelry and expensive ornaments for the home. They total cash and *prizes* of $350,000.

December 2000

Travis and Tricky rob five homes in five days in Orangetown, NJ. At the last home, fingerprints are found on an alarm system circuit breaker. The fingerprints come back to Travis and he is arrested, charged, and released on $35,000 bail.

The detectives obtain a search warrant for Sherim's office and confiscate a lot of jewelry. They begin to have victim's come in to identify their jewelry.

The dates of robberies are compared with the different times when any of their license plates were ran by an officer or stops when they were identified and let go.

February 2001

Chance is identified by a girl whose parents' house had been robbed shortly after she met Chance in a club and takes him home when her parents are away. A week later, her house is robbed and when the detectives ask her if she had met any new black men and she tells them of Chance, she identifies him from his mug shot. He will be charged on this when he is eventually brought in. They leave him on the street, waiting for him to hang himself, plenty more times.

Travis recruits one of his friends from high school to be a driver for him and Tricky. Chance is away on vacation with Junior and two girls so Travis and Tricky need a driver. While they are in the house, a patrol car stops alongside of Travis' friend and begins to question him. He says that he is tired and lost and felt himself falling asleep so he pulled over. The officer took his name and information down and made him drive off. He got scared and left and did not go back to get Travis and Tricky. He called Travis and told him that they left. They were stuck in the house. Travis called Chante, told her it was an emergency, and that he was stuck in someone's house. She rushed to get him before the neighbors came home. They came outside and jumped in the car with Chante, who blasted Travis in the car the whole ride back to drop Tricky off. Chante was pregnant again and was concerned about how Travis had let his company lag because he was too busy going on jobs with *the crew.*

Tricky was dropped off by his car, which was parked in a local supermarket parking lot. He called one of the two girls that he was involved with. Tricky was very selective with the people that he dealt with and let into his life. He did not like many people and a lot of people thought he was a little off because he always had conflict going on within himself that he would try to put on the people around him. Tricky called the young girl, the one who had no kids because his girl that had two kids could not get a babysitter. She was the whore that he tricked on, while the other was the girl that he cared for.

Tricky picked the girl up in his new Maserati that he was leasing and as soon as she got in the car, he put blindfolds on her. She was young, immature, and she knew what he did for a living. So he was not about to let her be able to tell someone how to get to his house or where he lived, because he knew that young girls always had to run their mouths to prove that they were messing with a "baller".

When they got to his townhouse in the affluent West Milford town, where he lived secretly and incognito, he didn't take the blindfold off until they were inside. Tricky paid the girl $1,000 to clean his house, wash his clothes, and suck his dick all night. He then made her sleep on his living room couch while he slept in his king size bed.

Tricky was emotionally detached, unaffectionate or uncompassionate, and skeptical. Tricky trusted no one and was overly suspicious of everyone.

August 2001

Travis and Junior robbed a Bridgewater home. While they were in the house, a neighbor noticed flashes of lights going around in the bedroom and called the police. Travis and Junior are met at the door by the detectives who arrest them without incident. They are given $250,000 bails each.

One day Chance is in the mall taking a girl shopping and he runs into Supreme who he hadn't seen in years. Supreme is in a suit and tie.

"Yo, what up, Supreme? Damn, long time no see. Where you been?"

"I got married and moved to North Carolina. I have two boys now." Supreme gave Chance a hug and a pound.

"Word? You all suit and tied up huh? You a good guy now?" Chance teased.

"Man, I left that trouble alone. I finished high school and got my shit together. I'm up here for a funeral but I own my own Audi/Volvo dealership down south. I had to get away from up here. Nobody wants to do right and I wasn't ruining my life. How are you man?"

"I'm good. Just taking my chick to get some wears you know. Well, take care of yourself man. Stay sucker free." Chance gave Supreme dap and took the girl's hand who he was with, Dana, and walked away. He thought about where he would be and what he would be doing if he had finished school and maybe gone to college. *I'd probably be married to Danielle right now,* he thought.

October 2001

Chance, Junior, Travis and Tricky go to Basking Ridge, New Jersey. They are in two cars. Tricky is riding with Travis and Chance and Junior are driving together. They approach four homes in a cul-de-sac. All four homes appear to be empty.

Junior goes into one home while Tricky and Travis go into another. Chance and Junior found $15,000 in cash and no jewelry. They approach the next home, where they find $5,000 and a small amount of inexpensive jewelry.

Tricky bursts through the back door of another home. He ran up the stairs with Travis right behind him, with both of their small flashlights leading the way. They ran up another flight of stairs to the master bedroom. Tricky was a few steps in front of Travis. As soon as Tricky turned to enter the room, "Boom!" his body flew back against the wall. His chest splattered all over the wall and his limp body dropped to the floor. Travis took one look into Tricky's lifeless eyes, turned around, and leapt over three stairs to make it to the first landing. As he turned to go down, he saw the shotgun pointed at him. He heard the next, "Boom!" and felt the air from the bullet as it flew past and missed his head while he jumped to the bottom of steps, missing all ten of the stairs. Travis flew out of the back door and began yelling into the walkie-talkie

The man with the gun did not chase Travis outside with the shotgun because he was naked. He and his wife were in their room having sex when they heard the door kicked in. He jumped up and grabbed his gun in enough time to stop Tricky as he entered the room. His wife had already called the police and the police were on their way.

Travis yelled, "They shot Tricky!" He continued running as he saw them running out of the man's neighbor's house. They all ran for their life back to their cars. Travis made it to his car, jumped in and took off. He made it home without seeing one cop car. He traveled the back streets out of town-a different way from the local highways, which he knew would be flooded with police cars looking for them.

Chance and Junior weren't so lucky. They were surrounded and forced off the main road. They were arrested and taken to Somerset County Jail.

When they were questioned, they were separated and interrogated by three detectives each. Chance was giving smart remarks and being cocky, so he was beaten up and thrown in a cell.

Junior sat quietly and kept yawning as the detectives took turns trying to get information out of him. The officers were frustrated by his quiet arrogance.

"So, Mr. Brown, you think it's okay to break into people's homes and take their hard earned possessions?"

"Sir, I will not speak without my lawyer; you're wasting your time. But, I will say this. You people sure live with a lot. I know people whose whole house is the size of some garages in this area. I doubt that these people need all those things to live. Now, again, please take me to my cell. I will not speak without my lawyer, sir." He turned, looked at the wall, and refused to look or answer of any of their questions. Before taking him to his cell, one detective made a promise to him.

"Mr. Brown, it seems that you and your friends have had quite a few tricks up your sleeves. Now it's our turn to show you what we've got. It's taken a while, but I think we've got a surprise for you."

Junior shrugged his shoulders and they took him to his cell.

Chance's and Junior's bails were set at a million dollars each. Neither could make their bails. They would have had to come up with $100,000 and no one that they knew, not twenty people put together, could vouch for that much money legally. The FBI stepped in and brought them up on all the charges they had been accumulating over time.

A big press conference is held and the news announces that the infamous Robbin' Hoods have finally been brought to justice. Travis was arrested at his and Chante's new house, which they had moved into a month earlier. He is brought in and charged with running an illegal enterprise of organized crime. His bail is considerably lower and he bails out to get ready for trial.

During interrogations, all three men follow the rules that were made by their deceased friend, Tricky. They do not cooperate with the police and the police are frustrated with the thought that *The Robbin' Hoods* might just get a few insignificant punishments.

Before trial even starts, Junior goes to the infirmary complaining of stomach pains. He is unaware that the nurse that works in the infirmary is the cousin to the man who shot Tricky. Junior is *accidentally* given a lethal dose of pills that kill him. His death is listed as natural causes and never investigated.

Chance begins to worry that he will also be killed. He is told by a CO that the guy who shot Tricky was a Basking Ridge detective who had been closely following The Robbin' Hoods case and very emotionally charged by it. He told everyone that, "if those punks come in my house they will leave in a body bag."

Chance was starting to stress out. He put in for a transfer to another jail and it was denied. He called Chante and told her that she had to get in touch with Danielle. He said to tell her that he would pay her anything she wanted but that she had to represent him. Chance couldn't wait to lay eyes on Danielle. He didn't like the condition that he would have to see her in but he knew that Danielle would put her heart and soul into saving him. He felt Danielle was the only person on earth that he could trust with his life.

The cops wanted blood. They had been after The Robbin' Hoods for six years and they had won small victories, but now they wanted Chance's head on a platter. They were going to try to torture him for all of the ones who died and got off easy. Death wasn't enough punishment as far as the white towns and police departments that took it personal that some niggers were able to take from them. They didn't want Chance to die-they wanted him to rot.

Danielle was there within two days of Chante calling her. When Chance was brought into the room to see Danielle, he felt her energy as soon as he walked in the room. Her eyes looked through to his soul. She was so disappointed to see him in an orange jumpsuit. The officer left the room and Danielle embraced Chance and kissed him softly.

She sat down and crossed her hands. She looked into Chance's eyes and he saw the glimpse of tears. Danielle was the only woman who ever made Chance feel like he could take his armor off. She softened him up.

"So, Chance. Will this finally be it? Will you choose life after this? Cause baby they are trying to give you twenty-five years."

"You would think I murdered somebody. You can murder somebody and get less time than that. All this country cares about is materialism." Chance held his composure. He was not going to blow his stack.

"And you bought into it Baby. First off, I'm so sorry. I didn't even say hi. Hi." Danielle flashed her smile in Chance's direction, which made his eyes light up.

"Hey, beautiful. Did I ever tell you how beautiful you are?" Chance wanted to touch her, caress, and hug her.

"All the time and, please, don't start, Chance. You are a womanizer and you will always be." Danielle opened her clipboard and begins looking over the notes she had.

"Oh, so your real feelings come out now huh? Well, you didn't want me."

"Chance, did you ever try? No, you only liked the easy girls. I was too much work for you."

"Damn, I wish I would have taken on that job. How I wish I could have had you."

"Well, you could have and we could have been happy but you couldn't see the forest for the trees. You always cared about the things that weren't important. The flash fizzles after a while Chance. Can't you see? Look at what you have gotten yourself into?"

"Well, if you really love me you will make sure you get me out of it, so we can be together."

"Chance, we can fight this but the evidence against you is pretty tight."

"So you want me to cop out? Damn, you don't wanna fight for me either, huh? Don't talk about me. But, I will do whatever you think I should do."

"Well, let me tell you all the charges they have against you. I'm gonna lay it all out for you and tell you all of our options."

"So you're hired? I got you Baby?" Chance grabbed her hand, held it, and looked into Danielle's eyes. He wanted to apologize to her. He wanted to tell her that he was sorry that he couldn't have been that ideal man for her.

"Yes, you got me, baby. I'm gonna fight like hell for you, too."

"That's what I want to hear. So what are we working with Diva?" Chance winked at her.

"Well, they have a total of 300 burglaries over the last couple of years but not all have The Robbin' Hoods' signature. All of the alarm systems were not disconnected. So, they really have a lot of work ahead of them. There are other people burglarizing homes, they can't just blame you guys for all of it. So, they are relying on eyewitnesses, the confiscated stolen property, any hair or fingerprint evidence, DNA, and the times that any of you were caught red-handed or with stolen property. Their best offense is the fences cooperating and they would love for you guys to rat on each other. That would really make their job a piece of cake."

"Well, that ain't gonna happen. We are loyal. We got each other's backs. So that's what they call us huh? The Robbin' Hoods? Yeah, we robbed from the rich to support our 'hood."

"Chance, you got caught up in the hype of the 'hood. You didn't have to take care of 'the 'hood' but 'the 'hood' will sure take care of you, in the worse way. Chance you have people telling the police about all of the money you would spend in the bars, and all the cars you guys had. There is no loyalty in those streets Chance. You don't owe anyone, anything. This is a sensational new story to them, but this is *your* life that's on the line. None of those people you splurged on are here to have your back. And those fences have no loyalty to you; you think they will risk their livelihood for you?" Chance shook his head.

"Yeah? People are rolling over on us?" Chance shook his head again. He had tried to do whatever he could for people and here they were cooperating with police for what? It wasn't like they were getting paid to tell. They were just telling.

"They have some of your DNA, hair mainly at a few of the locations. They have the jewelry that you were caught with on different occasions and they have witnesses who have identified you from other robberies. They have the fences that you sold the jewelry to and they confiscated stolen property from them as well. The fences are cooperating with the police in terms of the different meetings that you've had, money you've been paid, and jewelry you have brought to them. The jewelry ties you to the house."

"Yeah, but it doesn't put me *in* the house. They can't prove that I committed the robbery, just because I had the stolen property. I could have bought it from someone. Or I could have took it to see it for them."

"They have some girl named Nadja who has given information on you, too." *Damn, that bitch gon' tell on me just 'cause I stopped fucking her?* Chance thought.

"She's just a scorned woman, that's why she's telling," Chance said agitatedly.

"Chance, you have to understand the police will threaten people's lives. They will act like the person is facing time for their involvement and people get scared. I will interview her. I can't coerce her, but I can just tell her that they really have nothing on her; they are just using her to make their job easier. But, they have a pretty tight case, except for the houses where the stolen merchandise has not been found, where there is no DNA, or evidence. They have tried to put all of the robberies on you and Travis." Chance thought instantly about the promise he had made to his sister about not getting Travis into trouble. He rubbed his head.

"They are putting *all* of the robberies on me and Travis? We didn't do *all* of those robberies. There was Marquise, Star, Junior, and Tricky too. Just because they are dead or in jail doesn't mean they didn't do anything. How can they do that? Make us responsible for dead men's actions?"

"They can't. They are going to give you everything and hope that you cop out to it all for a lesser sentence. We have to go through every robbery. We have to see how many they really have you on. Then I can negotiate for you. When we go to court, you are going to plead not guilty. I am going to get all of the evidence and we are going to fight. Even if you don't go to trial, I have to get them to drop some charges so that the time that you are looking at will have to decrease. Some of those charges have to get thrown out because there were other participants. And that's good for us. There always has to be that reasonable doubt."

"So how much time are they trying to give us?"

"Twenty-five years. Six months for every charge."

Danielle looked at Chance and imagined him having reached his potential. Chance was very smart but he chose to use his mind to do criminal activity, instead of legitimate business. In her eyes, he was a King. He was a great man with a great mind. He just never knew it.

2002
The End

Danielle was able to get many of Chance's charges dropped. He ended up taking the blame for the charges that he could not deny and the charges that Travis had, except for the three of four times that Travis was caught red-handed with stolen goods. They could not be charged for robberies that they were not caught in the house for.

The FBI was able to charge Chance under the RICO Act. The Racketeer Influenced and Corrupt Organizations Act. It is a United States federal law that provides for extended criminal penalties and a civil cause of action for acts performed as part of an ongoing criminal organization. It meant that Chance was a person who profited from an illegal racket that he ran. This made him a crime boss, like a mob boss.

That made up for the charges that Danielle was able to have dropped. Under RICO, Chance would receive a mandatory 10 years and they added six years for every year he committed robberies from 1995 to 2001. So, he would be given 16 years in prison if he went to trial and lost.

To save taxpayers money and the possibility of him beating his case, they offered him 14 years to plead guilty instead of going to trial. Danielle managed to negotiate with the prosecutor for 12 years.

Danielle told Chance that he should take the 12 years instead of going to trial and possibly being sentenced to 16 years, since the prosecution had a tight case. Chance agreed.

Travis copped out to two years for the charges that Chance was unable to take.

Chance made a statement to the judge and prosecution when he entered his guilty plea.

"You can act like I'm scum and the lowest thing on this earth but those were just material things. I'm 32 years old. I have been surviving the best way I know how, from a child. Where are all the opportunities for men like me? This country values money more than people's lives. If you rich people would try to help the poor, then we all could live happy. I have kids; I want them to have the same things you rich people have. Why shouldn't my children enjoy 'The American Dream' too? Or is the attainment of that 'Dream' only possible for some?" They just looked at him and no one responded.

Danielle gave Chance a final hug and a long kiss, in front of everyone. She whispered, "We would have been great together," in his ear. She hugged him again and wiped her tears as she watched him be led to the back to the holding cell, where he would stay until being transported back to the county jail.

Chance paid Danielle $100,000 for her work and ended up with $300,000 in his stash. He told Travis to get his money from the house and give it to Chante to use to take care of Janet and the kids and his mother with.

Travis ended up with $1,800,000 in his stash that he would come home to in two years.

Chance was sent to Trenton State Prison to do his 10-year term. He had spent two years in the county jail, waiting for the case to come up and be over. When he got through receiving and was taken to his cell, he met his cellmate, Victor, who was lying on the top bunk, reading his Bible..

"Hey, buddy, nice to see you back. I have something for you." Victor highlighted a few lines, passed Chance the

Bible, and told him to read the highlighted text. Chance stood there for a minute, looking at Victor. "You can't deny the truth and the truth is the light." He humbly held his hand out and took the Bible and it read....*And you did he make alive, when ye were dead through your trespasses and sins, wherein ye once walked according to the course of this world, according to the prince of the powers of the air, of the spirit that now worketh in the sons of disobedience among whom we also all once lived in the lust of our flesh, doing the desires of the flesh and of the mind, and were by nature children of wrath, even as the rest...But God, being rich in mercy, for his great love wherewith he loved us, even when we were dead through trespasses, made us alive together with Christ.*

By grace have ye been saved – Ephesians 2:1-5

Epilogue

C hance's first year in prison was trouble for him. He got into a lot of altercations but he had a crew of ten that looked out for each other and were respected. He was angry and was always ready to take his frustration out with his hands. He was in the hole more than he was out. He felt that the system was a joke, so he didn't care. Chance didn't consider what he had chosen, but was infuriated that the "powers that be" were more concerned with putting another black man behind bars and materialism than human life. He felt that taking was the only way that he could survive; the people were rich and could replace those items. They were just objects to them, but a way to eat for him and his family.

Chance continued to lend a deaf ear to Victor's preachings, readings, and teachings. Victor continued to always be calm with Chance, but he would always make sure that Chance could hear him reading. Chance chose to listen to headphones most of the time, but Victor would just put the words in the air, praying they would penetrate Chance's brain.

After the first three years, a lot of the random visits from his many females started to die down and Janet was the only one still coming. Janet made sure that Chance had everything he wanted. His commissary stayed full and he wanted for nothing, but his freedom. Janet would drive the nearly two hours to see him, twice a month, and bring the kids the third weekends of the month. She was keeping his money well saved at the same time. She continued to work and take good care of the children with Vonetta and Chante's help. The family stuck close together and the women were there for each other in the absence of Travis and Chance. Vonetta moved in with Chante to help her and to be there for her grandchildren.

When Travis came home, he opened an auto body shop and towing service. He also started a messenger service that he would turn over to Chance when he got out. Corey ran the business and stayed out of trouble. Chante had a third child and was the accountant for Travis' and Chance's businesses.

During Chance's fifth year, he and one of his boys got into a fight on the yard. The guy, named Justice, was killed within feet of Chance. A gang member named Trigger took a shank to Justice's throat and was shot by a guard as he was about to stab Chance in his head. Chance was on the ground fighting when Trigger almost stuck him in his temple. The shot saved Chance's life. He went back to his cell after being in the hole and began asking Victor questions and asking him to read scriptures to him about different topics. For a whole year, Victor read the Bible to Chance.

The sixth year, Chance came out on a visit and, when he sat down, Janet knew something was different about him just from the look in his eyes. He looked into her eyes and got on his knees. He had already told the guard what he was going to do, so he was allowed to do it. He spoke to Janet from the heart. "Janet, I was a selfish boy. I was an angry, frustrated young man. I was a ruthless, harsh criminal. I didn't care about anything but my pain. I didn't care about anyone else's feelings, concerns, belongings, privacy, or dignity. I imposed on people's privacy and I used people for my advantage. I trashed women. I had fun and I loved it. But, I didn't love myself. I loved material things, danger, and destruction. And through it all, you loved me. I love you. I never knew how to love, but I love you, Janet, and when I come home, I will prove it to you. Can you show me that you trust what I am saying is true by marrying me? I want to marry you before I come home to show you that I'm not just talking. And then when I get home, we are going to have a wedding on an island somewhere. I'm gonna make this all up to you. Will you marry me?" Janet was shocked and overwhelmingly happy. She had loved Chance from the first day she made love to him and she believed in her heart that God would give him to her the right way when the time was right. She agreed and they got married a few months later.

Chance began going to church with Victor on Sundays by the seventh year and continued going and learning. He knew that he could have been killed that day on the yard and the day he was saved, he decided to change his life. He spent the next six years in a walk with God and taking classes and reading at the library. He prepared himself to take over his messenger service. Travis had a roster of a hundred local businesses that used his low cost service and had a good reputation, which kept his customers from using more expensive services, like UPS and FedEx, for local and domestic deliveries.

Chance came home and transitioned well. He kept on his path of living a righteous life. He did not return to the same people, places, or things that he had done 12 years before. He was 44 years old when he came home. He, Janet, their kids, and the rest of his family prospered.

An Author's Note

This story is very dear and sentimental to me. Since I attended junior high school, many of the boys who I grew up with and were friends with, began getting into trouble for criminal activity. We all know that boys are mischievous, but what started out for some as petty crime, became a lifetime of recidivism in jails and prisons.

Many boys were sent to juvenile detention centers and grew into men who did serious and lengthy time behind bars. This epidemic continues today for our black and Latino men. This is nothing new, but when do we ask why? When do we change it? When do we heal and solve this problem?

Why do boys drop out of school more than girls and go to jail more than females do? One large answer is due to education and the other great influence is socialization. Girls are socialized and raised to be good, smart, and obedient, while oftentimes, boys are allowed and left to raise themselves, fend for themselves, and be "men" too early. While men have always been raised to be providers for their women and families, in our communities, they are not given the proper tools or guidance to pursue scholarship. They are pressured to get things on their own and be "men" and the street idea of what being a man means, is detrimental to their health and well-being.

In my opinion, the breakdown of the family is the first problem. Many boys are the man of their homes. They are not taught how to be successful, progressive, or healthy-minded men. It is unhealthy for a boy to think that he must take to have, or kill to have, or to think that his only option in having financial empowerment is by choosing a life of crime. This does not only negatively affect their lives but, ultimately, the lives of the mothers, family members, women, and offspring that they love and who love them. This is a vicious cycle, which leaves their sons to raise themselves, with the same unproductive, dangerous, and unhealthy attitudes; while their fathers are dead or in prison due to their lives of crime.

I wrote this book for the men who have suffered this type of existence. I wrote this book to speak for them, because the newspaper articles with their names in them only demonize them.

It is time to heal our boys and teach them how to be great and successful! Without crime!

About the Author

Ericka Williams is a tour de force, a phenomenal woman. She is a compassionate person who not only cares about herself and hers, but she cares about humanity. All of her books are themed to show the unlimited access of human beings to redemption. She is a Christian, spreading the message that Jesus saves; no matter who you are, what you've done, or what other people think of you. She uses societal ills, her own experiences, and real situations that we all face, to show that there is a light at the end of every tunnel, if you take God's hand and let him lead the way. She may not fit the mold of a "saint", but she sure is a believer and she knows that we all only have the obligation to spread the Word, the way that we personally know how.

Ericka Williams is a mother of two, an elementary school Language Arts teacher, an actor, a director, and a producer of short films. She is currently in the cast of The Cartel Publications, feature "Pitbulls in a Skirt" movie being released in the Winter of 2011. She continues to write books, act, and prepare to fulfill her dream of having her books turned into films.

Ericka Williams is a humanitarian, a mentor, a public speaker and above all, a Child of God. You may contact her at erickaw.com, erickawilliamsinfo@yahoo.com, or (212) 201-9329. You may "like" her at Ericka Monique Williams on Facebook, or follow her on Twitter @AuthorErickaw.